C000274746

Anne Sebba

Anne Sebba read history at King's College, London. She is a biographer, journalist and former Reuters foreign correspondent. Her
five books including the best-selling *Mother Teresa: Beyond the Image*
and *Laura Ashley: A Life by Design*. She lives in London.

www.annesebba.com

The Exiled Collector

William Bankes and the Making
of an English Country House

ANNE SEBBA

JOHN MURRAY

First published in Great Britain in 2004 by John Murray (Publishers)
A division of Hodder Headline

Paperback edition 2005

1 3 5 7 9 10 8 6 4 2

A CIP catalogue record for this title is available from the British Library

ISBN 0 7195 6571 5

Typeset in Monotype Bembo
by Palimpsest Book Production Limited, Polmont, Stirlingshire

Printed and bound by
Clays Ltd, St Ives plc

Hodder Headline policy is to use papers that are natural, renewable and recyclable
products and made from wood grown in sustainable forests. The logging and manufacturing
processes are expected to conform to the environmental regulations of the country of origin.

John Murray (Publishers)
338 Euston Road
London NW1 3BH

For Imogen

Contents

Illustrations

The author and publishers would like to thank the following for permission to reproduce illustrations: Plates 1 and 7, National Trust Photographic Library/Christopher Hurst; 2 and 12, National Trust Photographic Library/Derrick E. Witty; 4 and 6, The National Trust/The Bankes of Kingston Lacy & Corfe Castle Archives, Dorset Record Office; 5, the Bankes Family; 8 and 9, National Trust Photographic Library/Angelo Hornak; 10, The Stapleton Collection/ Bridgeman Art Library, London; 11, National Trust Photographic Library; 13, National Trust Photographic Library/James Mortimer.

Bankes Family Tree

Owners of Kingston Lacy are named in Capitals

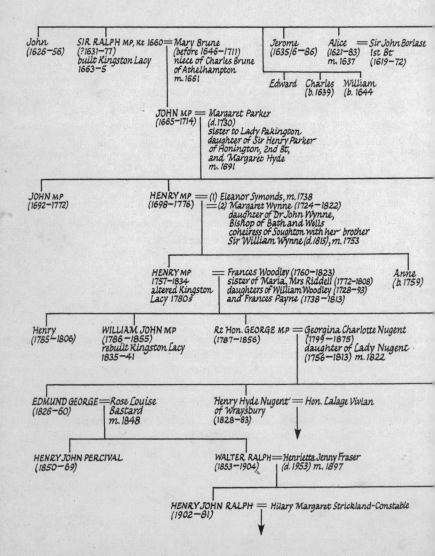

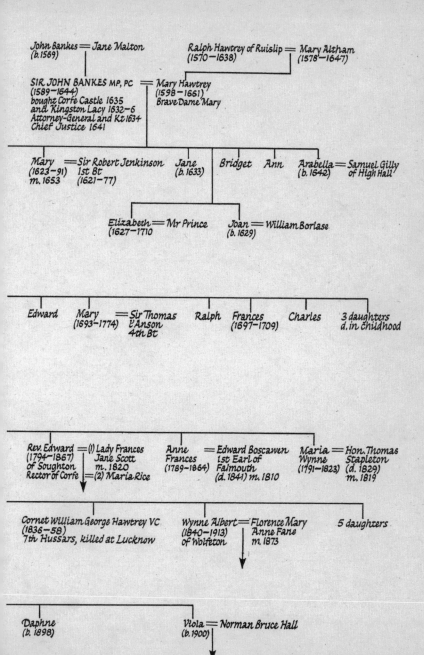

Introduction

~

O N THE BLANDFORD to Wimborne road in South West England there is a long avenue of mature beech trees lining the road on either side. Then suddenly a brown sign: Kingston Lacy. Just beyond is an impressive driveway. Take it, for it leads to an unexpectedly beautiful little Italian Renaissance palazzo hidden in the Dorset countryside. The house, now owned by the National Trust, is full of dreams and treasures collected by a man of extraordinary talent and tragedy, William John Bankes. Bankes planted the two-and-a-quarter-mile avenue of 726 trees in memory of his mother, living proof of one man's concern to leave his mark in this corner of the world.

William John Bankes was a traveller, archaeologist, artist and connoisseur. He was a handsome charmer blessed with a sensitive eye, a full wallet and an acquisitive nature who indulged his amateur and disorganised hobby of procuring Egyptian and European art all his adult life. But one night in 1841 Bankes, a former Member of Parliament, was caught with a guardsman in Green Park. In 1841 sodomy was a capital offence and men were still hanged for it. Bankes jumped bail, swiftly signed over his house and grounds – everything that he loved so much – and escaped into exile. The Government, taking advantage of an archaic law, declared him an outlaw, which gave it the right to seize his possessions.

He settled eventually in Venice, forbidden by law from visiting the house his family had owned for generations, his for a scant seven years. It was his one real and requited passion in life. And so he continued to embellish this house, transforming it by remote control from Italy. He bombarded his willing steward and two barely compliant brothers with constant directions. Meanwhile, he travelled all over Italy discovering stonemasons, gilders, carvers and other craftsmen, commissioning them to copy his drawings. Shipping home crate loads of alabaster, marble, stone and woodcarvings – several whole ceilings – became his obsession. There was too much for one house. Often the measurements were slightly out or shipments arrived with their contents smashed, causing deep anguish.

Collecting is intimately entwined with memory. The true collector acquires objects because of their excellence and beauty, but also because of their power to transport their owner to a time of real or imagined past. Most collectors take pleasure from living with their possessions and enjoying the memories they evoke. This pleasure was denied William Bankes during his fourteen years' exile. But his ferociously sharp memory enabled him to find others. Sending consignments home with detailed instructions about the objects' arrangement and display was his way of reminding himself of a time and place that meant so much to him. According to family myth, William evaded the law and did return occasionally, always between the hours of sunrise and sundown on Sundays. His descendants maintained that he landed his yacht on what had been his own property at Studland Bay and delivered to a waiting steward new treasures that he had purchased abroad. This was permitted, so the story went, because of an ancient indulgence to outlaws arising from the obligation of Catholics to hear Mass on Sundays.

The wayward son who cannot bear to abandon the ancestral home to which he has devoted his life, takes advantage of a legal loophole to continue transforming it as a fugitive from justice: it is a powerful myth, and, if I am honest, the silky strand of William Bankes's life history that ensnared me in its web years ago. But I no longer entirely believe the story. Historians insist there is no such 'ancient indulgence'. More likely, it was part of the process of romanticising William in Bankes's family history. Focusing on his secret visits was his family's way of understanding or avoiding discussion of his homosexuality. After all, the exiled ancestor who had created this exquisite country house could not be ignored.

Drawn to his story, I spent many hours burrowing among the surviving family papers – most, but not all, now in Dorchester, at the County Record Office – hoping to find evidence of visits home. What I found was tantalising, as I shall show later, if not the cast-iron proof I hoped for. More significantly, I slowly acquired a surer grasp of William's personality. He had, after all, wished for his letters and numerous scholarly memoranda on art and architecture to be preserved. This in itself was revealing since he had been amongst those who, although not directly consulted, had been in favour of the destruction of his friend Lord Byron's memoirs shortly after the poet's death in 1824. Occasionally he required his faithful manservant to copy essays of at least twenty pages to be preserved for posterity. Others he copied himself, or asked for letters to be returned to him. He begged his brother George and his sister Anne to keep his papers along with important memorabilia from his ancestors. It was his family in Dorset, nervous, conservative, sensitive to their position in society, who cut, deleted, tore, burnt or otherwise removed sections of his letters they considered embarrassing or criminally compromising. Particularly regrettable this, as it consigned Bankes to the footnotes of history, known, if at all, through the diaries and letters of those closer to the centre of power. This Bankes, more at ease with objects than people, appears as peripheral, slightly foolish at times, making little real contribution, often insensitive to those around him, embroiled in scandals and humiliations. His failure to publish an account of his travels led contemporaries to judge him as a lost hope, his early prominence dissipated in the froth of conversation.

But there is another William Bankes, who deserves a central rôle for his part in creating a beautiful and original house, his one true passion in life. Surviving letters and myriad memoranda reveal a man of courage, determined to continue the one task that mattered to him. He had been forced to leave England, aged fifty-four, with this unfinished and, as an outlaw with a threatened death sentence, was alive to the myriad difficulties he would face in completing this from Italy. That he found the resources within himself after the shock and humiliation of his arrest and the serious charges placed against him, communicated to me a man far more steely and interesting than one who would simply load his own yacht with treasures 'from time to time' and sail over to Dorset to install them. Always aware of the punishment hanging over him, he did not brood but did all in his power over the next fourteen years to make his family proud of him.

As I puzzled over the small, spidery handwriting in brown ink on tissue-thin cream paper in one erudite essay after another, I discovered a man neither embittered nor broken by his experience of an outdated law but, arguably, strengthened by it. I found a man whose youthful confidence had frequently veered towards arrogance but who matured under the strain of banishment, so that this confidence was transformed into the ambition to leave behind a glorious artistic monument. I saw a once flamboyant man, evidently attractive to women as well as to men, who allowed his obsession to collect for his house free rein as this was his life's work, but who never lost sight of what was possible. Here was a man in touch with reality yet always ready to take risks, who knew when he was mortally ill he had nothing more to lose by paying one last visit, perhaps two, to his home. Of this I am certain. This myth of William John Bankes is different, but no less potent or romantic, since his salvation came through one of the most notorious smuggling families of his day. Most of all, I discovered the pain and emotion involved in one man's creation of a unique English country house.

I

Ancestors

~

'An Exceeding Good House'
Sir Joseph Banks

OCTOBER 2000. KINGSTON Lacy is a house full of ghosts. The spirits of those who assembled this treasure house assuredly still lurk in its rooms. Today their presence is stronger than ever as everything that could be damaged by dust, dirt or damp is shrouded with white linen covers that will remain in place for the next six months. Each object has its own cover; even a painted velvet piano stool, while the marble statue of Sir John Bankes, founder of the dynasty, has his identity embroidered on his, with a bow tied around his waist.

Before anything is covered it is examined and cleaned with fine pony or hog's hair brushes to remove surface dust which is then vacuumed away. Furniture is inspected for woodworm; acid-free tissue paper is placed over gilding; centuries-old books are gently opened to discourage worm and silverfish. A Dictionary of Italian and English published in 1659, is being restored with a flour and water paste. Glass covered prints are wiped with simperonic, porous china is packed up to be sent away to a conservator, experts check rugs for carpet beetle before storing them for the winter. Carpets *in situ* are covered with thick druggetting.

After the hectic summer months, when hundreds of visitors come to admire this treasure house, it needs time to recover, to breathe, to rest. But for the National Trust conservation staff involved in 'putting to bed week', the repair and maintenance work which follows ensures that the winter months are the busiest.

As I wander from room to room, William's spirit is pervasive. The Golden Room, opulent setting for his Spanish paintings, best reflects his exuberant taste. Busy, flamboyant, camp, an excellent room for entertaining his gentleman friends. How William would have admired the present house steward's patient attention to detail, perching on scaffolding to inspect the magnificent gilt and coffered ceiling. William's own steward must have climbed countless ladders to take measurements, make templates or essay the effect of parts of ceilings.

In the grand saloon, I am beguiled by the richly disparate range of furniture, paintings and decorative objects reflecting William's wildly eclectic ideas. On the north side, between the windows overlooking the entrance driveway, stands a large composite roman baroque giltwood console on a bronzed base, with a pair of crouching athletes either side supporting a scalloped shell, dolphins and seated trumpeting tritons, flanking a figure of Flora with a cornucopia. Quite possibly, he never saw this concoction completed. Opposite, standing in marble niches, are a pair of eighteenth century giltwood candelabra in the form of a mermaid and merman holding putti, clasping cornucopia sprouting ormulu flowers which serve as lights. Bankes added tortoises for feet and had them regilded. Flanking the fireplace, a pair of bronze firedogs support satyr and sphinx-decorated candelabra, made in the Veneto in the sixteenth and nineteenth centuries. William assembled the late sixteenth century Venetian bases with finer tops, perhaps by Severo da Ravenna and his workshops, and shipped them to Dorset. Ample evidence of a man supremely confident in his own aesthetic judgement with an admiration for contemporary crafts unusual for his time. He believed the young men he 'discovered' in Italy were pursuing noble professions and, with his guidance, could transform raw materials into objects of beauty.

In the basement is a small museum of a room where once billiards were played. Here are the remains of Bankes's assorted collection of

Egyptian antiquities: shabti, amulets, scarabs and a 'Mark Antony' bust, the only addition he made after his return from Egypt. Once he began the remodelling process for the house his Egyptian treasures did not fit in with his decorative ideas and his preference for Western European art.

Among the most revealing parts of the house are those the public never sees: the passageway where a Tintoretto acquired by William hangs awaiting conservation; the attic stuffed with bric-a-brac and carvings mostly bought by William; the basement cellars created by William in the 1830s underneath the new terrace, still crammed full of stone and marble objects he despatched from Italy, many damaged or surplus. Two-and-a-half thousand objects are on display at Kingston Lacy but seventeen-and-a-half thousand are in store. Neither the Bankes family nor the National Trust throws anything away.

No doubt William Bankes, a conservationist almost before the word was invented, would have been delighted by today's team of experts and volunteers setting about their work. From Spain, he wrote to his father begging him not to have the paintings he had acquired cleaned in London. 'I am so afraid they will play tricks . . . and paint in the background . . . I would not have it touched for the world.'[1] In Egypt he painstakingly copied inscriptions inside tombs instead of ripping frescoes off walls, as others were to do; in Italy he preferred to commission new artists to make copies rather than remove ancient objects from their historical context. In the garden, too, William ordered wooden boxes to protect his garden sculpture from the damp English winters. These green covers are in place today. He also gave instructions for a special protective box for the most striking single object in the garden: the ancient Egyptian pink granite obelisk from the island of Philae. Magnificent in its simplicity, this souvenir of William's pioneering travels as a young man in Egypt at the beginning of the nineteenth century took years and considerable expense to transport to England. It became a national treasure. No cover was ever made for it, and today patches of moss grow in the cracks. But it still dominates its surroundings, as it once dominated the entrance to the Temple of Isis.

For most of the last three centuries, while this gem of a country house was in the possession of the Bankes family, such detailed care and attention was not lavished on its fine objects, although servants maintained the house and kept it clean. It was compact enough to be, above all, a family home, with children born and dying within its walls, meals cooked beyond its walls and brought in, parties and balls held in its fine reception rooms. Nor were visitors unknown. William Bankes was born into a family already renowned for collecting fine paintings, and important men considered the long pilgrimage to the wilds of Dorset well worth making in order to view them.

Kingston Hall was originally built in the 1660s as a restoration mansion for Sir Ralph Bankes whose collection of pictures – one of the earliest surviving by a member of the gentry – made the house famous. In 1739 Joshua Reynolds, accompanied by Samuel Johnson, paid a visit to Mr Banks [sic] of Dorsetshire. Reynolds is said to have remarked that he had never appreciated the genius of Sir Peter Lely, who was a friend of Sir Ralph, until he had seen the Lely portraits at Kingston Lacy. But Doctor Johnson was apparently little interested in the pictures and retired to a corner where, to quote Boswell, he began

> stretching out his right leg as far as he could reach before him then bringing up his left leg and stretching his right still further on. The old gentleman observing him went up to him and, in a very courteous manner, assured him that though it was a not a new house, the flooring was perfectly safe. The doctor started from his reverie, like a person waked out of his sleep, but spoke not a word.[2]

Sir Joseph Banks, no relation, also visited, some years later in 1767:

> Went this morn to Kingston Hall in the Vale of Wimbourne to see Mr Banks, my namesake, an old bachelor of 70 and more. His house is an exceeding good one but quite of the last age as there is not one sash in the whole. Its furniture, however, of pictures is very capital; a collection of Sir Peter Lellys portraits very fine; two Spanish boys eating fruit by Morellio, a landscape by Bergem, a copy or original of Rembrandt's Rabbi. But four pictures are remarkably capital,

perhaps Guido; they represent Pope Gregory the Great, the Great St. Augustine and two more of the fathers; but Mr Banks has no catalogue and knows very little about them.[3]

Sir Ralph was the grandson of one John Bankes, born in Keswick in 1569 of modest yeoman stock. But John's son, Sir John Bankes, born in 1589, rose to become a brilliant lawyer; as Lord Chief Justice of the Common Pleas, he was a key supporter of the King during the Civil War and first gave the Bankes name its lustre. Keswick was, according to William John Bankes years later, a place so beautiful 'I wonder how our ancestors could ever quit.'[4] But in 1635 Sir John bought Corfe Castle in Dorset, with all its manors, rights and privileges, from Lady Elizabeth Coke. No longer fortified, it was a fine example of medieval military architecture and came with land at Kingston Lacy, near Wimborne. This name derived from the ancient lords, the Lacys, Earls of Lincoln who once owned it, together with the Shapwick of Blandford. But Sir John had little time to spend there with his family as he was constantly in demand to advise the King.

His wife Mary, only daughter and heiress of Ralph Hawtry of Ruislip, County Middlesex, came from more aristocratic stock, through her maternal line, the Althams. The Hawtrys claimed Norman lineage. Mary proved her courage and endurance by withstanding two long sieges of Corfe Castle by parliamentary forces when Corfe was the only Royalist stronghold between Exeter and London. For months she managed with little fresh food and heating supplies, surrounded by the enemy, while her husband was in Oxford with the exiled court. After he died in 1644 the future of the Bankes family was entirely in her hands, but she was determined not to surrender. Only once she realised the extent to which she had been betrayed in 1646 – by treachery which enabled Parliamentary troops, in disguise, to enter the castle – did she demand a truce in order to save lives. The rebel commander, Colonel Bingham, in recognition of her fortitude over three long hard years, allowed her to leave in dignity and safety with her children, along with the seals and keys of Corfe Castle. All her magnificent possessions – tapestries, rugs, Elizabethan silver and furniture, velvet hangings and fine linens — were left behind.

After the surrender, Parliament ordered that the Castle be sacked. Far more was destroyed than necessary to make the Castle untenable, but not before the rebels had plundered it, dividing its sumptuous contents. Even timber and stone were appropriated by anti-Royalist county families, causing generations of hatred, as the Bankes family believed that many fine mansions in Dorset were built from the wreckage of the great fortress castle. Only a few pieces of furniture were traced and these events became seared into the family psyche. The ruined castle became a romantic symbol of the Royalist cause, and Brave Dame Mary, as she is known to history, a metaphor for Bankes determination and courage in the face of adversity. So powerful was the myth that George Bankes, William's younger brother not known for his literary leanings, wrote a history of Corfe Castle. William dreamed of rebuilding the castle as his home and his final artistic commission was to immortalise his ancestors in sculpture.

With the Restoration of Charles II in 1660 Mary's son Ralph Bankes, who, like many Royalists following Charles I's execution had spent much of the 1640s abroad, was knighted and appointed a Gentleman of the Privy Chamber as a reward for his family's loyalty. His mother and her children had paid large sums of money to regain the remains of the family property confiscated by Parliament. But on 11 April 1661 Brave Dame Mary died, coincidentally the same day that Sir Ralph married Mary Brune of Athelhampton, an heiress worth £1,200 a year. Her dowry helped his plans to build a new family seat some twenty miles from Corfe on the supposed site of a palace of the West Saxon kings. Like William in a later generation, he had not expected to inherit but his older brother, John, had died unmarried at the age of thirty in 1656.

Sir Ralph had trained as a lawyer and sat as an MP representing the family seat of Corfe Castle from 1658. His parliamentary duties often took him to London, and by the 1660s he was part of a cultured circle which Charles II attracted to the court at Whitehall which included Sir Peter Lely, the most fashionable painter of the age. It may have been while John and Ralph were travelling, mostly in France and Italy studying classical Roman architecture, that they met the gentleman-architect, Roger Pratt, who returned to England in 1649 with strong ideas about the inferior state of architecture in his country. Pratt built mostly for well-educated gentry like Sir Ralph, who understood the niceties of classical architecture but had fewer servants than the aristocratic country-house builders of the previous century and lived more domestically and privately. His first house, Coleshill in Berkshire, which burnt down in 1952, was considered his masterpiece and was widely copied. William knew it well and admired it. When Sir Ralph, his natural classical taste developed by his travels in Italy, had recovered his property and was ready to erect a splendid new mansion for his family, he turned to Pratt.

The house Pratt designed for Sir Ralph Bankes around 1663 was largely finished by 1665. Built of red brick with stone quoins, it was four stories high, comprising an attic, a basement and two main reception floors, with an impressive flight of stairs leading to the main entrance on the north side. There were three windows either side of this and the protruding front section with pediment also had three windows. Whatever alterations were subsequently made to the house, this external arrangement, in essence, was never to change. Pratt also included a round domed cupola and a rooftop balustrade. The interior was intended as a place to display works of art as Sir Ralph, like many a Royalist, was determined to display his love of beautiful objects, and the Great Chamber or Great Dining Room for entertaining was upstairs on the bedroom floor. This was probably not fully fitted out until 1665, by which time the family had managed to claim back some of the paintings which had hung in Corfe Castle, such as the four portraits by Van Dyck of Charles I and his family. All four were given by King Charles to Sir John. In addition, Sir Ralph invited his friend Peter Lely as his guest to Kingston Lacy when three of his seven sisters sat to the artist for their portraits. They were hung by Ralph in the library, where they have remained. The library's many other treasures are thought to have been purchased by John and Ralph on their travels during the

Civil War. Lely, born in Germany of Dutch parents, had already painted Sir Ralph himself in the latter 1650s as a youngish man with long golden curls and pale skin, sitting resplendent in his rich golden-brown coat with lace ruffles at the wrist. He appears as a man of grace and gravity, culture and elegance, which indeed he was. But Lely's fame derived from his talent at celebrating feminine beauty and his luscious portraits of women in mildly salacious poses. The Lely portraits at Kingston Lacy are judged to be among the artist's finest and that of Arabella Bankes, one of Sir Ralph's sisters, considered 'unsurpassed in Lely's career', according to Sir Oliver Millar, Surveyor of the Queen's pictures from 1972 to 1988. There is no portrait of Sir Ralph's wife, possibly because she was pregnant at the time of Lely's visit. Lely also helped Bankes to acquire the work of other artists from the Netherlands. Sometime between 1656 and 1659 Bankes bought *Two Peasant Boys Eating Fruit* by the then barely known contemporary Spanish artist, Bartolomé Estebán Murillo. Although no longer thought to be an original work this is still considered a fine quality copy, notable as the first of Murillo's images to arrive in England and one of the first examples of Spanish seventeenth-century painting collected in the country.* Other drawings and miniatures bought by Sir Ralph include two religious works: *Christ before Pontius Pilate* in the style of Simon Bening (c. 1525) and *The Last Supper* by a follower of Jean Bourdichon (c. 1500), and *Mars and Venus*, copy of a miniature by Peter Oliver after a painting by Titian. These fine works were the familiar furniture of William Bankes's boyhood.

Notwithstanding his wife's dowry, the Kingston Lacy enterprise had stretched Sir Ralph to his limits. In 1670 he sold his wife's inheritance and placed his own land in the hands of trustees. He was seriously in debt by 1675, when he wrote his will, which displayed a trait inherited by his descendant William nearly two

---

* Experts today consider that because of political strife between Britain and Spain at this time the copy is more likely to have been made outside Spain, possibly in Antwerp.

hundred years later, deep concern that his collection pass to the next generation.

'I will that my Study of Bookes, my mapps, my pictures, my medailes, and other Curiosities and piece of Antiquity shall be reserved for my eldest son and not disposed of by my Trustees amongst the rest of the Personall estate towards the payment of debts.'

When Sir Ralph died in 1677, his twelve-year-old son was obliged to let the house to the Duke of Ormonde, who died at Kingston Lacy eleven years later. This was the nadir of the Bankes family fortunes. Their gradual recovery owed much to the prudence and careful accounting of Margaret Parker, daughter of Sir Henry Parker of Honington, Warwickshire, who married the third John Bankes in 1691. Only three of her ten children survived into adulthood, sparing the family the burden of dowries and houses. Yet despite her careful recording of every purchase made to re-furnish and re-equip Kingston Lacy, money was always tight. Then disaster struck when her husband John, aged forty-nine, was shot in the head one morning when a loaded blunderbuss he kept by his bedside caught up in his dressing-gown and discharged.

The next Bankes heir, another John, was only twenty-two when he inherited. He lived until eighty and during his unremarkable fifty-year stewardship undertook some refurbishment of the house in the 1730s; in 1736, when the threat of structural collapse – caused by the removal of the 'pergolo' (a linking gallery) and the columns that were part of it, by his father thirty years previously- forced him to repair the roof. He had it rebuilt without Pratt's cupola, which then tilted eighteen inches, and balustrade. Apart from this, he acquired a reputation as a miser, eccentric and recluse who neglected his estates and died unmarried. His frugality had, however, enabled him to pay off some outstanding debts.

His brother Henry, William John's grandfather, barrister, MP, distinguished King's Counsel as well as Commissioner of Customs, took over the estate aged seventy-four. Although he had only four years in charge and already suffered from the painful, often untreatable ailment of kidney stones when he inherited, his dynamism appears undimmed, and over the next two generations the family situation moved from relative poverty to comfortable prosperity, largely thanks to actions he set in motion. His wide legal and entrepreneurial experience enabled him to negotiate proper contracts with his stewards, put tenancies on a businesslike footing and give notice to quit to at least thirty squatters. In 1773, having sold most of the government stock accumulated by his brother and himself, he was able to buy Shapwick Champayne, the estate adjacent to Kingston Lacy, for £26,500. This was more than double what his brother had spent in total during the previous fifty years on agricultural and house property combined and would not have been possible without the judicious second marriage he made in 1753. In that year – his first wife, Eleanor (née Symonds), having died childless – he married Margaret Wynne, daughter of the Rt. Rev. John Wynne, Bishop of Bath and Wells, nearly thirty years his junior. The Wynnes were a family of culture and wealth, both of which were to reinvigorate the Bankes family. In 1732 Margaret's father had bought the Soughton Estates in the County of Flint; he died there on 15 July 1743. Bishop Wynne had many sermons published but was best known for his publication of *An Abridgement of Locke's essay on the Human Understanding*, a book commended by Locke himself, which Margaret's brother, the Rt. Hon. Sir William Wynne, a judge of the Admiralty, Privy Councillor and Master of Trinity Hall would urge his young nephew, William Bankes, to read.

Even before he owned Kingston Lacy, Henry also took in hand the troublesome but potentially highly lucrative Bankes share in a northern England black lead mine. In 1622 Sir John Bankes, helped by his father-in-law Ralph Hawtry, had bought a highly speculative half share in a mine in Borrowdale, Cumberland. Lead, or wad, had recently been discovered in the area apparently after an ash tree had blown down in a gale and the soil around its roots had revealed a rich moss or sop of wad. Originally the wad – not called graphite until 1789 – was used for drawing a faint grey line when inserted into a quill. It was clean, dry and easy to use and if a mistake were made could be erased with a piece of bread. Locals maintained that a teaspoonful of black lead dust or powder in beer or milk was an infallible remedy for 'the chollick and constantly used for that purpose in the neighbourhood of Keswick'.

The high quality Borrowdale lead had another use that was to prove most lucrative: coating moulds in metal casting. It was a natural dry lubricant which could withstand intense heat without changing form. This characteristic had been long known and would become a vital strategic war material used for casting bombshells and cannonballs. But demand was slow at first and until a more scientific method of mining was discovered, it was expensive to extract. For much of the eighteenth century, according to a report made by the Bankes family, even professional and scientific miners and mineralogists admitted to inspect the works did not believe that regular veins existed on the hill or that the black-lead mines in the Manor of Borrowdale were commercially viable. Yet Sir John had taken a risk in buying and his great-grandson Henry, recognising that demand was increasing, was determined to exploit that initiative. His older brother John, faced with a long history of thieving and smuggling via a network of local receivers ensuring that little profit reached the proprietors, favoured selling off the family share. Given the distance involved from Dorset to Borrowdale, his reaction is understandable. Henry, however, was more single-minded. He commissioned a report which showed that a key reason why the proprietors were being defrauded was the iniquity of their stewards, who 'lay hold of every opportunity of opening the mines and every attempt to purloin the lead under the pretence of securing it from the thieves. Not only are they selling it on their own account but, to compleat [*sic*] their villainy, they conceal the quantity dug and what they sell for the proprietors is always sold in private and in a clandestine manner and to the most notorious dealers in stolen lead.' The year after this report, Henry steered an Act through both Houses of Parliament which made receiving black lead a felony, ensured that convicted robbers were to be transported and all sales were now transferred to London. He also made changes at the mine developing a guardhouse system to make access more secure and building a steward's house with clear views up to the mines.* Over the next twenty years he gained a controlling interest in the mines for the Bankes family and, when any objectors lodged claims, he fought them in the courts or found other ways to cajole them into submission.

By the time Henry died in 1776, income from the lead mines was much more secure. Towards the end of the century, as graphite became immensely more valuable, Henry's son took further initiatives to stop the pilfering. Thanks to these efforts, by the early 1780s the Bankes share of the black lead mines was worth £1,000 a year, which provided most of the working capital for the two great projects at Kingston Lacy that decade: the enclosing of the estate and the rebuilding of the house. Not until the French chemist Nicolas-Jacques Conte, forced by the exigencies of the Napoleonic Wars to come up with an alternative – ground graphite, mixed with clay and baked – was the Bankes family monopoly seriously threatened. Until 1815 they controlled the only source of pure natural graphite then known. Soon other technological advances allowed inferior graphite to be used in pencils and, by the mid-nineteenth century, the mine finally submitted to pressure from foreign markets and closed down. At its peak around 1810, when William was indulging himself at Cambridge, the family's share brought them £1,500 a year, sufficient for an artistic son to feed a habit of collecting beautiful possessions.

Henry and Margaret's first son, John, died in childhood. But in 1757, when Henry was nearly sixty and the Bankes line dangerously close to extinction, they produced a second son, also called Henry, followed by a daughter, Anne. Henry Bankes the younger inherited when he was nineteen and still at Cambridge but this did not prevent him indulging in a two-year tour of Italy. In Rome, at his mother's insistence, he sat to the most fashionable portrait painter of the day for English Grand Tourists, Pompeo Batoni, although he

---

* This building still stands and came to the National Trust along with Corfe Castle and Kingston Lacy in 1981 in the will of Ralph Bankes.

did not consider Batoni's portraits 'equal to those of Reynolds'.[5] 'I shall sit to Batoni tomorrow as you have determined on it,' he told his widowed mother in September,[6] noting that at least 'his daughter is an uncommonly fine singer.' The painting was ready two months later: 'I have had the greatest difficulty in making him keep it quite simple in a dark coat. It is certainly like me, but without any sort of Taste or good painting,' he wrote crossly.[7] 'I think it but a melancholy, cold picture whose only merit is being simple and having nothing offensive.'[8] He also met there two architectural students from the Royal Academy Schools who were studying in Rome, John Soane and his friend Robert Furze Brettingham. Conversations with them possibly turned his mind to the need for alterations to the ancestral home. At all events, in November 1779, Brettingham's gifted friend Soane, who became famous as the architect of the Bank of England and owner of a vast collection of Greek and Roman marbles who bequeathed his house and collection to the nation, drew up some plans for Henry. These were based on measurements sent out by Robert's uncle, Matthew Brettingham junior, for a new downstairs eating parlour as well as a suggestion for moving the kitchen from the south-east corner to the much larger great cellar in the centre of the north side under the saloon. Although Soane's not especially inspired proposals came to nothing, his enthusiasm to remodel the Pratt interior of Kingston Lacy may have encouraged Henry. Surviving correspondence between Henry in Rome and his mother makes no mention of his meeting architects or contemplating changes to the house, indicating that he had not yet decided what form alterations should take. When his mother complained of lack of information he replied tersely, if not cruelly: 'My dear Mother, there is no subject I would not discuss with you if I thought you were interested.'[9]

Returning home in his early twenties, he set about enclosing the vastly expanded estates, now stretching over some 60,000 prime acres from Purbeck and Corfe Castle in the south of the county to Kingston Lacy in the north – a work started by his father who employed William Woodward to undertake a survey, completed in

1775, as a prelude to enclosure. Enclosure in England was at its height from between 1750 and 1860, when small freeholders lost their ancient common grazing rights in the name of greater agricultural efficiency.

Henry also entered Parliament, representing the family seat of Corfe Castle from 1780 until 1826, after which he was MP for Dorset, a tradition of parliamentary service which had continued through five generations of Bankes. Henry was a good public speaker noted for his independent spirit who became a prominent Tory MP with a wide interest in issues of national importance. What friends might term stubborn others derided as reactionary. He also took seriously his duties as country gentleman and wealthy landowner and was active in local affairs.

On 11 August 1784, early in his parliamentary career, Henry married Frances Woodley. Frances's father William (1728–93) was a well-to-do sugar planter in the Caribbean island of St Christopher and was later appointed Governor of the Leeward Islands, a post he held until his death in 1793. The family never had a home in England but rented houses when they visited, and in 1781 the Woodley family was staying in Bath, where Frances 'shone in the first circles of fashion; she drew all eyes and warmed all hearts'.[10] Perhaps Henry was among those captivated by her 'beauty, ease, politeness and elegance'. In 1766 Woodley had commissioned Johan Zoffany to paint his young family. Frances, then a sweet looking six-year-old and the eldest of four, is handing a rose to her young brother. By twenty she was ravishing when George Romney portrayed her, three years before she married Henry Bankes, in a suggestively loose cream gown with her auburn hair piled high. Our notion of Frances as an oustanding beauty of her day derives partly from this celebrated image, although Romney was so popular as a portrait painter partly because he understood how to enhance natural beauty. Unlike most painters at the time he had had access to life models while training, and from this he learnt how to exaggerate the neck and limbs to brilliant effect, as he did in this picture. Not only was Miss Woodley beautiful, she also provided a dowry of £6,000 (approximately

£362,000 today), extremely useful for Henry's plans to modernise the house. Two years before the marriage, Henry had returned to Rome and invited Robert Furze Brettingham, the young architect he had met there earlier, to undertake the remodelling. Today Brettingham's fame rests largely on his designs for several prisons, notably those at Reading, Northampton and Poole. But he erected a number of well thought of country mansions as well as the classical Temple of Concord at Audley End, before retiring early in the nineteenth century, after his marriage to a wealthy widow.

Major alterations began just after Henry and Frances were married and lasted six years. Henry's main requirement was to establish a great dining or entertaining room downstairs, upstairs great chambers being by then out of fashion; the one at Kingston Hall had already been abandoned by 1708. Instead, a dining room was created downstairs in the north-west apartment with a new, larger kitchen outside the house, also on the north west side. In addition, Brettingham added a pretty pergola to the south front and designed a new basement entrance with an Ionic porch in the east front of the house, on Pratt's stable yard. This led up new internal stone stairs to the centre of the house, which took up the space of Pratt's great back staircase. Brettingham divided the magnificent Imperial staircase, which no longer had its ceremonial significance of leading to the great chamber, between a less impressive but adequate family stair and a new all-purpose service stair to replace Pratt's back stairs and stairs in the closets. Other changes included new sash windows everywhere, with those in the ballroom being extended down to floor level and including a new central one replacing Pratt's front door. Henry also commissioned an icehouse, completed in 1790 at a cost of 11 pounds, 3 shillings and 3 pence.

During these years Frances was creating a family. In all, she gave birth to seven children; the first five arrived in quick succession while the building and decorating works were in progress and were largely taken care of by Mrs Hills and Nurse. Henry, the eldest, was born on 30 July 1785, William, 1786, George, 1787, then Anne in 1789 and finally Maria in 1791. Edward was born three years later in 1794 and Frederick, who died in infancy, in 1799. Clearly extra sleeping accommodation was needed and a new bedroom was duly added over the new stone stairs.

To celebrate the house's first major alterations for a century, the Bankes gave a grand ball on Monday, 19 December 1791 to which a hundred and forty guests were invited. Had Pratt's windswept north front door still opened directly on to the ballroom, a winter ball, freezing the ladies in their decolletage, would have been risible. So perhaps Frances and Henry were enjoying showing off to their guests, who had been instructed to arrive on this cold winter's night 'exactly at eight' and who came in via the new basement level entrance door and ascended the new stone stairs to the door of the ballroom, which was fastened open for the evening. They turned left so that Frances and Henry could receive them first in the library, newly 'fitted up in yellow', proceeded to the drawing room and either went directly to the ballroom or could take refreshment first from a long narrow table erected in Frances's bedroom. The Bankes were offering tea, white and red wine negus (hot sweetened wine and water), orgeat (a cooling drink made from barley or almonds and orange flower water), lemonade 'and everything that people usually call for upon these occasions'.[11]

Frances had worked with determination to make the evening a success and fancied that she had triumphed as she wrote to her mother-in-law, Margaret, soon after the 'Fete'. Important local families had been invited, such as the Bonds, also Members of Parliament, with whom it was understandably important to make a good impression. Frances was evidently sophisticated enough to realise that what might be necessary to impress London society was not necessarily demanded in the country. She told her mother-in-law she had placed on her new dressing table powder puffs, powder and lavender water and left the room opened and well lit 'and tho' it is a common thing enough in London yet I found it struck people in general more than many article attended with greater expense.

'We had ten ladies' maids who waited at the tea table and they all happened by accident to be dressed exactly alike in pink and white, which had a very good effect.' Later, for dinner, the Bankes borrowed all the men servants out of livery in the neighbourhood, 'who were particularly clever and attentive in waiting, and I really believe that not a single creature had occasion to call twice for any one thing, which is a great deal to say in so large a company.'

The tea makers, she explained, 'could go in and out for everything they wanted without disturbing the company and people in general must have been better off than usual from having a place to go where they were sure to find a constant supply of Cakes etc during the whole evening.'

Constantly boiling water was kept on Mr Bankes's dressing room fire. In conclusion, Frances said she flattered herself 'there never was so large a company better supplied with hot tea and Negus. I likewise saved my new carpets very much by having nothing of that sort handed about.'

Guests entering the ballroom would have been struck by the beautiful coved ceiling 'with a noble lustre in the middle' painted the previous year with delicate neo-classical motifs by Cornelius Dixon. This was offset by white and gold cornices, a frieze and white and gold curtain boxes over the windows from which hung delicate pink curtains – like entering Aladdin's Palace, as one guest gushed. Here the visitors were entertained by musicians from Salisbury and the dancing lasted until one o'clock when the eating rooms and north parlour doors were opened to display a 'very handsome supper' (Frances had made a small economy by serving no dessert other than ices). Immediately after supper the dancing began again and lasted until about seven in the morning without a break. This success, according to Frances, was because they had a much greater number of young men than young ladies, 'by which means the ugliest women in the room were sure to dance every dance unless they preferred sitting still, which kept them all in high good humour'. From seven until eight thirty breakfast was served, after which everyone left, and the house guests, those who had travelled furthest included Frances's own mother, also called

Frances (née Payne), her younger brother and his wife, finally retired to bed.

Frances – a difficult employer by her own admission – then summoned her servants and instructed them not to retire until the house was thoroughly cleaned and returned to order 'as if nothing had happened'.

Imagine the children's excitement that night. The 'five brats' had tea at four o'clock in their upstairs sitting room, were made to sleep for two hours and then dressed up, but ordered not to come down until Frances, impatient to show them off, rang for them. Mrs Hills, who seems to have fulfilled the role of nanny, and Nurse then brought them all into the ballroom, ranged in a row, so that 'it was a very pretty sight and they all enjoyed it more than I should have imagined'. Maria, the baby, alarmed at so many people, was returned to bed within half an hour. William, aged five and his just older brother Henry, rather tired towards the latter end of the evening, were taken up by Mrs Hills who retired to bed at the same time. Three-year-old Anne, protesting her energy even at midnight, begged that she might sit up as long as the other ladies, so it was Frances who took both her and George to bed.

'You may guess I have had very little leisure this week,' Frances recounted to her mother-in-law. Frances, evidently fond of Margaret Bankes, who lived in Duke Street, London until her death aged ninety-two in 1822, shared every detail of the occasion with her 'knowing you are interested in whatever concerns us', but begged her not to divulge the contents of the letter with anyone else to whom 'so circumstantial an account must be horrid tiresome and perhaps not very intelligible'. She told Margaret that she hoped to see her next month in London with all the children. 'It is so long since they have been in town that every thing will be new to them and a matter of wonder.' She saw little of her own parents since they never bought an English property.

The changes to the house seem to have satisfied Henry and Frances, who concluded that no further improvement projects were required. Yet their son William, as soon as he grew old enough to be critical, was indeed so. He continually urged further changes on his father, and suggested other architects. He drew his authority from his belief that what Brettingham and his father had done in obliterating the Pratt interiors was to leave a house 'that was neither old nor modern . . . but a bad mixture of both'.[12]

2

Education

~

'The Father of all Mischiefs'
Byron to John Murray

FRANCES DOTED ON her flaxen-haired second son, William John. Born on 11 December 1786, just seventeen months after Henry, and baptised the following month, he seems from the first to have persuaded her to single him out among her children for his special sensitivity and talents. Both godfathers were chosen from his mother's side, two William Woodleys – grandfather Woodley, the colonial Governor, and the less distinguished cousin Woodley of Eccles in Norfolk – like his godmother, his grandmother Margaret Bankes (née Wynne). William was a baptismal name given to every first-born son in the Woodley family since 1620, and a Wynne family name, although the two Wynne uncles, John and the Rt. Hon. Sir William, had stood as godfathers to the first-born, Henry.

Frances noted in a baby journal that William at birth was 'to all appearances quite as stout and as healthy a child as his brother. He was indeed so perfectly free even from any of those little disorders of the bowels to which children are so very subject that I never gave him any medicine whatever. Hunter [presumably John Hunter, 1728–93] inoculated him the 23 feb 1787 . . . but after the operation he desired that the wet nurse might only have the porter allowed her that she normally drank and she was to eat no butter.'[1] Although Frances went through days of worry before he was fully recovered, she was following the best available medical advice in having him inoculated against smallpox. The procedure was not universally successful as the lightly inoculated child could infect others around him but it was still recommended as safer than risking uncontrolled infection. Jenner's much safer vaccination process was introduced only in 1798. According to their grandmother, the five eldest children, despite Hunter's inoculation, had smallpox, whooping cough, scarlet fever, chicken pox, mumps and 'all the disorders under the sun excepting the plague'. In April 1799, when William was thirteen, his newborn brother Frederick was inoculated but died of the illness a few weeks later. If William was away at school he probably never saw this brother, who lived only a few months.

Frances appears to have been a modern mother in her attitudes to discipline as much as medicine. The two became closely linked in the late eighteenth century; as improved obstetrics and reduction of diseases such as smallpox dramatically reduced infant mortality, interest grew in education and childcare. For the first time, a child was seen as a being with rights and privileges of its own. The Wynnes were likely to be in the vanguard of such progressive ideas, given the family interest in the philosopher John Locke. Locke's *Some Thoughts Concerning Education*, published in 1693, must have been known to Frances, perhaps suggested by a helpful mother-in-law. The *Ladies Library* published a version which went through eight editions between 1714 and 1772. Several other manuals appeared, mostly by doctors or medical men, with advice on food and clothing as well as the education and management of children. Breast-feeding, a natural process, was encouraged for all mothers. But Frances's reference to a wet nurse indicates she did not breast-feed her children herself.

Although she had help from Nurse and Mrs Hills, from whom she expected modesty and diffidence in conduct and manner of dress, she clearly relished having a close relationship with her young children. They were not permanently banished to the day nursery, a bright room with two large windows overlooking the south lawns doubtless filled with sturdy wooden toys not so different from those today. Sometimes Frances allowed her offspring to run around noisily in the main reception rooms, close to her, distracting though they were. When guests were present Mrs Hill's job was to keep them in order and prevent them being rude or troublesome. But an avid follower of child care fashions would know that the mother herself had to oversee important issues of education and manners, including teaching children to read.

The Bankes children led an outdoor life. In summer they went for walks, learnt to ride donkeys and occasionally visited Brownsea Castle where they spent happy hours on the beach. Other times, they went to stay in London with their Bankes grandmother, of whom they were all extremely fond. Once, when William was nine, after a small problem of sibling rivalry Frances had to write to her son Henry pleading for understanding: 'William, to please me, will I am sure break himself entirely of his fondness for singularity. We are few of us exempt from faults but I am very desirous you should all of you have as few as possible.'[2]

William's childhood was one of security, material comfort and maternal adoration. The girls were taught at home – a curriculum that included embroidery – and William, who formed a close bond with his sister, Anne, and his brothers evidently profited from the lessons given by the drawing master. There was probably a visiting music master, too, as William's aunt, Anne Bankes, had been taught by the renowned Dr Burney, (father of Fanny) and household accounts in the 1770s record lessons with another music master as well as bills for Bach's concertos, Shobert's sonatas (*sic*), tuning the Piano Forte and tickets to the opera. From the first, emphasis was put on developing the children's visual talents – not surprising as Frances herself was a gifted amateur artist, who made pastel copies of works by Hoare, Reynolds and Greuze and enjoyed teaching her sister-in-law, Anne Bankes. A folder filled with dozens of unsigned sketches survives, and it is tempting to presume that the best of these were executed by William.

In 1795 he must have felt some of this comfort and security evaporate when, aged nine, he went to Westminister School, along with his older and younger brothers, Henry and George, and like their father before them. Westminster is a medieval school of monastic foundation in the heart of London. The study of ancient Greek and Latin was at the centre of their schooling and the Latin Plays, the first of which was performed for Queen Elizabeth I, were one of its most notable winter features. But the curriculum was wide and the study of Hebrew and Arabic as well as ornithology, architecture, astronomy and mathematics were all encouraged. By the seventeenth century it was considered the most distinguished school in the country. The great aristocratic families started sending their sons there and a high proportion of leading statesmen, scholars, poets, philosophers and politicians emerged through its doors. John Locke was a pupil during the 1640s. By the eighteenth century, the school had four hundred boys and was considered superior to Eton. But by 1790 the balance of MPs educated at Eton was once again greater than those from Westminster. William's father's contemporaries included Samuel Bentham, brother of Jeremy, Charles Abbot, Lord Colchester, later Speaker of the Commons and George Leveson Gower, 1st Duke of Sutherland, a politician and supporter of the Reform Bill and Catholic Emancipation. Old Westminsters were known for their confidence and style; the school, it was said, encouraged in its pupils a certain arrogance bred from a healthy disrespect for mere convention.

For all that, life was disagreeably uncivilised at Westminster in the late eighteenth century. Food was scarce, bullying rife and dormitories were chillingly cold and rat-infested. Lady Mansfield visiting her son, who was ill, is said to have found only one chair in the room upon which the sick boy reclined. 'A friend who was with him was sitting on the coal scuttle. When Lady Mansfield entered the room the lad who was sitting on the coal scuttle got up and, with perfect natural politeness and good breeding, offered it to her ladyship to sit down upon.'[3]

Young gentlemen were sent to this establishment to be hardened almost as much as educated. Frequent fights, not only between boys but also with and between masters, were described as 'a beautiful exhibition of manly form and skill'. Many of Wellington's best officers were Westminster educated. A sensitive boy must have found this hard life excruciating; scarcely surprisingly William neither excelled academically – he failed to win one of several closed scholarships available to Westminster pupils – nor wrote about his days there. He did, however, produce a more than competent drawing of the headmaster, William Vincent, now in the British Museum, indicating that his artistic skills were not neglected. Vincent, headmaster from 1788 to 1802, had a reputation for severity and the school declined under his headship. Perhaps the most useful knowledge William acquired during eight years was an intimacy of the surrounding neighbourhood, in which unspeakable slums encroached on the Palace of Westminster itself.

Apart from family tradition and the school's high intellectual reputation, the family owned an impressive if not especially pretty five-storey house, Number 5, Old Palace Yard, just a few yards away from the school and the medieval Palace of Westminster. This would have enabled Henry, William and George and later Edward to avoid being boarders at Westminster School and, during Parliamentary terms, to see something of their father. It seems they stayed also with their grandmother during term time, as Anne wrote to her of how 'we miss our poor brothers sadly and long already for the Christmas holidays. You must be very happy to have them with you.'[4] Frances more often had to remain in Dorset with the younger children. When not at school, William would have had a fine view of the wide carriage track depositing politicians at the Parliament House from the front of his own home at Old Palace Yard. To the back was, and is, the remains of the medieval jewel tower, built by Edward III in 1365 to house his personal treasures, with a moat dug around it for extra protection. Westminster boys who were the sons of MPs were allowed occasionally to attend a House of Commons debate sitting in the Stranger's Gallery. William would have spent his formative years listening to great orators of the period including Pitt, Fox and Sheridan.

When Henry bought a lease on Old Palace Yard – his name first appears in the rate books in 1794 – the immediate environs were not as grand or smart as, for example, St James or West Mayfair. Old Palace Yard houses, built in the mid-eighteenth century, were conven-ient and moderately priced in a relatively mixed area. Some houses here would have been owned, some let for the season and some government houses. Almost all Henry's immediate neighbours were MPs, often with second homes in the country, and they included William Wilberforce, who became a close friend; Henry, Wilberforce and Wellington were so often in each other's company that they were sometimes described by contemporaries as a political trio. Henry's purchase of Old Palace Yard is a reflection of how much he loved Parliament.

For William, after nearly eight years enduring Westminster's rough discipline, escape in 1803 to the tranquility and privileged life of Trinity College, Cambridge must have afforded much relief. The links between Trinity and Westminster were strong; between 1695 and 1803 five head or under masters were Trinity men. Nonetheless, William's father and brothers all went to the older but smaller Trinity Hall, Cambridge – George winning a scholarship – where the boys' great uncle, Sir William Wynne, was Master. Only William, singled out for special treatment perhaps to separate him from his brother Henry who was already at Trinity Hall, went to Trinity. Founded by King Henry VIII in 1546, Trinity was and remains the University's largest college and one of its richest. Isaac Newton came up in 1661 and did most of his important mathematical work there. By the end of the eighteenth century, Trinity began to earn a reformist repu-tation for leading the University in the teaching of new scientific subjects and introducing examinations. But when sixteen-year-old William arrived, Trinity, like other colleges, was still struggling to emerge from a period of decline and intellectual decay where lectures were few and the pursuit of pleasure predominant.

Trinity today looks much as it did in Bankes's time in the early nineteenth century. The Great Gate still leads into the Great Court, with its magnificent 1601 fountain and cloistered surround in Tudor Gothic style and the Wren Library, with its delicate Grinling Gibbons carvings, is breathtakingly beautiful. Bankes's five or so leisured years in these surroundings surely helped to mould his aesthetic sense. He always admired Gibbons's work and decades later was praised for the way he encouraged Italian craftsmen to copy the master's designs for Kingston Lacy.

William soon gained a reputation at Cambridge, if not for academic excellence in his chosen subject, classics – he also attended 'very good' mathematics lectures – then for his singular taste in interior decoration and exuberance. Here, at last, he could indulge his own artistic ideas and decorate his Great Court rooms in high Gothic style with 'an altar at which he daily burned incense.'[5] Sir William Wynne encouraged him, sending him prints of Exeter and Durham cathedrals, with a comment: 'I apprehend what you have already . . . will supply you with as many Gothick ornaments as can well be employed in the intended improvements of your rooms.'[6] According to a Trinity contemporary, Bankes 'fitted up some of his rooms in imitation of a Catholic Chapel and used to have the Singing Boys in dress suitable to the occasion, come and sing there for him, and it was constantly asked "what the devil does Mr Bankes do with those singing boys?"'[7] William had three rooms at Trinity: a large drawing room – 'about the size of one of the front rooms in Palace Yard. It is uncommonly neatly, though not expensively, furnished, and my bedroom is very suitable to it with all its accoutrements,' he told his grandmother. 'I have also a third room which has no fireplace and I use it rather as a light closet than a dwelling room. Three of my windows look into the quadrangle and one looks backward with a view of Caius College, Trinity Hall and King's Chapel . . . My library is a very great and very useful ornament to my rooms, which are now as well furnished as any in college.'[8]

From the first opportunity, William cared about his own immediate surroundings and was acutely observant of others'. He never entirely shed his fondness for the Gothic, a taste possibly influenced by the notorious multi-millionaire homosexual, William Beckford, whose scandal involving the whipping of a young boy had erupted just about the time Bankes was born. Beckford, maverick collector and generous patron of the arts, was also the precocious author of the oriental tale *Vathek*, written in 1782 at the age of twenty-two, and whose celebrated Gothic creation, Fonthill Abbey, was famously under construction just as William went up to Trinity. By the time Beckford moved in to the unfinished Abbey in 1807, the nation was gripped by 'Fonthill Fever', a curiosity and excitement to see the Gothic folly that, in the public imagination at least, was imbued with elements of secrecy, mystery and darkly brooding extravagance. In an undated letter to his grandmother around this time William tells her that he has recently visited Montacute and was delighted by that house 'as it has two of the most magnificent Gothick fronts that I have ever met with'.

In the autumn of 1805 William, well settled and already notorious, was introduced to a new undergraduate from Harrow School: George Gordon sixth Lord Byron. William, at nineteen, was older, wealthier and far more confident of himself than the seventeen-and-a-half-year old Byron, who was as painfully aware of his relatively impoverished and uncertain family circumstances as of his deformed foot and corpulence. According to John Cam Hobhouse, the future Whig radical politician Lord Broughton, in a note in his copy of Moore's *Life*, the Rev. Thomas Jones, Byron's tutor, effected the introduction. Hobhouse, notable for founding the Cambridge Whig Club, came from a well-off Bristol family and had been an exact contemporary of William's at Westminster. He was to become Byron's most intimate friend and travelled with him to the East in 1809. Bankes, to whom he owed the friendship, he never liked, considering him arrogant and pretentious. Perhaps he also sensed a fatal recklessness in Bankes and, wishing to protect his friends and himself from what he feared might be a baneful influence, was at pains to distance himself and his friends from this rich and charismatic charmer.

'I was miserable and untoward to a degree,' Byron later described his state of mind at this time. 'I was wretched at leaving Harrow, to which I had become attached during the last two years of my stay there; wretched at going to Cambridge instead of Oxford (there were no rooms vacant at Christchurch): wretched from some private domestic circumstances of different kinds, and consequently about as unsocial as a wolf taken from the troop,'[9] he reflected shortly before he died. He may have exaggerated his unhappiness in later life but there is no doubt that Bankes, long before others were magnetised by Byron's fame and beauty, was immediately responsive. Many assumed the pair must have been at school together as the immediate friendship was not an obvious one. Byron, the aristocrat wearing distinctive nobleman's robes who worshipped Napoleon, and William, the gentleman commoner, son of an arch Tory whose family was close to Wellington, found what drew them together rather than that which separated them. But relations were at times edgy, perhaps fostered by Hobhouse.

'I know the Mr Bankes you mention,' Byron once told a friend, 'though not to that *Extreme* you seem to think, but I am flattered by his "boasting" on such a subject . . . for I never thought him likely to boast of anything which was not his own.'[10] Yet they continued to correspond until Byron's death in 1824 – a correspondence of honesty and warmth on both sides – and the relationship provides an important key to understanding Bankes in his youth.

> I suspect that I am one of the very few that are left to you, [Bankes wrote in 1822] who, much as I admire your writings, do not when I think of you, approach you exclusively with them, nor with your fame, who continue to feel towards you just as I did before you ever published, and to think of you, as, had I the fame that you have, I would wish that you should think of me.[11]

During his first university year Byron was somewhat in awe of the more sophisticated and critical William Bankes, whom he described as 'my collegiate pastor, and master, and patron . . . good-naturedly tolerant of my ferocities.' Byron soon became part of a Cambridge 'fast set', comprising, in addition to Hobhouse, his old Harrovian schoolmate Edward Long, who acted as swimming and riding companion and Charles Skinner Matthews, a brilliantly wild – if indolent – homosexual ('man of Method') whom Byron met chiefly in Bankes's rooms. Later there was Scrope Berdmore Davies, a witty

womaniser and compulsive gambler six years older than Byron.
Eventually Matthews, Hobhouse, Davies and Byron formed an exclusive quartet of which Bankes was not part. But initially it was Bankes
who, in Byron's fond words of later life when the intense relationships of his youth came into sharper focus, 'ruled the roast – or
rather the roasting – and was father of all mischiefs.'[12]

These 'mischiefs' – partly drinking and carousing – must also have
been connected with Bankes's homosexuality noticed, even if largely
ignored and in the unforgiving climate of the day never publicly
discussed. Years later, Bankes reminded Byron of the time spent in
this little chapel – 'an architectural folly' which 'must recall to both
our minds some singular, some pleasant, some bitter associations'.[13]
But there were peaceful activities too: Byron discovered the poetry
of Sir Walter Scott while sitting in Bankes's rooms, a discovery for
which he was to thank Bankes.

Who was initiating whom in 'mischief' is not obvious. When they
met Byron was probably the more experienced in sexual encounters even though he described himself as 'the humblest of your
servants' while at Trinity.[14] Bankes always believed he had played an
important role in Byron's Cambridge life. And although Hobhouse
comments scathingly that 'Bankes attached himself to Byron's
coronet', he admits that Bankes 'was also of that band of profane
scholars'.[15] Shortly after the poet's death Bankes maintained that he
'was almost the only person Lord Byron was ever much attached
to; that he had implicit confidence in him and used to confide all
his iniquities to him. In early youth they lived very much together
and, in spite of all his vices and though . . . he wd. not have trusted
him with his own sister, yet his genius, his enthusiasm and even his
caprices rendered him so attractive that, though he knew him so
well he could not help liking him.'[16]

For three years at least, Bankes swaggered rather aimlessly at
Cambridge. Few undergraduates, unless impoverished, considered
studying should take precedence over pleasure and the traditional
Bankesian legal career never held any appeal. Sir William, who took
a keen interest in his great nephew's progress, urged him for another

letter 'not quite so laconick as your last . . . One maxim I am sure I am not mistaken is that the way to be happy is to be fully emploied and Cambridge, which to the diligent and studious is of all places I know the most delightful, is to an idle man the dullest and most intolerable.'[17] Yet for all his lack of ambition and apparent bravado, Bankes still sought acceptance as a privileged insider of the Cambridge elite. He was excluded from the private, possibly secret, debating society – later the Cambridge Union – set up exclusively for the entertainment of St John's and Trinity undergraduates, and a document has survived, endorsed by Henry John Temple, the future Lord Palmerston, which shows how much he minded. 'Latin lines by WJ Bankes at Cambridge upon his being caught listening at the door of the Speculative Society.'[18] Perhaps this element of the outsider in Bankes, enforced or not, gave him the sensitivity that brought him occasionally close to Byron. Hobhouse, jealous no doubt, and wishing continued exclusion for Bankes, wrote revealingly to Byron: 'William Bankes is here at the Master's Lodge, Trinity Hall, living in state so he tells me – he told us yesterday that he wanted to buy a horse for hunting – we asked him, Why? "Oh," said he, "you know in Dorsetshire I must hunt for popularity's sake!!!" Is not this complete Corfe Castle all over?'[19]

The freshness and tension of the Bankes–Byron relationship derives largely from Bankes's willingness to discuss Byron's poetry frankly and even criticise it. A risk. In January 1807 Byron arranged for the private printing of his *Poems on Various Occasions*. He did not send a copy to Bankes: to have done so would have forced Bankes to compliment him, he argued. Byron explained with some irony that it was also because 'I know his *talents as critic* to be far superior to mine as a *rhymer*, that I would have rather passed the *ordeal* of an Edinburgh *review*, than offered my unfortunate "*juvenalia*" to his inspection. He has too much of the *Man*, ever to approve the flights of a *Boy* and I await in trembling suspense my crucifiction from his Decree.'[20]

Bankes borrowed a copy from Long and in an unsolicited letter told his friend he found the quality uneven, some parts more pleasing than others, 'which is perhaps no bad ingredient as it is the certain antidote to mediocrity'.[21] Although Bankes was known more for his caustic wit than his literary insight, Byron insisted he was not offended by his remarks. In fact his was a most valuable letter since it was the only response 'in which flattery has borne so slight a part . . . I feel no hesitation in saying, I was more anxious to hear your critique however severe, than the praises of the *Million*.'[22] But he also told Bankes he had a better opinion of his judgment and ability than his feelings and then, somewhat defensively, pointed out how few of the best poems in the language would stand the test of minute criticism. 'Johnson has shown us that No poetry is perfect but to correct mine would be an Herculaean labour; in fact I never looked beyond the moment of composition and published merely at the request of my friends . . . we shall never quarrel on the Subject,' he assured Bankes, 'as poetic fame is by no means the "acme" of my Wishes.'[23]

He then sent a copy anyway, which gave Bankes an excuse to launch into further discussion of the poems. After apologising for not having thanked him more promptly as he was busy trying to gain his degree – 'the empty privilege of calling myself BA' – he wrote: 'A longer acquaintance has reconciled me to some particulars which appeared blemishes at first . . . the stanzas on the death of Cromwell are both vigorous and sublime.' Fully aware of the degree of presumption involved, he goes further and proposes an alteration: 'After all this preamble what will you not expect what mangling, what amputation, what cruel and distorting operation on your works?' Finally, Bankes tells his friend the line he is concerned with: '"By that remember'd or for e'er forgot." In so short a composition the turn should be more pointed and antithetical and such a contraction as e'er, for ever which is almost always integral, should not stand in so conspicuous a place especially where it adds so little force to the expression.' He begged forgiveness for his comments which showed how much he had thought on the matter.[24]

Byron, polite or concerned enough to preserve Bankes's friendship, thanked him for his remarks – even said he wished they were more frequent – and assured him there could be no greater respect for his alteration than by immediately adopting it; 'This shall be done in the next edition.' Privately, Byron could not resist complaining to Long about this 'epistle or Dissertation of 2 large double sheets . . . a *bad* custom, I say.'[25]

Bankes had asked Byron to burn this 'tedious letter', written while he was in extremely low spirits. The reason for his depression, he explained, was the sudden death of his older brother, Henry, who had recently drowned in an accident at sea. Ensign Bankes was on his way to Sicily to join his regiment, the 35th Foot, when on 20 October 1806, his ship, *L'Athenienne*, struck the Esquerries rocks near Tunis and was lost. Many took to a lifeboat and were saved, but Henry apparently refused, believing it safest to remain in the ship. He was last seen trying to swim to a floating fragment of the wreck.

'If you imagine that I have no feelings I do not ask your pity, look upon me with the eyes of the world, consider rather the aggrandizement of my inheritance than my loss of comfort and think me happy.' Drawing a melancholy comparison with the fortunate outcome of Byron's recent lawsuit and consequent increase in his property he commented 'your wealth is not chased by affliction, nor made a mockery of grief by pretending compensation – you have no brother to mourn for and to succeed.'[26]

The sudden death of William's 'dear and affectionate brother' Henry, only one year older, was to change everything. Although at different colleges, William and Henry were close and had seen each other frequently at Cambridge, breakfasting together most days. William, at twenty, was now destined to be head of the family, heir not only to the magnificent Kingston Hall estates but also to those of his elderly great uncle, the Rt. Hon. Sir William Wynne of Soughton Hall. The Wynne Estates, which included the properties of Soughton Hall and Dol-y-Moch and 3,000 acres of hill farmland in the county, would now pass to an unprepared William. As Sir William's heir he also acquired a useful double inheritance and an income of £8,000 a year (approximately £500,000 today) even during his father's lifetime, which though healthy was not outstand-ingly enormous for landed income.* But it also meant he could not play the role of indulged second son for ever. Responsibilities and duties were now his lot. He had not been brought up to expect this. There is a deep sense that the tragedy took from him in the long term far more than he could possibly gain, although the agony of loss which his parents suffered is not mentioned in surviving correspondence. A few months later Joseph Farington wrote in his diary, perhaps unfairly,[27] 'Mr Bankes was extremely affected by the loss of his son; it appeared to make a stronger impression on him than on Mrs Bankes.'

Meanwhile the erudite Sir William, who had always taken great interest in his namesake even before he was his heir, now urged William to remain at college for as long as possible, to show a more serious attitude to his studies, to learn Cicero and to find a method of committing all he learnt to memory. 'I could have wished you might have been a candidate for some of the university prizes in classical learning . . . I hear some of your poetical effusions which do you great credit; why are you so shy of communicating them?'[28] Since William's father had been awarded the Chancellor's Classical medal in 1778 his great uncle and benefactor's none-too-helpful reminder must have rankled. He moved back to London for a time to be with his unhappy family, but decided to spend at least one more year at Cambridge postponing decisions about the rest of his life. He gained his BA in 1808 and his MA in 1811.

---

* By the 1790s the really great Grands Seigneurs like the Dukes of Bedford, Bridgewater, Devonshire and the Egremonts, Shelburnes and Rockinghams had incomes approaching forty or even fifty thousand pounds and were richer than many of the small continental rulers. The houses they built, Petworth, Chatsworth, Wentworth, Woodhouse and Woburn, were palaces. On the other hand almost fifty peers not invariably of the Scottish and Irish variety, derived incomes of less than £7,000 a year from land. (Information from *Creating Paradise* by Richard Wilson and Alan Mackley, Hambledon and London, 2000)

3

Travel

~

'Opportunities which will not occur again . . .'
William Bankes to Henry Bankes

I N 1810, SOON after he came down from Cambridge, twenty-four-
year-old William did what was expected of him and entered
Parliament. He did not have to stand for election; the dying system
of rotten boroughs enabled him to accept one of the Truro seats
which his sister's prospective husband, Edward Boscawen, 4th Viscount
Falmouth, could offer him. Boscawen, who sat in the Lords and was
a rare close friend of William's, hoped that by using the patronage
available to him and returning supporters of the administration he
would be granted an earldom. He was, eventually, in 1821. In turn,
William had to vote as required; but as he never professed strong
political ambitions his lack of independence seems to have troubled
him less than the long hours in the House.

The Parliament he first encountered was consumed by the issue
of the continuing war against Napoleon. Spencer Perceval, previously Chancellor of the Exchequer, had just taken over as Prime
Minister from the Duke of Portland; the Foreign Secretary was
Marquess Wellesley, older brother of the then Viscount Wellington
and the new Minister of War was Lord Liverpool. It was a Tory
government which gave full support to Wellington, now in the throes
of spectacular successes in his Peninsular campaign. It was also a
Parliament where William's father Henry had been active as the
Member for Corfe Castle for the last thirty years and knew everyone

who mattered. The Speaker was Charles Abbot, Lord Colchester, an old Westminster friend.

Henry had launched his political career by opposing the American War of Independence which, he declared, was not in the best interests of the nation which had been deceived into it, and the Americans had been compelled, in self-defence, to have recourse to arms. These views had made him an early supporter and friend of William Pitt – he even voted for Pitt's first parliamentary reform proposals in 1783, but not his second two years later. Henry Bankes was considered a good orator, a man of high principles, probity and calm solidity if lacking in originality and brilliance. Nathaniel Wraxall wrote of Henry Bankes: 'His enunciation, slow, formal, precise and not without some degree of embarrassment, was nevertheless always controlled by judgment, caution and good sense. No man displayed more rectitude of intention, independence of mind, and superiority to every private object of interest or ambition.'[1]

Henry's unwavering independence had earned him a seat on the cross benches, which became known as 'Bankes' bench'. His friend William Wilberforce, godfather to William's younger brother George, glossing his predictability, described him as a man 'from whose general principles one may anticipate pretty confidently how they will act in given circumstances.'[2] Henry's main tenets were control of public spending, which led to his campaign for the abolition of sinecures, and the rationalisation of administrative costs; over the years he became an advocate of the parliamentary committee as well as an expert on parliamentary procedure, worthy yet deeply unexciting. He also deplored the cost of the war with France, a high-minded stance for one whose family fortune partly derived from increased use of graphite in wartime. Clearly, Parliament was an arena where William would find it hard to outshine his father.

By 1812 Henry's prestige was such that his voice was heard in almost every debate of importance. But with age, and following the death of his first son, Henry Bankes became increasingly reactionary. He had voted for the abolition of the slave trade in 1796, but in 1815 voted against its international abolition. He believed that popular education and 'the new state of knowledge' endangered the country's stability. He was, true to form, against industrialisation, parliamentary reform and Catholic Emancipation – three burning issues of the day. By 1813 he had become so militantly anti-Catholic that he was nicknamed 'Protestant Bankes'. He lacked charisma and his son's friend John Cam Hobhouse, possibly unfairly, called him a 'dull dog'.[3] Henry was after all civilised and cultured, 'one of the most accomplished gentlemen in England'.[4]

By contrast, young William made an inglorious debut. His only speech during two years in office was in his father's shadow on the subject of liberalising the anti-Catholic laws. Bankes, who waited nearly two years before giving his maiden speech in April 1812 and worked on it painstakingly beforehand, said he doubted whether the time was ripe to give full rights to Catholics and considered the pro-Catholic 'party' dangerous to political stability. By one account he 'floundered' in this speech 'whilst deep in a rhetorical allusion to the Lake of Geneva'. A fellow MP likened his performance to a 'ranting, whining, bad actor in a barn speaking a full tragedy part, and mixed up with the drawls and twangs of a Methodist preacher.'[5] But perhaps William Wellesley-Pole, brother of the Duke, who made the jibe was getting even as a few weeks earlier he himself was said to have cut a 'miserable figure' in the debate on the Catholic issue; in May Wellesley-Pole changed his mind and aligned himself with more liberal views.

Bankes was more successful making a name for himself as a wit in London society than inside Parliament. In 1812 William was good looking with reddish golden hair, darker eyes, pale skin and rosebud mouth, as reflected in a miniature of him by George Sandars; this portrait showed him as more pretty and sensual than handsome, but he was also amusing, intelligent and rich. He went about occasionally with Byron, whose celebrity since the publication of *Childe Harold's Pilgrimage* in 1812 gave him a glittering entrée to the salons of many a Whig society hostess. Ladies Holland, Melbourne and Jersey all courted the aristocratic poet and, sometimes in his wake, his eligible and attractive friend Bankes. But Bankes, impatient to make changes to Kingston Hall, not yet his, easily tired of salon life in the capital and also went about the country, as was the fashion, visiting and comparing other grand houses. He drew up lists of intended purchases. 'There is in a shop near Leicester Square a noble carved bedhead, charge £250 pounds, and pieces of heavy oak furniture to correspond. It would be worth my while to offer two hundred pounds for the three,' he noted in his book. There was also 'a vast deal of old oak carving' in Salisbury, indicating his still dark and Gothic tastes. He bought some of this for his mansion in Wales, Soughton, where he took to staying 'quite alone. . . sharing with the rats', rambling and riding about the surrounding countryside, long before he owned it.[6] His great uncle, who survived until 1815, seems not to have minded William treating the house as if it were his already and issuing invitations to friends.

'I am invited by Wm Bankes to "*one of my places in Wales*!!!" but which of all these places this Deponent knoweth not . . .' Byron commented caustically to his friend Scrope Davies.[7] 'One would think Corfe Castle had perched itself upon Penmanmawr – I have heard of Purse = pride and birth = pride and now we have place = pride.' He clearly found his own joke so amusing that he repeated it to Hobhouse and even Bankes himself, who as the relationship with Byron subtly altered, often fell into the role of supplicant. 'Why do you call me a man of many residences and never stir a step to see me in any of them?' Bankes asked.[8]

In 1812, as Parliament was dissolved, William gave up his seat and decided to travel, enticed by the insistent lure of the Orient. The tolerant atmosphere and ready availability of beautiful young men would have been well known to the small circle of Cambridge 'Methodists', especially after Byron and Hobhouse had returned from their travels to Greece and Albania discreetly boasting of the 'paradise of boys' they had discovered. By contrast the atmosphere of repression and hostility to homosexuals in England was graphically illustrated by the Vere Street affair in 1810. The police had raided a tavern in Vere Street, well known as a meeting place for homosexuals, and of several men arrested and charged with 'assault with the intention to commit sodomy', six were sentenced to be pilloried in central London. Greater discretion than ever was now demanded of Bankes and his friends. Shortly afterwards, the brilliant Charles Skinner Matthews, Cambridge intimate of Bankes, Byron and Hobhouse, was found drowned in the River Cam, possibly the result of suicide.

In addition, William had just been rebuffed by the only woman to whom he ever proposed marriage. William's mother Frances was said to be 'indefatigable' in searching out suitably brilliant matrimonial alliances for her children, the constant pre-occupation for women of her day. The first marriage Frances arranged was for her twenty-one-year-old daughter Anne to Edward Boscawen, Viscount Falmouth. Judging by her portrait by Sir Thomas Lawrence, Anne, with her thick golden curls, was almost as beautiful as her mother had been, so perhaps arranging this marriage was not difficult. The families had longstanding political connections. When William first made the three-day journey from Dorchester to Truro in 1808 he wrote to his mother that Tregothnan, 'was an old [house] patched at different times and very indifferent'. But the two young men became lifelong friends, and a year before Anne's marriage toured Wales together, including in their itinerary the celebrated 'virgins' of Llangollen: Lady Eleanor Butler and Miss Ponsonby. The lesbian duo, who had eloped together and wore masculine dress, were a well known attraction to visitors.

The Boscawens were a distinguished and courageous Cornish naval family who could trace their ancestry at least to the thirteenth century. According to some, Falmouth was a most reluctant bridegroom. After the wedding on 27 August 1810, he refused to drive away from the church with his bride but banged on the carriage door and proceeded on foot to the reception at the Bankes's London house in Old Palace Yard. It was reported among the wits of society that 'the Falmouth cutter had run aground on Mother Banks'.

The friendship between Edward and William was undisturbed by the marriage and Edward was to remain William's staunchest supporter. Strong male friendships, with no sexual overtones, were not unusual then. But it is also possible that Edward was of a similar sexual persuasion to William yet, following the mores of the time, decided to marry. At all events on 8 July 1811 Anne gave birth to Henry, the Falmouths' only surviving child. By contemporary standards, a marriage that produced only one child could hardly be deemed successful even if it were happy.

When William made his own proposal to Anne Isabella Milbanke his action might simply have been an act of filial duty. If so, considering all the more suitable matches his mother might hope to make for him, why did his eye alight on this confident, self-composed but naïve intellectual? What was it about Miss Milbanke, the blue-stocking, the 'Princess of Parallelograms' as Byron was unforgettably to describe her, which elicited from William Bankes his only marriage proposal? Did he know, in his heart, that she would reject him? Or did he hope, like others of his inclination at the time, that she might provide an acceptable front behind which he could hide his homosexuality? Bankes's own silence on this subject is to be expected; he may have considered that marriage, even fathering a child, since it was expected of him, was feasible.

Anne Isabella (Annabella) Milbanke, the extremely rich and well-connected daughter of Lady Melbourne's brother, Sir Ralph Milbanke, was not entirely unsuitable. The family was granted its title by Charles II in 1661 along with the Bankes, and Annabella's intelligent mother, the former Judith Wentworth, was a descendant of the sixteenth century Wentworth Barony. Annabella was an only and much wanted child who was born after her parents had been married for fifteen years and flourished in their ancestral home in the small Durham village of Seaham. Her opinions were, from earliest days, uncritically indulged. Annabella herself was a child prodigy, not bad looking and now, aged nineteen, in her second London season, at the centre of one of her aunt's intrigues. The cynical and manipulative Lady Melbourne had decided that a marriage between her niece and Lord Byron was the best way to ensure the poet ended his scandalous liaison with her daughter-in-law, Annabella's cousin, Lady Caroline Lamb.

Historians and novelists have dealt harshly with Annabella in the aftermath of her disastrous marriage to Byron in 1815; she has been considered smug, priggish, obsessive, provincial, formidable, mean and chilly and a vengeful bully. But she was also an innocent caught in a web of corruption, a fierce moralist who fell in love and one aspect of her love for Byron was her need to be a redeemer. 'I have no desire to be better acquainted with Miss Milbank' wrote Byron in 1812. 'She is too good for a fallen spirit to know or wish to know and I should like her more if she were less perfect.'[9]

Perhaps Annabella's pious disapproval of the social world which was exploiting her acted as an obscure attraction for Bankes, much as it may have done for Byron. No doubt Bankes half-hoped she might redeem him, too, or at any rate offer him the respectability which at one level he craved. His proposal to her was genuinely meant. At another level, the coincidence of the two men proposing to the same woman was possibly a variation on the subconscious sexual rivalry between them. Byron tells Annabella, after she has left his own proposal dangling, the amusing story of how his equally unlucky friend W. Bankes paid him a visit one evening the previous winter 'with an aspect so utterly disconsolate that I could not resist enquiring into the cause. After much hesitation on his part – and a little guessing on mine – out it came – with tears in his eyes almost – that he had added another name to our unfortunate list. The co-incidence appeared to me so ludicrous that not to laugh was impossible – when I told him that a few weeks before a similar proposal had left me in the same situation. In short, we were the Heraclitus and Democritus of your suitors with this exception – that our crying and laughing was excited not by the folly of others but our own – or at least mine – for I had not even the common place excuse of a shadow of encouragement to console me.' Byron is probably not telling young Miss Milbanke quite how much the two men must have laughed at the coincidence of their 'common grievance'.[10] But according to his version of events neither man had been aware of the other's intentions.

Byron's chiselled account of Bankes's dejection at her refusal may well be accurate. Annabella, who prissily maintained she took no pleasure in flirting, was nonetheless juggling several suitors. Yet for William Bankes, she insisted, she never felt the slightest affection. 'One of my smiles would encourage him but I am niggardly of my glances,' she wrote to Byron. Nonetheless, it seems unlikely that Bankes would have persevered in his courtship, visiting her house and leaving so many calling cards that she had 'some idea of returning them for his own pocket's sake',[11] if she was genuinely so discouraging of his suit. She allowed Bankes to lend her his copy of *Childe Harold's Pilgrimage*, but to her father she wrote: 'I was tormented by that impudent Bankes, who seems really to consider me as his property and will not understand any rebuffs.'[12] When Annabella and Byron finally announced they were to be married two years later, she wrote: 'I am afraid he [Bankes] will hear of US with pain yet he cannot *lose* hope for I never allowed it to exist.'[13] We have only her word for it.

But by this time William was abroad, all thoughts of marriage with Annabella banished along with any ideas he might have indulged of becoming an orator and a statesmen and even 'perhaps a baronet'.[14] Delighted to find himself at large and free of duties, he allowed travelling to occupy his mind. It is not clear when William first made plans to go to Spain, Portugal and Sicily. By 1812 he admitted he was dreaming of the Alhambra and the 'cross-legged knights of Malta', as recommended to him by Byron. Not for him the French-Italian track of earlier Grand Tourists, well beaten by his father, grandfather and countless others of his class but which war with France made impossible.

Curiosity is a key Bankes word. William used it often to explain his desire to 'tourify', Byron's word, and his generous great uncle, Sir William Wynne, who had sent him a draft of £500 travelling expenses, urged him not to hurry back to England 'as all the world is now open to the curiosity of the traveller.'[15] Learning that Spain was William's first destination, he cautioned him that the French invaders would have left dreadful marks of devastation wherever they had been. He was well informed: Spain had been ravaged ceaselessly by marauding French armies, which had left an appalling trail of pillage and destruction behind them.

Spain and Portugal had attracted other travellers before Byron, most notably William Beckford, whose Gothic taste had so influenced William at Cambridge. Beckford's name was still synonymous for homosexuals hounded out of England. Although Beckford, 'apostle of pederasty',[16] had travelled in Spain and Portugal between 1787 and 1788, more or less at the age Bankes now was, his travelling journal was not published until years later so is unlikely to have influenced William. Yet he was clearly in Bankes's thoughts as he began contemplating his itinerary.

In December 1811 Bankes had 'the greatest curiosity' to see the magnificent Fonthill Abbey and decided to pay an uninvited visit. First he wondered how he could breach the four-mile wall which enclosed it on all sides, only to discount that when he realised it was ten feet high with spiked palisades sloping outwards from the top and covered with nails and tenterhooks. He then found the gates, watched over by a trusty old woman, and tried to persuade her to let him in; but she was not fooled by his stories. No stranger has been allowed in for five years, Bankes learnt. By this time 'very obstinately bent upon my project . . . I changed clothes with a poor labourer and put on a smock frock and a ragged hat and trousers and in this masquerade climbed the wall and pales; my hands were so much torn and bloody with clinging upon the hooks that I thought I might have been taken up for Mr Marr's murder.'

However, having succeeded in getting himself inside the grounds, he proceeded to walk confidently all over the place. 'I took the abbey in every point of view. I was questioned and spoken to over and over again by servants and workmen. I always asked for work and offered my services in ditching or banking or something of that sort and was often advised to go about my business.'

Discovering that Beckford himself was out driving about the grounds, Bankes grew bold enough to venture inside the house. Finding neither bell nor knocker, he pushed the open great door – it was almost 30 feet high – and found himself in the great hall, rather like that of a large college with windows on both sides topped by a rich gilded oak roof. On one side was Alderman Beckford's tomb. Facing the entrance was a long flight of stone steps with a stone balustrade which led to that part of the house

> under the tower which is an octagon and runs up the whole height near 200 feet. This forms the centre of the grand gallery . . . with windows on both sides which had crimson blinds and all the other furniture crimson to correspond. Beyond this at one end is the chapel.
>
> I saw his dinner laid out in a low moderate room to the south, a profusion of gilt plate but only one knife and fork. When I had seen all that I could hope with any safety I walked out again after not having encountered a single servant, although he keeps so many . . . one to snuff his candles and another who rides before him wherever he goes but is not a groom.

In addition, Bankes learnt that there was not a single bell in the house 'but that a dwarf lies on the rug in the room where he sits to answer the purpose and that the cook always brings up the first dish dressed in scarlet.'

As Bankes made his exit he saw Beckford drive up to the door in his 'charriot' – or so he told his Grandmother and anyone else to whom he recounted the adventure. It made for an exciting ending to the story, which no doubt improved over the years with the telling. 'I took advantage of the workmen coming away to get out in the crowd at the gate, and could not resist afterwards dancing and shouting around the old woman who was so determined I should not come in. I afterwards gave her half a crown for being so trusty to her master.' How typical of William Bankes: at once boastful, generous, observant, adventurous and curious in this account of a schoolboy escapade. Only William was no schoolboy. He was twenty-five.[17]

What else might have influenced Bankes in his decision to travel to the Peninsula? Only a handful of Englishmen who had visited the Peninsula during the latter part of the eighteenth century had written short accounts of their travels. The Duke of Wellington, his father's friend, was still fighting a war there and 60,000 British troops, among whom must have been some of Bankes's school or university friends, faced difficult and unpleasant conditions. They endured fifteen-mile forced marches over rugged terrain in heavy rains or, in summer, intense heat and dust. At night they were plagued by mosquitoes, gnats, midges, lizards and scorpions. In the early part of the war some troops had to bivouac, but Wellington encouraged the use of billets for his men – ranging from an onion loft to a nobleman's palace. In this way the Spanish, grateful for British help, grew accustomed to accepting British soldiers as their houseguests. Few billets were free of vermin or fleas; but the best and most frequently used billets were religious houses, disbanded by the French, often with as many as two hundred empty cells.

For five and a half years, since the 'Dos de Mayo' of 1808, when the people had risen in unanimous revolt against Joseph Bonaparte and the occupying French army, the Spanish had been engaged in an exhausting struggle. Spanish guerrilla bands, who viciously harried the large numbers of well-equipped French troops, were of inestimable help to Wellington with his much smaller forces. As late as 1811, desperate and indecisive battles – such as those of Fuentes de Oñoro and Badajoz – were still being fought. But on 22 July 1812, while Napoleon was mired in his Russian campaign, the British won a decisive victory at Salamanca. This signalled the turning point for Wellington. The following month British troops entered Madrid in triumph. Although they faced another retreat to the Portuguese border after this, by spring 1813, after months of careful preparation, Wellington opened his brilliant offensive campaign. In August the frontier fortress of San Sebastian fell; two months later, Pamplona. The war as far as Spain was concerned was virtually over.

William Bankes made his plans in the wake of Salamanca. He may even have read some of the military memoirs which started appearing at this time. It is inconceivable that the country, which had suffered so much under French occupation, would not have made a strong impact on the British imagination. The British found plenty strange enough to write about, nothing more so than the food – macaroni 'poisoned' with saffron, a salad mixed with 'lamp-oil' or *gaspacho* laced with the ubiquitous garlic – 'this simple mixture which is the universal food of the peasantry'.[18]

For travellers such as Bankes, for whom risk was a key element of adventure, the appeal lay in the unknown and the wild. Spain was warm and romantic, its people brave, especially its folk hero guerrilla leaders who sometimes brutally resisted the French army of occupation. According to one account 'a captive Frenchman might be buried with only his head above ground, to be used as a pin in a bowling match. As alternatives he might be hanged by his feet, sawn apart between two planks, skinned alive, boiled alive, impaled and then grilled over a campfire or crucified upside down.'[19]

On 20 January 1813, William set sail from Portsmouth, en route to Lisbon, a journey of at least six days.

In the few minutes left before the departure gun was fired he wrote one last note – to Byron, of course. He who had popularised Spain in the first part of *Childe Harold*, and had armed Bankes with three letters of introduction, was now cajoled to join him in Albania in the summer 'and buffoon with me in Palestine and Egypt'.[20] But remember, added Bankes, not to come without '<u>our Benjamin</u>, or I shall send you back to fetch him or Joseph and his good natured brethren.'[21] It was not the first time Bankes had tried to entice Byron to join him. 'It would be delightful to visit Egypt together,' he had suggested a month earlier, promising mirth and merriment at the tomb of Godfrey de Bouillon. 'What could hinder you?'[22]

Bankes was carrying an early form of passport, of doubtful use. It was a large single sheet issued by Charles Stuart, British Ambassador in Portugal, to Lord Strathaven announcing that William John Bankes and two servants would be travelling in the area; scribbled on the back is one of Bankes's poetic 'effusions' in Latin. But his note begged Byron for further introductions. 'Do think what turban'd people ... will be useful for me.'[23] Byron sent him some suggestions, and hinted to Bankes and others that travel was on his mind, but never came to visit. Nor did he send Benjamin or Joseph, nicknames presumably for boys they had known at Cambridge. That relationship, although rekindled in Italy in 1819, was never re-established. When the letters Bankes longed for failed to arrive he responded: 'I doubt the dead letter office somewhere will be quite choaked with their accumulation.'[24]

Bankes went first to Portugal, 'a fine country, the climate delicious'.[25] He made some moderate excursions, extended his route northwards as far as Torres Vedras, crossed the Tagus and eventually reached the convent of Arrabida, where he was entertained and slept. He loved the isolation and wild aspect of this corner of the Peninsula. 'There is not an evergreen in our gardens, nor a flower in our greenhouses but is there and all this close upon the margin of the Atlantic with not a house nor an inclosure to interfere with the prospect. If ever I abjure the world it shall be at Arrabida,' the twenty-six-year-old wrote home. Nonetheless, he was ready to move on although constantly aware that his movement depended on the progress of the Army.

James Hamilton Stanhope, meeting Bankes in Oporto, commented perceptively that he was

> a very extraordinary young man ... I never saw so singular a compound of eccentricity and judgment, of trifling and study; of sound opinions about others and wild speculations about himself, good talents applied to no future object and a most wonderful memory prostituted to old songs and tales of Mother Goose ... I like the man much for he appears to have an excellent temper, a good heart and a certain degree of freshness and independence in opinions which I do not think the travellers who come to this country generally possess.[26]

The Spain of 1813, when William Bankes arrived, was unsettled, dangerous, snake-infested and almost bankrupt – the bandits who had once attacked the French so cruelly now turned their gaze and their weapons on any hapless traveller. But despite poor roads – most were tracks passable only by horse or mule – and lack of bridges over rivers – in the rainy season travellers often had to wait for swollen rivers to subside – the country was not altogether unwelcoming, as Milord Bankes found. Wherever he went he began sketching and painting, as well as keeping jottings on scraps of paper.

He spent some time at Wellington's headquarters, more camp follower than aide-de-camp, thanks to the great man's friendship with his father. Seventeen years older than William, the Duke was well known for encouraging high-spirited young men with dashing style to work on his personal staff. William Bankes, with no military training, was not looking for a post; he had no official duties, and his presence is not officially recorded, but on occasions he was in the thick of battle. On 14 November 1813 he sent an account of Wellington's success 'upon passing the Nivelle above fifty pieces of cannon and several hundred prisoners taken'.[27]

To this time in his life can be traced his excitement at collecting art. Possibly the idea of buying paintings was one factor in his decision to go to Spain. His ancestors had often bought art while on their grand tours. William was at ease with Spanish painting, despite its religious and Catholic subject matter, having grown up in its presence; he was serious, too, about what to collect. In previous years he had visited other English grand houses and made sketches or jottings about their interiors and design. At Okerver Hall in Staffordshire he made copious notes on a painting there attributed to Raphael and, in addition to marginalia in catalogues, kept a journal in which he honed his artistic taste. He had a strong visual memory and had been 'getting his eye in'.

Plunder and profit were rife during the Napoleonic Wars. Almost as soon as Napoleon had installed his brother Joseph Bonaparte as King of Spain he wrote to him, inducing him to seize all the paintings he could find from confiscated houses and suppressed convents and to make him a present of fifteen masterpieces. Joseph himself assembled a collection of paintings, partly with the idea of creating a museum of Spanish painting, and rewarded his generals with major works of art. When the French were in Seville, until the summer of 1812, they seized hundreds of paintings from the sacked religious foundations of the city, intended by Joseph for his public museum. But the best of these passed into the personal possession of the rapacious Marechal Soult, Napoleon's Commander-in-Chief in Spain, as everyone knew. Later William Bankes asked his father to try to buy one of these.

Art dealers grabbed the opportunity offered by this flood of paintings released on the market, many of them never seen before. William Buchanan, then a young Scotsman who had made many acquisitions in Italy, sent his agent, the landscape painter George Augustus Wallis, to the Peninsula. Wallis wrote: 'Of the Spanish School we have no idea whatever in England. If they could see the two or three best Murillos of the St Iago family and some of the fine pictures of Velasquez, Alonzo Cano, Pereda, Zubaran, Carreno and del Greco, really first-rate men whose works are quite unknown outside of Spain, some estimate of the high excellence of the School might then be formed.'[28] Bankes bought neither a Goya nor an El Greco, the latter a painter scarcely appreciated in England, though neither were completely unknown – an El Greco is recorded in the seventeenth century collection of George Villiers, the Second Duke of Buckingham, while in August 1812 Wellington sat for his portrait by Goya.

In the spring of 1813, just before the campaign that culminated in the victory at Vitoria, there had been a major outbreak of looting. Wellington himself commented that the night before the battle, instead of being passed in getting rest and food to prepare for the following day, was spent by the soldiers in looking for plunder. Napoleon's brother Joseph had fled in haste, leaving his own carriage behind and with it a priceless group of paintings, including Velasquez's *The Water-Seller*, from the Spanish Royal Collection, which fell to Wellington himself. Wellington had these shipped back to England. Although delighted by their capture, he was nervous of keeping them as personal trophies of war, aware of the criticism he would attract. But King Ferdinand VII graciously allowed the British commander to retain them: 'His Majesty, touched by your delicacy, does not wish to deprive you of that which has come into your possession by means as just as they are honourable.'

The treasures and spoils spilling out of King Joseph's coaches were legendary. In addition to many rolled canvases, chests and hatboxes were torn open to reveal doubloons, dollars, watches, jewels and trinkets. The 14th Light Dragoons acquired thus Joseph's lordly silver *pot de chambre* which they christened 'the Emperor'.* Wellington had a keen eye and was not immune to the pleasures of acquiring fine art for his own walls, but was shocked by the sheer volume of treasures looted by the French and tried, after 1815, to return much to its rightful owners. Most of his Napoleana collection was either bought in post-war Parisian sales or occasionally commissioned.

Bankes himself appears not to have been involved in the plunder of Joseph's carriage but some of his pictures were acquired by irregular means. In the main he was a shrewd and opportunist collector, benefiting from the general confusion and abandonment of property following military campaigns to acquire some fine examples of Spanish painting at a time when it was far from fashionable in England. He was an absentee collector, buying for a house that was not yet his. He sent his trophies home to Dorset but a well-worn anecdote in the Bankes family recounts that when Wellington realised how many treasures William and others were acquiring, he addressed his officers thus: 'Gentlemen, I will have no more looting; and remember Bankes, this applies to you also.' The reprimand had little effect; from then on Bankes found it amusing to send his art home addressed to Lord Wellington at Kingston Hall.

In the autumn of 1813 he was living 'in disguise' at Pamplona, one of the last pockets of resistance, besieged by the English until November 1813. According to a story he told later to Princess Lieven, he went to dine with the French commanding officer, 'who regaled him with a meal of rats washed down with strong drink, and after dinner obliged him to buy a Raphael, which he had stolen from the Sacristy of the Escorial, and a donkey, which I don't think he had stolen from anybody.' Bankes spent all his money on what he believed with good reason to be a Raphael, and a few days later had only just enough to pay his passage on the boat which was to bring him and the donkey to which he was greatly attached, back

---

* Their successors still use it at mess functions for drinking champagne toasts, after which the pot is ceremoniously placed on the drinker's head.

to England. When he presented himself on board with the animal the captain declared, 'the jackass should pay like a gentleman.'[29]

The 'Raphael', *The Holy Family with the Infant St John in a Landscape*, was one of the finest pictures William ever bought, though now believed to be an Italian work by one of Raphael's pupils. Previous owners marked by brands on the back are Vincenzo Gonzaga, 4th Duke of Mantua, and King Charles I of England, who bought the bulk of the Gonzaga collection in 1626–8. Provenance was already an important consideration for Bankes. But Princess Lieven, recounting the story of how William acquired it nine years after the event, must have been mistaken, since William remained in Spain until 1815 and then did not return immediately to England. The ass's fate is not recorded; probably William used him to travel around Spain.

Bankes explored the rugged grandeur of Granada in Southern Spain, travelling mostly on foot or on mule-back. He was sufficiently hardened against dirt and stench to bed down where he could when he was not based at Wellington's headquarters, avoiding, or occasionally hunting, wild boar and wolves. By this time he was accompanied by a Portuguese manservant, Antonio da Costa, about whom little is known apart from his devotion to Bankes. He remained in his service for the next seven and half years, following him obediently.

Few letters survive from William to Frances Bankes. With his father he discussed money matters and purchases of art. For his mother's amusement he chose an anecdote about a house whose owner was a lady of rank, where he was plied with chocolate and such personal interest that the good lady was often to be found in his room, 'both after I was in bed and whilst I was getting up . . .' a habit he found most annoying. He preferred to stay in monasteries, sleeping in a cell and conversing with monks. He travelled through one small village where the locals had never met an Englishman and was trying to find a guide when two brothers emerged and invited him back to their home. Bankes was enormously impressed with their hospitality and 'charming rustick life'.

They made a special broth for him and gave him some new straw as a mattress to sleep on with very clean sheets in the corner of their bedroom. 'The room was full of spinning wheels and the whole family slept in the same corner of the room.'[30]

Perhaps news of this episode had reached Annabella Milbanke from her friend Miss Montgomery, also staying in Granada, for she told Byron in October 1814: 'I have heard more of Bankes at Granada – he is living there in a beggarly, eccentric fashion.'[31] It was not what an aristocrat was accustomed to, but many British officers had for some time now grown used to this gypsy mode of life.

Bankes wrote a list of pictures he bought in Granada which clearly explains how he was spending his time and money.

> The good shepherd by Murillo that was in the door of the Sagrario of the nuns del Angelo
> The Virgin receiving the sceptre from the hands of the almighty belonged to the same nuns by Alonso Cano
> St Francis visited by an angel from the convent of S Diego by A Cano
> S. Bernardino d++ do.do.
> The Virgin and Child half length by Cano was in the possession of some who had been servants of Cano
> Sta Rosa by Murillo with his name from the collection of the Marquis of Diezma
> El Venerable Roelas de Cordova. Cano
> El Conception a sketch by Murillo from the Cartuxa it was presented to the Cartuxa by Mr Wall of the Soto de Roma. I suspect this served for the model of the great one in the Convent of S Francis of Seville.
> Samson & the Lion & Moses and the burning bush by P. Orrente
> An Old Man's Head much in Rembrandt's manner bought of the widow of an artist who had a large collection.
> Heads of a man and woman bought of the same I think the man's is by Murillo.

For an Englishman to choose to spend his money on Spanish painting in the early nineteenth century was rare. Apart from a Mr Rose Campbell, who had lived at Cadiz and assembled a Spanish collection, there is no record of any previous Englishman setting out to build a substantial representation of Spanish art as Bankes did. Campbell sold his collection at Christie's in July 1814 while Bankes was abroad, but evidently he took an interest in the sale as an undated memorandum survives in the archives, written by William probably after his return to England in 1821, which refers to the Campbell Collection.

Spanish art was distinctly dark, with many images that must have struck the English as 'popish'. As late as 1853, the *Art Journal* attempted to explain why the Spanish School of painting had few admirers in England: images of 'saints and martyrs, attenuated ghastly-looking monks and nuns, innocent of "damask cheeks" do not constitute the most pleasing pictures, and are certainly not those which our country-men would choose wherewith to decorate their mansions: living flesh, smiling faces and joyous sentiment are much more in accord-ance with their tastes and feelings.'[32] Bankes, aware of this senti-ment, did not expect that a newly purchased Zurbarán would please in England. Yet it delighted him as 'an example of a singular effect of light'.[33] Murillo, though also a painter of religious scenes, was more popular for his genre painting, whose appealing colouring and livelier scenes often involved children.

Perhaps the most striking aspect of Bankes's attitude to collecting was his idea of making a display of paintings from one country, including examples by lesser-known artists as well as star names. The Spanish artist Pedro Orrente two of whose pictures Bankes bought, *Moses and the Burning Bush* and *The Boy David and the Lion*, was so little known outside Spain that the German scholar Dr Gustav Waagen, Director of the Royal Picture Gallery in Berlin, learnt of him only through visiting Kingston Lacy in the late 1850s. 'I know of no other collection in England containing so many valuable pictures of the Spanish school,' Waagen wrote. By October 1814 Bankes had sent at least three packing cases of pictures back to England from Cadiz. 'You are already in possession of the list of them,' he wrote to his father from Alicante, 'and what I wished to say respecting them. I have several here among which there are three Murillos, one Velasquez and many of Alonso Cano, which I have bought from Convents in Granada and the interior, they will remain here probably a twelvemonth more before they are shipped off.'[34]

Some months later he commented to his father:

> Though I could have wished that they were all good, I am pleased to find that of the pictures from Cadiz, the three which you admire are the very ones which I esteemed by much the best; the Sleeping Child is in my mind a most delightful picture. It is the very best manner of Alonso Cano, the next best of all the Spanish school to Velasquez or Murillo. He was superior to either of them in drawing, particularly of hands and feet. The little angel by Murillo was cut out by the French of one of his most famous pictures the Jubileo della Porciuncula in the Capuchin convent at Seville . . . The Spagnolet is quite of his best, it belonged to Philibert Duke of Savoy and is out of the Cathedral at Placencia.[35]

In fact, the little angel fragment is now no longer thought to be by Murillo since the altarpiece from which it would have come, now in the Wallraf-Richartz Museum in Cologne, lacks no such section. The inscription that Bankes subsequently organised for the cartouche over the picture says: 'Cut out by French soldiers and applied to the covering of a knapsack.'

Bankes was desperately keen for his father's approval of the Velasquez, 'which I flatter myself will be the finest in England, though not a finished picture.' He described it as 'a middle-sized picture, with eight or nine figures, all portraits and a dog. I was a long while in treaty for it and was obliged at last to give a high price.'[36] He concluded from Henry's silence about it that it had not yet arrived. Bankes thought he was buying a Velasquez sketch for the extraordinary painting *Las Meninas*, then barely known, created in 1656 for King Philip IV. Although this is now believed to have been painted by the artist's son-in-law, Juan Bautista Martinez del Mazo, this makes it almost as rare as the original; it was the only copy of a masterpiece hidden from public view in the private apartments of the Royal Palace in Madrid. Believing his acquisition to be 'the glory of the collection', he entrusted this picture to Wellington's brother Sir Henry Wellesley to bring home personally. It was thanks to this confident purchase that *Las Meninas*, now one of the most famous examples of the Golden Age of Spanish painting, was known in Britain. Bankes knew and admired Sir Henry, having gone with him to see the deposed King Ferdinand VII at Valencia, probably in 1814 when Wellesley prevailed on Ferdinand to forswear the Bourbon alliance and recognise the new status quo. Bankes was, like many of his countrymen, euphoric at the way Wellington had won victory in Europe and destroyed France as a military power and wished to see his country's saviour amply rewarded. 'Surely we cannot do too much for the Duke of Wellington,' he suggested to his father. 'As it may be difficult to purchase him an estate if not of the extent, at least of the dignity that is suitable, it strikes me that . . . the handsomest thing we could do would be to take the Derwentwater estates from Greenwich Hospital, giving an annual revenue of equal amount out of some funds and present them to the Duke in lieu of the grants of money with a palace upon the Keswick Lake or at Dilston, the old seat of the Earls of Derwentwater.'[37] Nothing came of this idea.

Bankes consulted various sources for advice during his three-year shopping spree in Spain. He used Palomino's *Lives of the Artists*, as can be seen in his comments on the Murillo *Good Shepherd*, as well as Cean Bermudex's *Diccionario* of 1800. He also probably relied on certificates of authentication of dubious accuracy. He bought the Ribalta *The Virgin and Child with Musical Angels* in 1814 following 'the opinion of several good judges . . . for all the court was in Valencia at the time'. It had been one of several paintings by Francisco Ribalta adorning the Goldsmiths' Chapel of St Eligius in the Parish Church of St Catherine the Martyr. William was sorry his father did not think more of it.[38]

After Bankes had left Spain in 1815, he urged his father, who was shortly going to Paris to see the 'ill-gotten spoils' from Napoleon's conquest, to look for a painting by Juan de Juanes – 'the only master wanting to my collection and very rare'. Bankes had failed to acquire one of these himself – he mentions specifically pursuing Juanes's *The Assumption of the Virgin*. But he also urged his father: 'Do not neglect to inquire particularly what is become of Soult's pictures (for they must now come upon sale). He has the famous Murillo of *the Birth of the Virgin from the Cathedral of Seville*. Say nothing of it for perhaps it will not be much noticed and if after seeing it and liking it you could buy it for 3 or 4 or 5 hundred pounds I beg that you will do it on my account . . . I beg of you to do this commission for me if you can. These are opportunities which will not occur again and Heaven has placed me in a situation where I am not likely to feel the loss of £500.'[39]

His father, with whom he was in close discussion throughout his trip and who paid for some of the works, was also an important source of advice, often consulted.

> You mention that you wish I could have sent home a fine specimen of Murillo. I offered £500 for one belonging to a Canon in Seville but could not get it. However of the four I have collected (which are all genuine pictures) three are very good and one a most delightful one, it is small but there is nothing better by his hand . . . It is the Good Shepherd that was on the door of the Sagrario in the nunnery of El Angel at Granada. It was unfortunately cut into a half-length to disguise it when it was carried from there . . . The Santa Rosa was in the collection of the Marquis de Diezma and has the name upon it, it is in his grey manner and in spite of its bad condition I consider the little cherub that I left with those at Cadiz in his best manner.[40]

Tactfully, but in two separate letters, Bankes asks his father not to have the pictures cleaned, showing sensitivity to the need for careful conservation in advance of his time.

> I have observed that Spanish pictures in general are not the better for being cleaned . . . there is a rawness in the colouring which that tone which they acquire from age tends to soften a gloss over and the most part of those in the palaces at Madrid where they are in very good order are quite without varnish. Mine however have been all knocked about so much that the only difficulty will perhaps be with some of them to find a person who will undertake them.

In another letter he comments:

> Do not have it cleaned till I come. I am so afraid they will play tricks
> with it and paint in the background, which has a mellowness that is
> quite remarkable in a plain grey colour. I would not have it touched
> for the world.[41]

Not all the paintings which Bankes bought in Spain can now be
traced. Possibly some never arrived in England. More likely, some
were sent to Soughton, others to Old Palace Yard, yet others stored
pending his inheritance of Kingston Hall or sold at a later date. But
what remains is a fine, interesting and idiosyncratic collection of
Spanish art, much of it revealed for the first time in European history.
An undated but detailed hanging plan for his pictures at Kingston
Lacy still exists; it records a space for the Juanes he was negotiating
for in Spain, so the plan was probably for the then North Parlour.
Later, when he started altering the house, the room which became
the Spanish Picture Room was the old 'eating room', symmetrical
to the North Parlour. Assuming the hanging plan was made while
Bankes was in Spain, it is a clear indication of the way he viewed
his embryonic collection from the start, even though he had no idea
when the house would finally become his. His entire life was marked
by the uncertainty of inheritance.

4

Exploration

~

'He has dedicated his whole time to Learning and the Arts'
Henry Salt to Mrs Bessy Morgan

IN DECEMBER 1814 William left Spain. He spent a few months visiting Italy, Sicily and Malta and might have remained longer had his father made more money available to him. Although nearly thirty and financially independent, he berated Henry for not having set up better arrangements for him, causing him both inconvenience, 'as it throws me into the hands of low shabby merchants in the different towns which I have to pass through', and expense as commission was charged upon commission. He listed the various commissions he paid and calculated that 'of the £800 which I have placed as a fund, I make no doubt that £600 will never come into my hands. Can there be a more mortifying way of losing money than this when it might have been all saved by a few papers from a Banker in London?'[1]

Henry was entreated to 'have the goodness' to get more money out to him regularly: 'it will be better to tell them [Child's Bank] that after Constantinople my route will be through Greece and Albania to Ancona and so to Venice and Bologna and Milan and Florence and all the North of Italy, Switzerland and France . . .'[2] Bankes would eventually visit some of these places. But in the late summer of 1815, when he sailed to Alexandria then wrote so irately to his father from Cairo, he had no idea that he would be gripped for the rest of the decade by a serious interest in the Middle and

Near East. In 1815 he was still little more than an educated tourist, hoping to meet up with his family, whom he missed, in Paris in a few months, shopping for trinkets and gold chains for his sister Anne in Malta and writing from there to his other sister Maria that he thought a short stay in Egypt would be enough to see the Pyramids. Yet by 1820 he had earned his reputation as a traveller for his explorations, adventures and discoveries in Egypt, Nubia and beyond. 'Salute Him,' charged Byron of his publisher, John Murray. He is one 'who has done miracles of research and enterprize.'[3]

In 1815, when his father told him there was a vacancy for him in Parliament if he wished it, he begged to be allowed to decline 'if it is not disagreeable to you'. Even were he able to return to England the following year, he told his father, he would want a little repose and quiet after so much rambling abroad. In truth, as he recognised, he had had enough of public life and parties. He was uncertain how long he could postpone his inevitable return. The years in Spain had, to an extent, been filled with the pleasures of idleness. But they had also shown his ability to endure living in primitive conditions without the luxuries with which he had grown up. Now he was also to demonstrate that he could work intensively under extreme conditions and genuinely engage with 'the foreigner' – not given to all Englishmen of his class and age. These years were a vital part of his voyage of self-discovery and provided him with the ballast that maintained his equilibrium later. He began to understand the deep need within himself to take risks and to push himself to his limits; he acquired a confidence that occasionally appeared as arrogance.

And so in September 1815 William Bankes is living *en grand seigneur* in the maelstrom of Cairo, with a 'vast apparatus' which does not please him, but which he accepts as necessary in preparing for an expedition beyond the cataracts into Nubia. He has organised workmen and machines so that he could, if the situation arose, remove a pyramid or the statue of Memnon. 'I have a noble barge with a cabin,' he told his father.[4]

While waiting for his transport arrangements to be finalised, Bankes made a brief overland exploration of the Sinai Peninsula, an adventurous move for one new to travelling in the East. Roads into that desert were hardly used and its few inhabitants, almost wholly Bedouin, were not known for their friendliness to Europeans. But Bankes had determined upon seeing Mount Sinai and St Catherine's Monastery. Accompanied by da Costa, the faithful Portuguese, as well as an Alexandrian Egyptian, Khalil, who acted as interpreter, he set off in August. At the Monastery he was hauled by rope over a garden wall and, according to the journal of the British diplomat and traveller, William Turner, who met Bankes in Cairo and heard of his exploits at first hand, then rummaged in an astonishing library of 2,000 dusty volumes including several manuscripts and ancient works in Greek and 'brought away' several volumes. Perhaps the monks allowed him, or Bankes decided to help himself. One volume is today in the library of Kingston Lacy, a 1503 copy of Euripides annotated on the flyleaf: 'Brought from the convent of St Catherine upon Mount Sinai in August 1815 by Wm. John Bankes'. If he removed (or was given) others, they were apparently returned.[5] Turner was clearly in awe of his fellow Englishman, who had made the difficult round trip in a record sixteen days when other travellers needed twenty-five. Bankes's courage and intellect were another factor. 'His publication will teach us more respecting the East than that of any traveller who has yet described it; for he goes everywhere, fearing neither danger nor fatigue, collecting more information than any other man could obtain, and never forgetting what he collects. I freely own my own anxiety, that my humble journal, if printed at all, should appear before his return, for I should not expect any one would read it after the publication of his.'[6] On Mount Sinai, Bankes admired the beautiful fig and mulberry trees, which reminded him of his mother, a keen gardener. One of the most exotic places on their itinerary was Serabit el-Khadim, site of the ancient turquoise mines, where a temple to the goddess Hathor, worshipped as 'Lady of Turquoise', had a large number of hieroglyphic inscriptions. Almost immediately Bankes demonstrated not only his scholarly interest in recording what the ancients had written but also his skill in copying texts whose form and content were unknown to him.

Egyptology was a new science, stimulated by the Napoleonic campaign in Egypt and especially by the work of the Commission des Arts et des Sciences, whose 167 members travelled throughout Egypt for three years drawing, cataloguing and recording all the ancient monuments. Their enormous and extraordinary work, eventually published as the *Description de L'Egypte* (the first volume appeared in 1809) may have helped distract French public attention from the failure of the military campaign; it also excited enormous public interest in the history of the ancient land and in contemporary customs and culture. A key member of this expedition, launched in May 1798, was Dominique Vivant Denon, the great French aristocratic draughtsman, diplomat, author of erotica and, later, Director General of the Louvre. Denon, then more than fifty, displayed great energy and youthful vigour as a traveller and was among the first to focus on the architectural details of Egyptian temples. His book *Voyage dans la Basse et la Haute Egypte pendant les campagnes du Général Bonaparte*, published in Paris in 1802, inspired a new generation of adventurers. In England curiosity was fuelled by the discovery of the black basalt slab known as the Rosetta Stone, confiscated by the British after the capitulation of the French. Its arrival in London in 1802 along with other Egyptian antiquities was a cause for celebration and a sudden vogue for all things Egyptian. The belief that, after centuries of ignorance, decipherment of the ancient Egyptian scripts was imminent provided the greatest single stimulus to travellers and copyists, scholars and artists who went to Egypt in the wake of the French defeat. Until then, knowledge of ancient Egypt was limited to what could be gleaned from classical writers and the Bible. The philosophy, morality, religion, system of government or culture of the peoples of ancient Egypt could only be guessed. There was little or no understanding of the enormous span of Egypt's history, of the significance of the pyramids, the Great Sphinx and other wonders described by the few hardy travellers of the seventeenth and eighteenth centuries. The mysterious hieroglyphic script, known from the few antiquities such as the obelisks in Rome which had been moved to Europe and puzzled over by many a grand tourist, held the key. But no one knew what the script meant and this, together with the difficulties and dangers of travelling in the country, only added to the romantic fascination of this strange and distant culture.

For an Englishman such as Bankes, nourished on the classics and familiar with classical texts on Egypt and Nubia, this was a thrilling time to be in Egypt. Bankes had resources to pay for equipment and guides, insatiable curiosity to understand other peoples and their history, and a love of adventure and danger. He also had humour, patience, warmth and a personality that made him an ideal travel partner.

> Of all the men I have ever met with I consider [him] as being gifted with the most extraordinary talents; born to family and fortune, he has dedicated his whole time to learning and the arts, possessing a fund of anecdote and good humour, which renders his society the more agreeable and entertaining than can be conceived.

So he was described by British Consul-General Henry Salt, who came to know him well at this time.[7]

Bankes was not only a pioneer Egyptologist. He was something even newer, an epigrapher – though the term 'epigraphy' was not used until the mid-nineteenth century. These text collectors (sometimes called traveller copyists) could not themselves decipher the hieroglyphs (although Bankes had a good understanding of Greek) but were keenly interested in the decipherment debate and understood the need for new material and for accuracy in copying inscriptions on stone. Bankes recognised that the acquisition of linguistic and historical information through laborious copying of texts as well as recording of ancient sites and picturesque ruins could be more important for preserving the heritage of ancient Egypt than the glamorous but often destructive excavation and plunder of antiquities. Although he succumbed to sending home some acquisitions he was not a methodical collector and the quantity he acquired was tiny compared with real antiquity hunters. Denon, for example, amassed a collection of 265 items of Egyptian antiquities; Sir John Soane only slightly fewer, including the prize possession of the alabaster sarcophagus of Seti I, for which he paid two thousand pounds when the British Museum turned it down because the price was too high.

The short trip to Sinai successfully completed, William wrote to his father from Cairo warning that he might be incommunicado for several months; his family should not worry, as any bad news would be conveyed quickly. He reassured his father that he was helped by the protection of Mohammed Ali, Pasha or Viceroy of Egypt since 1805, 'to whom somebody has puffed me, I do not know why, does everything for me that I can wish and I shall travel with great advantage and perfect security.' The Pasha – a title conferred by the Sultan of Constantinople, Egypt being still nominally part of the Ottoman Empire – was a soldier of Albanian origin, born in Macedonia in 1769, who had decided that the future success of Egypt lay in greater openness towards European influences. A small man with lively eyes, a long beard and a sharp political understanding of the realities in the region, he considered that expanding his Empire – he founded the city of Khartoum – was as important as attempting to modernise his own country, Egypt. To this end he relied on the technical advice of European experts. In return, he allowed them special permits to excavate certain archaeological sites. This led to a systematic plunder of the country's archaeological heritage with priceless treasures ending up in museums in London, Paris, Mantua, Stockholm and elsewhere as well as private collections. But for the present Bankes noted that the Pasha 'continues shut up in the citadel afraid of his own troops' – there were dangerous rumours that his attempts to modernise his army was threatening a mutiny – 'and the alarm among the Christians here is so great and so foolish that I am glad to get away.'[8]

Bankes embarked on 16 September 1815 on his first Nile journey. He headed a small party, augmented by an American-French gentleman, François Barthow, 'who is perfectly acquainted with the country and the people and who was to act as a guide'. Barthow in turn introduced Bankes to Giovanni Finati, the most important member of his group. Finati accompanied his 'English Gentleman of Fortune' for the next four years, acting as fixer, interpreter, dragoman and janissary – Finati's preferred way of describing himself. Subsequently he dictated his life history to Bankes who, already fluent in Italian by the time they met, translated and edited the memoirs and eventually arranged for their publication by John Murray in 1830 under the title *Narrative of the Life and Adventures of Giovanni Finati, native of Ferrara, who under the assumed name of Mahomet made the campaigns against the Wahabees for the Recovery of Mecca and Medina and since acted as interpreter to European travellers in some of the parts least visited of Asia and Africa.* It was, however, widely believed that Bankes was largely the author of Volume Two.

Finati was pivotal to Bankes's success in Egypt and it is easy to understand why such an unusual character would have appealed to him. By the time they met, Giovanni Finati had led an extraordinarily eventful and Candidesque life. Contrary to his family's wishes, he had joined the French army but deserted twice; when captured the second time, he was sent to prison where he faced a death sentence. But instead of execution he was transported with other troops across the Adriatic and forced to fight, ending up in hospital in Spalato (nowadays Split). Luckily, he made contact there with some Albanian merchants from Scutari (Shkodera), who helped him, in his desperation, to escape army life for the third time. He then converted from Christianity to Islam, took the name Mahomet and fell in love with a young lady called Fatima, but left her when she became pregnant with his child. In March 1809 he arrived in Alexandria, along with hundreds of ragged pilgrims en route to Mecca or other adventurers: 'Here a new scene of life opened to me.'[9] At the time he met Bankes he was unemployed and his incalculable usefulness as a guide self-evident. He was familiar with the geography of the area, personally acquainted with many influential Egyptians and fluent in their language. 'My connexion also with the Egyptian army was no small point of recommendation.'

In the course of the first Nile journey, as Finati noted, the party stopped only at such sites as were considered of paramount interest, or when the wind failed, which was rare on the way up, but antici-pated for the way down. On the twelfth day they arrived at Thebes (modern day Luxor) and anchored for ten days. Then William fell ill; according to Finati: 'the ophthalmia depriving Mr Bankes totally out of sight during that time.' This illness was a frightening hazard for travellers in the region at the time and later attacked William again. But he seems to have recovered sufficiently to face the next impediment, a swarm of locusts, with his customary equanimity. This biblical scourge settled on the vessel and totally covered everyone's clothes. Even the natives were screaming and vainly slinging pebbles at the insects.

The original vessel was too big to proceed further up the Nile. The party then managed to hire a smaller one from the Nubians, 'for so are called all who live beyond Assouan [Aswan],' by walking to the island of Philae, where a rudimentary craft was prepared for them. This consisted of planks pegged together without nails, with a ragged sail of blue cotton, and in place of a cabin a mat of palm leaves bent over as an arbour. The space was so small only Bankes slept on board. Both he and Barthow wore European clothes, which Finati recognised drew attention to the party – not always un-welcome. One old man approached them with a gift of prime locusts which he cooked for them. 'First pulling off the wings, then frying the remainder in butter, which we found crisp to the taste and not wholly unlike a shrimp.' They went as far as Wadi Halfa, the second cataract, by boat then travelled on by camel to Wadi Aumki. Few European travellers had penetrated so far south. 'I soon grew so accustomed to see Mr Bankes drawing and noting (from any vestiges of antiquity) that I began to take some interest in the sight of them myself,' Finati admitted.

There were ruins to be explored near Wadi Halfa, but much was buried under the sand. Finati describes the discoveries of Abu Simbel, where the great temples of King Ramesses II had recently been noted by the Swiss-born explorer Jean-Louis Burckhardt, whom Bankes was to meet in Cairo. The dimensions of the four great colossal figures were so vast that 'when I stood upon the level with the necklace I could hardly reach the beard ... Mr Bankes had a longing desire to have uncovered more of this monument at this time and often spoke of it afterwards,' wrote Finati. Bankes, only the second European traveller to visit the site, was utterly captivated. Abu Simbel was 'the most astonishing remains of ancient architecture and sculpture that are to be met with above the cateract. There could be nothing more vast of conception in Egypt or the world than the façade of the Great Temple', he wrote at the time.[10] But when in 1817 Belzoni finally managed to clear away the sand at the entrance there was disappointment at not finding any objects of interest.

The party spent several days on the sacred island of Philae, where Bankes became engrossed in examining the ancient temple to Isis which dominates the island. Here he discovered a fallen obelisk, dating from the fourteenth century BC, which must once have stood at the entrance to the temple. Probably Bankes, who immediately saw the obelisk as an adornment to his house in Dorset, knew of its existence through the writings of earlier travellers. It was most likely raised around 116 BC by priests of the temple at Isis to commemorate Ptolemy VIII's Act of Justice in remitting an unfair tax, according to its Greek inscription. Immediate steps were taken to move the great monument but, lacking suitable equipment, Bankes and his group soon abandoned the effort.

They were not the first Europeans to be enchanted by the beauty of Philae and its fallen obelisks. The island, south of Aswan (the ancient city of Syene) and upstream of the first cataract, had already captured the imagination of the French Commission. One of the most beautiful plates published in the *Description* is of the temple on Philae. Denon himself spent three weeks there, making numerous drawings of the monuments and obelisks, and carried out a reasonably accurate survey of the island. Before that, in 1738, a Danish sea captain, Frederick Norden, in Egypt on a fact-finding mission for King Christian VI, had written about two obelisks, one standing, one upon the ground; in 1801 William Richard Hamilton, the diplomat and antiquary sent to Egypt by Lord Elgin who was present at the handing over of the Rosetta Stone, noted them; in 1813 Burckhardt saw them and suggested to the British Museum Trustees that they should try and procure them. They demurred. Three years later Belzoni formally claimed the prostrate, unbroken obelisk in the name of the British Consul. But it was William Bankes who took decisive action, determined to reclaim it from the water and bring it to England. It was not a simple task.

Bankes, with almost childlike excitement, established himself in a small temple and, working through the night by candlelight, soon found an inscription never previously observed. This referred to two Cleopatras, successive wives of Ptolemy Lathurus, the same who were addressed on the granite pedestal of the obelisk which he also identified for the first time on this short trip. The pedestal, inscribed with twenty lines of Greek, was quite submerged but Bankes and Finati – Barthow had returned to prepare the boat for their return – worked out its probable position from that of the obelisk. Bankes was a patient observer. He would often rise silently at dawn, eager to discover the source of the famous sound, alleged to emanate from the colossal figures. He believed that the noise, more like a plucked harpstring than a voice, was caused by a change of temperature in the stones cracking as they warmed or cooled. These were heady times – even more so when they tasted a fermented and intoxicating drink called Booza, made from grain and rather like beer.

But one day while Bankes was drawing the portico of the principal temple, an angry Nubian demanded payment at knifepoint for the privilege. A crowd quickly gathered. Finati, knowing that his companion went unarmed, drew his own pistol, but Barthow saved the day. At the critical moment he returned on the opposite shore accompanied by the Cashief of Aswan and a body of soldiers who came on the Pasha of Egypt's recommendation to meet the stranger from England. The crowd immediately disbanded, some throwing themselves into the water fully clothed and swimming for their lives, whereupon Bankes, Finati and Barthow mounted the asses which had been brought for them and rode back to their vessel, left in the charge of the faithful Antonio. It had been a useful reconnaissance trip; not only had Bankes identified and initiated his claim to the obelisk but also, at Thebes, he had purchased two massive lion-headed seated figures of black granite and a remarkably large papyrus, 'which had the singularity also of never having been rolled, but only folded on the breast of the mummy'.[11] He seems ultimately not to have sent the figures home, although the Papyrus – a late copy of the compilation of religious funerary spells called *The Book of the Dead* – is now in the British Library. Bankes did make one significant collection of antiquities which is still at Kingston Lacy – a group of Stelae, or small limestone inscriptions, mostly votive, set up by the privileged workmen employed to excavate and decorate the royal tombs in the Valley of the Kings. Scholars believe these formed the first substantial body of material acquired from the workmen's village at Deir el Medina.

Although he was alive to international rivalries in the search for trophies, Bankes often seems to have been unconcerned about his rôle as a player in a larger game. Danger was a greater incentive for him than rivalry with fellow collectors. At Thebes, his party met a snake charmer who offered to make others invulnerable to the teeth and stings of reptiles, as he was. Bankes, amused, volunteered first. Some white powder was rubbed on him, some words muttered and then the creatures were let loose on him. Sure enough, their bites drew blood but caused neither pain nor swelling afterwards. Finati, concluding later that the reptiles must have had their venom extracted, was impressed as much by Bankes's intellectual curiosity as by his light-hearted good humour. He was energetic and generous, handsomely rewarding those who part in his expedition: an engaging mixture in a travel companion.

By mid-December 1815, exactly three months later, Bankes was back in Cairo, resting in his quarters in the Catholic convent. He had fainted at Giza (not unusual for foreigners) while exploring the inner passages of pyramids by torchlight. He now cemented a close and important friendship with Burckhardt, who fed him advice and stories about his years travelling as a Moslem in the region. Two years older than Bankes, Burckhardt had studied at Cambridge, but although the pair overlapped it is unlikely that they met there. Yet in the Cairo of 1815, few of whose 250,000 inhabitants were European, Bankes would have been compelling company for Burckhardt. Similarly Burckhardt, who was sent in 1809 to the Near East by the Association for Promoting the Discovery of the Interior Parts of Africa, charged with learning Arabic perfectly and adapting himself to Moslem life, was keen to encourage young men in whom he espied serious purpose. Known as Sheikh Ibrahim, he adopted Turkish dress and urged Bankes to do likewise. Burckhardt had been the first European to visit the ancient Nabatean city of Petra; then he went up the Nile to Nubia and discovered the Abu Simbel temples. Before Bankes set off on his next trip he armed him with several letters of introduction, including one to Lady Hester Stanhope, the intrepid woman traveller living in Lebanon. 'You will no doubt find him a very pleasant and extremely well informed man of distinguished talents, and no less suavity of manner,' Burckhardt wrote to her.[12] The two men corresponded over the next two years but Burckhardt died of dysentry at Alexandria in October 1817, aged forty-one, his commission to explore regions south of the Sahara never completed.

Bankes remained in Cairo preparing the next stage of his travels to Syria (a term used by Bankes and his contemporaries to mean the Holy Land and surrounding regions). According to the scholar Dr Patricia Usick, the first journey was 'both a personal encounter with the Orient and redolent of the old antiquarian concerns: the second represents a leap towards a scientific approach to ancient Egypt and archaeology'.[13] Waiting for 'safe passage' letters from the Pasha was one reason for delaying; growing his beard was equally important. Once satisfied by its length, he donned a turban and oriental dress, which he wore for the next two years. Antonio, embarrassed at first, eventually agreed to wear a similar outfit provided by Burckhardt. Splendidly attired, the party departed, waved off at the Great Gate of Cairo by Burckhardt and others, this time without the company of Barthow and Khalil but soon augmented by two Germans on foot. Why Bankes agreed to travel across the desert with this pair – a cabinetmaker and a veterinary surgeon – is unclear. They were an encumbrance. Every hour or so Bankes dismounted from his dromedary so that they should have a rest from walking. Antonio and Finati occasionally did the same. But the Arabs considered the Germans as a baleful influence on account of their western clothes and, according to Finati, 'seemed to take a pleasure in witnessing the fatigue and shifts that they were reduced to'.

For the first three days, as their track ran parallel to the Nile, the group slept in the open air or in a tent. For another three days as they moved further into the desert they saw no sign of habitation. Little in the way of antiquities tempted Bankes to stop. At El Arish the Germans became drunk on some alcohol they had found in Bankes's luggage, angering the Moslems. According to Finati, no one else in the party ever touched alcohol and henceforward carried nothing with them to cause offence. But during the stop Bankes had noticed an object which he 'coveted very much', a drinking trough made of dark granite engraved with lines of hieroglyphs. He obtained written permission from the Pasha to remove it, but apparently never did so.

At Gaza Bankes was invited to dinner at Government House and took great interest in a mosque which had formerly been a church. 'The number of churches that remain in Syria, built by the Frank kings, is truly astonishing, when it is recollected that all must have been constructed in less than a century. This at Gaza is a fine specimen and exactly similar to the Gothic churches of Europe at the same period. I have detailed drawings of many of them,' Bankes was to write in a footnote to Finati's book. Architecture fascinated him above everything. But the customs and appearances of the local people attracted his attention too, and he observed everything that was strange and new, from the habits of Nile Turtles to a fine botanical watercolour of a Sudanese 'apple' plant. He was intrigued to discover that a hippopotamus was killed within four hours of Damietta, watched the whole procedure of skinning and stuffing the creature with a mixture of horror and fascination, and was instrumental in recovering the bones.

> Can anything be more surprising [he asked his father] than that so bulky and voracious an animal can have made a journey of more than a thousand miles between a continued chain of towns and villages without ever having been seen by any person? It seems to bear decisive evidence that it does really travel under water and feeds altogether in the night.[14]

Bankes's party travelled from Gaza to Jaffa and thence to Jerusalem, where they lodged in another convent and finally managed to rid themselves of the troublesome Germans. Bankes, insatiable, wanted to visit all the holy sites: the Mount of Olives, the Vale of Jehosophat and the Tombs of the Kings before moving on to Bethlehem and the Church of the Nativity. He insisted on seeing the small underground room celebrated by both Greek Orthodox and other Christians as Christ's birthplace. But there was an 'immense throng of people . . . the women sitting squatted on the floor and the men climbing and straddling over them so that there were sometimes screams and generally loud disputes and even blows going on in some part or other of this little sanctuary all night long.'

Arriving next at the Arab village of Ribha, ancient Jericho, they felt dangerously exposed when their Christian guides left them. The Bedouins warned they could offer no protection against gangs of brigands. But they were offered beds at the Convent of the Nativity, where Bankes learned that the son of one of his guides was imprisoned in Jerusalem. He quickly arranged the young man's release by pleading his case in person with the local chief and presenting him with a silver telescope and some pearls. Bankes won enormous respect and gratitude for this; in return, the father procured safe conduct for the 'Christian strangers' to the ruins at Djerash, which Bankes hoped to identify as one of ten major cities of the Decapolis region, created around 64 B.C. as a Greco-Roman federation, mostly to the East of the Sea of Galilee. The area was an important site for a number of New Testament stories. Bankes also insisted that on the eve of their departure they partake of a feast and spend one night as his guests.

After four days' journeying Bankes and his group arrived at Djerash. Finati commented that the ruins there exceeded expectation: 'not massive like those of Egypt but, for the most part, light and slender and beautiful with almost innumerable columns standing in rows and others curved into a great open circle'. Bankes, deeply immersed in drawing plans, elevations and views of the noble city, failed to notice when his horse, tethered during the afternoon, suddenly collapsed and died after consuming poisonous oleander. This put him in a quandary, for he was far from having completed the work he wished to do. By sacrificing a beautiful pair of scarlet boots, a present from some Abyssinian friends at Jerusalem, he persuaded the Arab guides to let him stay longer. When he had finished they managed, by sharing the three remaining horses, to move on to Oomkais (ancient Gadara), another great ruined city overlooking Lake Tiberias.

Here the group encountered a wild looking, bearded Englishman by the name of James Silk Buckingham. Buckingham was a Cornish adventurer born to a seafaring family of little means. Quick-witted rather than clever, he had left a wife and children at home to search for fame and riches abroad. He was carrying letters for a mercantile house to India overland by the most direct and expeditious route, an aspect of his contract which clearly did not concern him too much. He was to cause Bankes endless trouble in the years ahead. He was, according to *Gentleman's Magazine*, one who when he achieves good fortune claims 'it has been by power of his own wit and far sightedness and when adversity has come upon him it has been through anybody's fault but his own'.[15] Finati noted tersely: 'He took no part either with his purse or with his pencil.' Bankes added later: 'He never made a single sketch.'[16]

Bankes, easygoing as ever, did not trouble too much about the credentials of the convincing newcomer who 'begged to be permitted to accompany me, offering to be any use to me in his power by taking down notes or memoranda or ascertaining bearings for me.

I consented to this, specifying distinctly that there must be no publication on his part.'[17] Together they visited Djerash and at Acre were introduced to Solyman Pasha and Malem Haim, 'a rich Jew' who was his banker and Prime Minister. In the Pasha's palace they were entertained with tales of poisoning and massacres to rival Scheherezade but Bankes fearlessly asked for permission to visit the mosque and the public bath, which was lit up expressly for their use.

On they moved to Tyre, Sidon and finally Mount Lebanon, where they were the guests, as arranged by Burckhardt, of the redoubtable Lady Hester Stanhope. Buckingham did not stay but returned to Nazareth, whence he had the audacity to write to Burckhardt that, 'Mr Bankes has pressed me into an union with himself under the idea that you also would contribute your share to a work on Nubia, Egypt and Syria, particularly the countries east of the Jordan.'[18] Buckingham, admitting this was not an immediate proposition, went on: 'His drawings are numerous and accurate. I have myself the most ample geographical details for a map of the country and notices of the geological features of the same. You could furnish the best material regarding the manners, peculiarities etc so that the union would perhaps be advantageous.'[19] Advantageous certainly to Buckingham.

Meanwhile Bankes was enjoying the hospitality of Hester Stanhope. Stanhope had left England aged thirty-four, following the death of a brother and would-be lover at the Battle of Corunna in 1809, to travel alone in the East. Born in 1776, she was the granddaughter of Lord Chatham, niece of Prime Minister William Pitt, relation of the Grenvilles, Campbells and Hamiltons, and must have been known to the Bankes family if only peripherally. William Bankes would not easily have passed up an opportunity to meet this courageous eccentric, a six-foot tall aristocratic heroine with the same spirit of adventure as himself. They would have had much to talk about and much to disagree over – especially Byron, whom Lady Hester had met in Athens. They disliked each other intensely, he making fun of 'that dangerous thing, a female wit', she considering him an affected poseur. The relationship was not helped by the fact that Lady Hester's latest lover, Michael Bruce, one of the Cambridge circle that had poked fun at Bankes, subsequently fell under Byron's spell.

She lived for a while in Turkey before finally settling at Mar Elias, a small former convent on the slopes of Mount Lebanon where she spent the last twenty-five years of her life. Here she became a legend and a curiosity as much for her habit of wearing male attire as for her sharp tongue and religious beliefs. William stayed in Mar Elias with Lady Hester, then aged forty, for some three weeks in March 1816, rarely venturing out as the weather was so bad, except to her beautiful summer residence at Abra, near the summit of the mountain. Antonio and Finati found rooms in the nearby village.

To Bankes she wrote after his departure: 'I have scolded you a great deal, as I do everyone when I think they deserve it, but yet I am much interested about you.'[20] She gave a quite different opinion to others, including her lover, Michael Bruce. 'He has been very civil to me but he does not suit me, he bores me, tho' thought vastly agreeable by Europeans . . . After all his talk he is naturally very mean, he wishes to see everything and wishes it to cost him nothing.'[21] To the naturalist Sir Joseph Banks she wrote: 'As to your namesake Wm. Bankes, I cannot endure him and wish I could pass a bill for him to be obliged to change a name which such a character can have no right to; if you have that one at least . . . He told Napoleon he was your relation; it is impossible.'[22]

When Bankes's party left, en route for Damascus and some sites of specific interest recommended by Burckhardt, Lady Hester offered a couple of Syrian servants and further letters of introduction. This was particularly dangerous countryside – twice Bankes had his purse stolen in the night – and snow hampered their progress to Aleppo, so he contented himself with finding some sarcophagi in burial places and copying inscriptions. He soon discovered that Lady Hester's act of kindness was not all it might have been. Sometimes her letters of introduction to local Bedouin sheikhs bore two seals if she considered the traveller merited special care; on this occasion the letters had only one. The Englishman had annoyed Lady Hester in a number of ways. She disliked his habit of talking so much, which rivalled her own. Perhaps Bankes, so charming and engaging to others, had not done enough to reassure her he would tell the 'truth' about her lifestyle when he returned to England.[23] She was further irritated when he changed his itinerary without discussing it first with her. But Lady Hester's change of heart concerning Bankes was largely caused by her jealousy over an offer he had made to her English physician, Charles Meryon, part of her household, whom he invited to join him as secretary for a forthcoming trip through Italy. Ostensibly, she objected because he offered to pay only Meryon's expenses and not a salary. But surely what rankled most was his insensitivity to a middle-aged woman's fears, when in his letter seeking permission to make the offer to Meryon he referred to rumours that Meryon was thinking of leaving her and settling in Italy.

Bankes told her frankly about his 'miserable indolence about writing [which] grows upon me every day', and his need for help with 'many notes and memorandums which it was almost a duty in me to have made in my travels'.[24] He believed Meryon could act as an invaluable amanuensis, but insisted that if she did not like the proposition she was not to scold him 'and whatever you do I rest perfectly satisfied'. He went on to tell her how he had been spending the days plundering the famous Cedars of Lebanon 'and have brought down with me a small log of which I propose to make some little box or cabinet and little sack with about twenty cones which I hope to sow in England.'[25]

Cedar trees were hugely fashionable and still relatively rare in the gardens of English country houses, some dating from the seventeeth century, and saplings supplied by Lee's Nursery at Hammersmith were prohibitively expensive. William Bankes would have wanted those at Kingston Lacy to be original Cedars of Lebanon. He begged Lady Hester to do him 'the greatest kindness in the world by asking the servant who carries over your horses to take charge of them and deliver them [via the consul] to my father'.[26]

Lady Hester, clearly vexed that Meryon might leave her for

Bankes, passed on his request with bad grace. She told the doctor: 'Your vanity, I know, will jump at travelling with a rich man' but warned him of 'plenty of mortifications' in store if he accompanied Bankes 'for he is a man who will go about saying that you scribbled your way home for your passage . . . as far as I can judge there is nothing to be gained but a great deal of trouble and little profit.'[27]

She did, however, ask Meryon to organise the forwarding of Bankes's possessions, including the cedar cones. 'For I will not keep one of his things another day in my house – impertinent fellow that he is! But he shall learn who I am . . . so off with frescoes, drawings and packages.'[28] Meryon decided to decline the invitation to travel with Bankes but did forward his belongings, mostly packed on mules. Eventually the precious cones reached Kingston Lacy, where William's mother Frances sowed and nurtured many of them successfully.* The correspondence between Bankes and Lady Hester does her little credit. Bankes, having been forced to negotiate safe passage himself with the sheikhs, had nonetheless written playfully to his former hostess: 'By and bye, when we are both respectable old people, we will sit at Kingston Hall under the shade of our cedars and fanning ourselves in spite of the difference of climate.'[29] But having turned against him, she became implacable in her criticisms.

In addition to her other complaints, she now began reprimanding Bankes for not having shown Buckingham, whom she persisted in considering a clever man, more sympathy. Buckingham, in no rush to complete his commission from the bank, was determined not to lose touch with Bankes. 'From having so recently enjoyed the pleasures of a companion I was doubly alone after your departure from hence for Acre,' he had written in February from Nazareth.[30] He feared separation from Bankes, who was extremely useful to him, and being forced into different routes, 'which I should regret more

---

* On 22 September 1821 William wrote to his father: 'I hope that my Mother will not forget that I have yet 18 cedars for which proper places are to be found, but if not planted this season they should be shifted into larger Pots.'(DRO) This implies that they were sizeable and that some had already been planted out.

than any event that could happen'.[31] He intended, he said, to travel to Baghdad and hoped to meet up back in Nazareth. In March he had written to Bankes, then still at Lady Hester's house, of his 'disappointment and anxiety' at not finding his new friend at Damascus, explaining how he had attempted the journey eastward, but the disturbed state of the country together with his own lack of money, clothes and letters of introduction made it impossible for him to proceed further. At the end of April a further message from Buckingham anticipated meeting Bankes at Aleppo, or overtaking him in time to set out for Palmyra together.[32] Bankes's replies to Buckingham have not survived. But there is every reason to suppose that in mid-1816 he still considered Buckingham an interesting fellow countryman who might provide amusement. He remained unaware for some months that Buckingham was taking advantage of every introduction his fellow traveller might have offered and several of those he had not.

Yet Bankes's suspicions must have been aroused within months of their meeting, for by May Lady Hester was writing to him:

> There has been a sad business respecting Mr Buckingham, as you will hear if the poor man is innocent. I am sure you will feel very sorry for not having assisted him. In case that you should hear how I have acted towards him and not understand exactly I must tell you. Upon his asking me if he should get a little money at Said's (which I knew he could not) I said I have just received some and gave him enough to get to Aleppo ... You know I cannot afford those sort of things but I cannot bear the idea of the poor man's future prosperity being blighted for want of a little ready money to carry him on after the journey. Do not say anything about it. I have no merit in having done what I have for having been a beggar myself I can feel for others more strongly than you rich men can probably do. I tell you this in confidence merely in case that you should hear a blind story at Aleppo.[33]

A month later John Barker, the British Consul at Aleppo, informed her she had been badly duped and that the rascal Buckingham had abused the confidence, squandered the money and sacrificed the interests of his benefactors 'to the vanity of becoming an author or to the expectations of a great profit from his book'.

Barker tried to make her see things as they were.

That Mr Bankes pressed him while at Aleppo to accompany him to Palmyra but that his sense of duty was so strong as to overpower his ardent desire of exploring the only remaining antiquities of Syria which he had not visited, while I know that Mr Bankes had no desire of his company and Mr Buckingham knows full well that I should have refused to advance him a piastre if he had really attempted that journey, think of the absurdity of a man in Bankes' circumstances endeavouring to make such a case . . . Oh, I retract my opinion of his abilities being superior to those of Mr Bankes and am quite ashamed that I could for one moment make the comparison or have believed him to possess common sense.[34]

But Barker's intervention did little to assuage the bad feeling between Bankes and Lady Hester. 'Queen Zenobia, or Semiramis as You like to call her,' Burckhardt teased Bankes,

is dreadfully angry with You for having slighted her advice, and is making very free with your name, almost as free as she did with mine, alledging as ostensible reason, your little liberality to Bedouins. The latter are a fine nation, but certainly very greedy; and Lady Hester is ridiculously mistaken if she indulges in the supposition to have acquired thorough knowledge of the manner to treat the Bedouins and still more if She prides herself upon exercising any influence over unruly sons of the desert.[35]

Bankes, some months after he had been her guest, made no secret of his conviction that she was 'not at all a woman of talent, an opinion that is never to be forgiven', and cannot have been surprised at the way relations between the two deteriorated. 'She wants, I know, to do all that she can to thwart and obstruct me but . . . I believe I may safely defy her to do her worst. It is not my intention to go near her.'[36]

5

Discovery

~

O N 26 JUNE 1816 Bankes and da Costa sailed from Suadieah, near Antioch in Southern Turkey, to Cyprus. They then moved on to Asia Minor to 'the islands of the Archipelago and Adriatic, Constantinople and all Greece, with Albania and the Roumelia [northern Greece and Bulgaria] and even Maina [the Southern Peloponnese].'

Bankes temporarily dismissed Finati, whose lack of sea legs and scant knowledge of Greek made him of little help, and seems to have had no clear idea of where to travel next. He was even contemplating returning home to England at the end of the year, prompted partly by news of the death in December of his great-uncle and benefactor Sir William Wynne, perhaps also by the fact that he had now passed the milestone age of thirty. He was still resisting his rôle as the eldest son. But he had already arranged to have a haphazard collection of some of his treasures shipped to Kingston Hall – statues, tablets and other antique stones – when he received a long and serious report from Burckhardt on progress with the removal of the colossal granite bust of Rameses II (the younger Memnon), from the Rameseum, the magnificent mortuary temple in Western Thebes, for ultimate presentation to the British Museum. Although the French first found the great head in the courtyard of the Ramesseum, their efforts to remove it were in vain. The English poet Shelley lyrically transformed the statue into Ozymandias, king of kings.

Burckhardt advised Bankes:

> Do let this be a Stimulus to Yourself, not to bury your treasures at your country house, where they can never be generally admired. Why not present the beautiful tablets from Thebes to the nation, after having taken drawings of them etc. They would serve to fit up the Egyptian room in the British Museum better than any thing else. They are, together with the colossal head, the finest specimens of Egyptian workmanship now extant and in so far better calculated for a public than for a private repository. And would you count the honour for nothing to be a donor to the Museum?[1]

Ancient Greece was a powerful magnet for a classicist such as Bankes, but without either Meryon or Finati as secretary, his movements are difficult to piece together from surviving scraps of paper. On 23 April 1817 he was in Athens where he hosted a ball at the house of the pro-consul.[2] He then toured various islands, bought a number of Greek vases, medals and trinkets, visited Mount Olympus and sketched some hilltop monasteries. Yet Bankes could not quell the urge to return to Egypt and Syria. What tempted him must have been partly the pace at which new antiquities were being discovered. Abu Simbel was now open, the tomb of Seti I had been discovered at Thebes and other excavations were taking place at Thebes and Giza. As he wrote to Burckhardt:

> You'll be surprised at my resolution of making a second journey through a part of Syria. I should have been surprised at it myself had it been pre-told to me six months ago. Upon the approach of winter I began to dread it and . . . to suffer from cold at Athens. However, there are some points in Syria which I did not sufficiently examine . . .[3]

It was the examination rather than the acquisition that was pulling him.

Another factor rekindling Bankes's interest in Egyptian antiquities was the arrival in 1816 in Egypt of Henry Salt, British Consul-

General. Son of a surgeon from Lichfield and trained as an artist under John Hoppner,* Salt became a diplomat, archaeologist and fearless collector. But his skills as a draughtsman gave him his first opportunity to travel in 1802, as official artist to Viscount Valentia on a long voyage to India and the East. He was tall, handsome and charming. Ladies in English drawing rooms were said to swoon at tales of his endurance and exploits, especially in the Abyssinian hinterland. Burckhardt, too, was immediately impressed and told Bankes that Salt was doing pioneering work collecting and drawing hieroglyphics. Burckhardt believed that Salt, with 'an excellent classical and modern library of whatever concerns Egypt,' would do more towards their explication than had ever been done before.

> As he goes very coolly and earnestly to work we may expect a sound
> work on Egypt from his pen and pencil.[4]

And so Bankes returned to the Levant in early 1818, reunited with Finati, who had been working for Salt, and determined to visit as many new sites as possible. Touchingly, Finati wrote of 'his earnest desire to be once more attached to the master who, both while I was with him, and since his departure, had always proved himself a kind friend to me'. They were joined by other English explorers, including the Earl of Belmore, as well as the extraordinary Italian, Guiseppe Battista Belzoni, a former circus strongman turned archaeologist-engineer and his English wife, Sarah.

Belzoni, 'the giant of Padua', is a key character in the story of early nineteenth century Egyptian exploration. Born in 1778, he started working life in his father's barber shop. He soon realised he was not suited to the work and travelled to Rome, Paris and the Netherlands, studying hydraulic mechanics along the way. Arriving in England when he was twenty-five, he progressed via Spain, Portugal and Malta before moving on to Egypt in 1815. Almost seven foot tall, he was a man of enormous physical strength and initiative who

---

* Hoppner's son Richard Belgrave was the British consul in Venice who, with his Swiss wife, was to look after Byron's daughter Allegra in 1819–20.

had developed a new water pump to replace the traditional water wheel used for irrigating the fields. It was rejected after a minor accident occurred during the demonstration to the Pasha, but he decided to remain in the country and devote himself to archaeology, and soon met a number of other Europeans, including Burckhardt, who introduced him to Salt.

As Salt's agent he was responsible for bringing down the great bust of Rameses II from Thebes, a feat he eventually achieved in 1816 'with a daily labour of 110 men to move it 80 yards'. He helped Salt acquire further antiquities, by excavation and other means, and was responsible for many achievements. In 1816 he made a first unsuccessful attempt to penetrate the Abu Simbel temple by removing the sand blocking the entrance. He made a second attempt, with better equipment, the following year and thus became the first person for centuries to enter the temple. A true amateur in the age of amateurs, he had initially assisted the French Consul, Bernardino Drovetti. But they had a spectacular falling out and Belzoni subsequently refused to mention the Frenchman by name, other than with the initial D. Belzoni's change of allegiance compounded the rivalry between Salt and Drovetti and by 1816 Thebes had become something of a battle zone.

Drovetti, a former officer in Napoleon's army who had enjoyed a brilliant military career, had been appointed French Consul-General in 1810 and established a close relationship with the Pasha after helping him organise the army more efficiently and improve agricultural methods. In 1814, following Napoleon's downfall, Drovetti was dismissed from his post, but he remained to continue further, largely unscrupulous, exploration on his own behalf. Henceforth, with a team of agents and scouts, he amassed a vast collection of antiquities, some of which ended up in Turin where he settled, forming the core of the Museo Egizio.*

By the time Finati and Bankes met up with each other again in

---

* A second, equally enormous Drovetti collection, comprising more than 600 objects, can be seen today in the Louvre.

Jerusalem in the spring of 1818, 'a very joyful day to me', as the former wrote, Bankes was in the company of two British naval captains, Charles Irby and James Mangles, Mrs Belzoni, Mr Legh and Lord Belmore and his family. The group amused themselves at the Dead Sea where the non-swimmer Bankes was able to float. Then, in Jerusalem, Bankes turned to more serious pursuits as he wished to excavate a vault in a complex of tombs known as the Tombs of the Kings. He had already taken measurements some months before and, convinced that other entrances and possibly additional chambers must exist, applied to the Military Commander of Jerusalem, the Aga, for permission to excavate. When this was refused he decided to dig anyway, secretly, at night by lantern light. That he persuaded his companions, plus servants, to join in with this dangerous escapade bears witness to his persuasive powers. He bought pickaxes and directed his accomplices to leave the town at night, singly, from different gates to avoid suspicion and assemble at the rendezvous after dark. The ten-strong group divided into two watches and with one servant acting as sentinel, continued the work for several nights, stopping only at daybreak. They heaved the stones, some extremely heavy, one by one until their hands were worn and rough. But just when they thought they had found a probable opening, the suspicious governor gave orders to fill up the hole. They abandoned the project and Bankes next threw his efforts into organising a long desired visit to the legendary lost city of Petra. Other than Burckhardt, now dead, no living European had ever seen the magnificent rock-cut city.

According to Finati, 'Bankes also entertained great hope of discovering somewhere by the way the palace of a Jewish Prince [Hircanus], which he had read of, a fortified temple [called Carnaim], and the tomb and town of King Herod; two former attempts had failed; and it was now arranged that both Mr Legh, and the two sea captains, and their servants, should join us in the expedition.' He travelled as an Arab known as Khalil (to which Bankes sometimes added the title el Beg, the prince) with Abdallah (Captain Irby), Osman (Mr Legh) and Hassan (Mangles) and many bribing presents. Bankes and his party passed many ruins both interesting and insignificant on their expedition to Petra. They were treated with respect and esteem by the people they encountered, most of whom required high tribute for ensuring safe conduct onwards, a system which seems to have worked for Bankes. He may have taken pouches of the new gold sovereigns, introduced in 1817 as part of a major recoinage under George III, which were a boon to travellers but made them well worth robbing. Although dressed in authentic Arab clothes, the travellers had their money 'concealed in leathern belts round the waist next the body'.[5]

Petra, today in Southern Jordan, is situated in the Wadi Mousa or Valley of Moses, named after the myth that here Moses struck the rock to secure water for his wandering people after the flight from Egypt. The rose red necropolis suddenly appears after a narrow winding pathway between lofty cliffs and Bankes was mesmerised by the red sandstone remains. He spent hours drawing the carved façade of the Treasury, a Nabatean tomb almost 40 metres high hewn out of the cliffside, while the rest of his group waited patiently in a nearby clump of oleanders. He was the first European traveller to make drawings of Petra: when Burckhardt rediscovered the fabled city in 1812, he had been dressed as a Moslem pilgrim, which made even simple note-taking more difficult. But Bankes was not so over-awed that he lost his critical faculties in matters of architectural good taste, as Irby and Mangles, impressed by his classical knowledge, discovered. They quote his opinion of one building as having

more the air of a fanatical scene in a theatre than an architectural work in stone; and for unmeaning richness and littleness of concep-tion, Mr Bankes seemed to think, might have been the work of Boromini himself, whose style it exactly resembles, and carries to the extreme. What is observed of this front is applicable more or less to every specimen of Roman design at Petra.[6]

After two days sketching and measuring in Petra, all their nervous guide felt he could safely allow them, the group had to move on. Through methodical copying and observation, Bankes hoped to find new revelations. At Petra his discovery of a Greek inscription on a tomb provided proof that Christianity had been established there. At the next stop, Beit el Karm, Bankes rediscovered a building which he believed to be the Temple at Carnaim mentioned in the Maccabees. But the trip was fraught with constant danger as different tribes threatened extortion. One armed Arab 'stole upon my master unawares as he was mounting and, after cutting at him with his sword two or three times, contrived to snatch away his cloak from off the hinder part of his horse and to run off with it'. Insects had been a constant source of trouble; in addition the travellers also now suffered from such disgusting food, and swarming vermin in tents and houses, that they were happy to return to Lake Tiberias and then Acre, where they found passage to sail to Jaffa. After the privations of the previous six weeks Bankes gorged himself on fruit – especially watermelons and mulberries – and as a result suffered a violent fever. According to Finati he quickly declined, was often delirious and soon in great danger. Finati, distraught, rode off to find a Spanish monk who, although possessing meagre rudimentary medical knowledge, agreed to return and treat the patient. Bankes recovered slowly, but having been dangerously ill for several weeks, he was left severely emaciated and extremely irritable.

Mangles believed that although Bankes could not have made such a journey without the others, 'still he has the merit of being the first European who ever thought of extending his researches in that direction; and from his profound knowledge of ancient history as well as his skill in drawing he was by far the best calculated to go on such an expedition'.[7] Scholars today think that the 1823 volume eventually published under the authorship of Irby and Mangles was at the very least a collaboration with Bankes, and probably contained several large passages dictated by him. Besides Bankes's wealth, he possessed important leadership qualities based on his superior knowledge and skills, that made him a desirable travelling companion.

As soon as he was well another adventure beckoned. He shaved off his beard, leaving only a moustache, donned an Albanian outfit that, mysteriously, he had ordered Finati to buy in the market and, with pistols in his belt, ordered Finati to ride with him to Jerusalem.

A master of disguise, Bankes covered his face with a large hand-kerchief when they met strangers on the journey and instructed Finati to say that he was suffering from a dreadful toothache which accounted for his silence and inattention. As he recounted the story later, he played the role of a half-witted beggar. Only when they reached Jerusalem did Bankes disclose his real aim: to penetrate the Dome of the Rock, one of the holiest pilgrimage shrines in Islam forbidden to non-Moslems on pain of death. Finati, half guessing what was behind his master's desire for Albanian dress, admitted that if Bankes had been more honest with him, 'I doubt I should have gone forward at all.'

He added tellingly: 'But this at least I can say more positively, that for no other human being in the world would I have done it.' Finati knew the escapade posed a far greater risk for him than for Bankes who, as a British subject and man of substance, might have been merely threatened with extortion and released. He, Finati, would have been made the ultimate example as one conversant with their religion, laws and customs. Bankes must have understood this, too. Nonetheless, aided by Finati's Arabic, they were allowed inside this hallowed site, built between 687 and 691 to commemorate Mohammed's 'night journey', written of in the Qu'ran. They were shown the place where the skull of Adam was said to have been found, where Cain killed Abel and several other sacred spots. Still not satisfied, Bankes insisted on a souvenir: a signed and sealed certificate confirming their visit. Finati suffered heart-stopping agonies during the long minutes it took to prepare this beautiful document. He knew it should then be placed, as a mark of respect, on the crown of the head, but if his master had removed his cap his full-grown hair would have betrayed them both. Finati quickly placed both certificates respectfully side by side on his own shaven scalp.

When they returned to their muleteer it was clear that his talk had aroused suspicions. Yet Bankes, caring more for such risky adventures than for owning objects, yearned to see more historic sites. Finati knew better and the pair bolted off on their mules, riding back as fast as they could to Jaffa. However, their adventure was by now known to the Turks and they deemed it necessary to flee the country. They hired a boat to take them to Damietta, stopped for a few days at Cyprus – Bankes was pleased to see again the great sculptured vases of Limasol – and eventually returned to Cairo where Henry Salt gave the pair a warm and entertaining welcome. 'Mr Bankes,' Salt told his friends in England, 'is the most delightful companion, from his extraordinary powers of memory and the opportunities he has had for observation.'[8]

Henry Salt's warm respect for Bankes was genuine and fully earned. The British Consul-General admired the younger man's hard work and genuine talent as well as his naturally engaging personality. He considered him not simply 'high-bred and well informed' but 'possessing an inexhaustible fund of humour'.[9] Salt was keen that his next trip to Upper Egypt should be in the company of this unusual Englishman.

William took weeks to recuperate fully from his illness. He was so weak, he told his father once he had recovered, that he needed support to stand. But the enforced rest in the summer of 1818 was useful, enabling him to prepare and provision for the next, most serious expedition he had yet undertaken. Salt and Bankes, joint organisers, both had the highest standards when it came to the accurate copying of texts, and the party was carefully chosen. The two were sharing expenses, but probably not on an equal basis: Belzoni, who joined them at Thebes, was there at Bankes's specific request to supervise the removal of the obelisk at Philae. The team was probably the strongest privately organised epigraphic team that had until then set out to copy and draw at ancient sites. In addition to Bankes, Finati, Salt and his secretary, Henry Beechey, son of Sir William Beechey, the portrait painter, it included an eminent Prussian naturalist, Baron Sack. Bankes had much good-natured fun throughout the voyage at the expense of the elderly Dr Sack's devotion to insects and other small creatures. Sack had more or less invited himself to join the party but proved good value as he entertained them all with his 'little anecdotes of armadillos, flamingos, field mice and monstrous snakes . . . withal very credulous, and permitting himself to have a goose's egg foisted upon him for a crocodile's . . . infinitely amusing and good humoured'. He was the odd man out among all the artists who 'really vied with each who should produce the best sketches; being generally hard at it . . . from nine o'clock in the morning till dark.'[10]

The party was divided thus:

> A large canjia with fourteen oars was engaged by the month for Mr Bankes; a more roomy, but less manageable vessel, called a mash, for Mr Salt, an inferior sort of boat for the baron and a fourth for riding-asses, milch goats, sheep fowls and such conveniences as a journey made quite at leisure might admit of; for Mr Bankes increased his suite very much during this last voyage, having engaged Dr Ricci, a native of Sienna, both as physician and draughtsman . . . and a young French midshipman, Monsieur Linant, who had offered himself also as assistant draughtsman and to take observations, besides some inferior attendants.

Belzoni, in his account of the voyage which embarked in October 1818 (*Narrative of the Operations and Recent Discoveries in Egypt and Nubia*), referred sarcastically to the high level of comfort enjoyed by those fortunate enough to be afloat with Bankes. Others who encountered them also remarked upon the cabin in the stern (shared by Bankes and Salt) 'being large enough to contain comfortably two travelling bedsteads lighted by lattice windows on each side, before which is a white linen hanging as protection from the wind'.[11] There were two small lateen sails (triangular sails typical of an Arab dhow) and the twelve-man crews could lay to the oars when the wind was contrary.

But, whatever their relative comfort, the entire party worked extremely hard, none more so than Louis Maurice Adolphe Linant de Bellefonds, only nineteen when he joined Bankes's expedition. A naturally talented artist with a quick intelligence, he had begun travelling at the age of fourteen with his father, a Breton Naval officer, visiting the United States and Canada. He joined the French Navy as soon as he could and was part of an expedition of artists and

scientists which arrived in Egypt in 1818. He had already decided
to remain there and explore the interior when he met Bankes.
Alessandro Ricci, a doctor, was known to Belzoni as he had been
employed in copying hieroglyphics for him in the tomb of King Seti
I, which Belzoni was excavating. Disparate as the team members were
in age, class and nationality, the expedition apparently coalesced most
harmoniously. It was the sort of semi-institutionalised, democratic yet
hierarchical male grouping in which Bankes flourished. Salt wrote:
'There was such infinite variety of matter to be found at all the principal ruins that our curiosity was never sated and almost every day
brought us a new discovery.'[12]

While Finati's memoir is written with great gusto and momentum,
the trip itself was unrushed. 'The progress up the Nile was very
slow, for every quarry and every tomb in the ridge of the Mokattam*
was examined and explored,' commented Finati. This led to discoveries, the most significant being 'the curious picture which represents the removal of a colossus as large as those at Thebes, upon a
sledge drawn by a multitude of men, and of a bas-relief, in which
the same sledge is applied to the transport of an immense stone
from the quarry and drawn by oxen.'

These tomb scenes had already been noted by other travellers but
Bankes was the first to have them copied 'by means of the ladders
and quantity of candles with which we were provided'. Apparently,
Bankes subsequently improved upon this technique with 'a new
contrivance for giving light within the temple'[13] – perhaps some
form of mirror or light reflecting surface.

By the time he had finished in Egypt, Bankes had covered some
1,500 well preserved sheets of paper of different sizes, colour and
quality.[14] Many are untitled, unsigned and undated but the unpublished drawings have escaped the subtle Europeanising and distor-
tions of the engravings and printing process, described by Beechey
as sometimes giving 'a fanciful effect, destructive of the character of

---

* J. G. H. James says he means the hills ranging the Eastern bank of the Nile not
just the Moqattam Hills by Cairo.

the drawings'. Bankes, aware of their value, had two cabinets made for their storage at Kingston Lacy, with the words 'Egyptian Drawings' painted in black on the fronts.

The drawings and sketches, now stored elsewhere, can still be viewed. In general, Bankes drew up a site plan or map – he was particularly strong on architectural details and anything requiring perspective – while paying others for more general views and reproductions of hieroglyphs.

However cohesively the group may have worked together, clearly this was more than a boating party of English amateurs. Bankes himself was well equipped with two paint boxes and all the necessary apparatus for producing detailed architectural plans. He copied inscriptions, annotated with well-informed comments, and painted some excellent botanical watercolours. His notes have the freshness and quality only possible from first-hand observation, revealing a man whose attention was constantly drawn to the strange and the new, especially the customs and appearances of local people and creatures. He was also keen to contradict the French wherever he could. He wrote about the Esna Temple in Upper Egypt, between Luxor and Aswan:

> The front of the temple very low and small in proportion to portico and the door narrow, its construction is quite distinct and the portico may have been grafted on it, not a single stone intermingling, the 2 side doors very small, only one visible, certainly out of Temple and possibly to a Peristyle, but the French should have expressly stated which were those [?] walls and their researches that confirm this conjecture. They have represented the capitals incorrectly.[15]

The party must have been travelling with a small reference library, probably Salt's, as Bankes's notes, with his plan on the Temple at Luxor, refer specifically to errors made by Denon in his *Voyage dans la Basse et la Haute Egypte* of 1802, which he presumably had to hand. Later he was critical of the larger multi-volume *Description de L'Egypte*, whose volumes appeared between 1809 and 1828. In a footnote to Finati's comments about the nine noble columns of the portico at Gau (Qaw al-Kabir) he said: 'Unfortunately the details given of it in the great plates of the French Institute are, as usual, highly inaccurate.' Correcting the French certainly gave Bankes pleasure but was less than a guiding motive compared with his genuine desire to study and record – and of course, to remove, with Belzoni's help, the Philae obelisk. He also understood that a breakthrough in deciphering the hieroglyphs was imminent and that careful copying of inscriptions, especially bilingual ones, was important to the English scholar Thomas Young, with whom he began a lively correspondence. The question of whether hieroglyphs had a phonetic element was still undecided. Might the temples, tombs and palaces, built as testaments to the desire for immortality, also have stirred in him a desire to celebrate, if not perpetuate, the Bankesian dynasty?

Belzoni had claimed the Philae obelisk at least three years earlier in the name of the British Consul-General and had been assured by the Aga of Aswan that it was being guarded for him until he was ready to take it away. Salt surrendered his claim to Bankes and Belzoni, who had recently suffered a violent physical attack by Drovetti's agents, was happy to see it go to an English home. But the French had already attempted and failed to remove the obelisk and Drovetti had not given up. He tried to bribe local officials at Aswan into believing he had a prior right to ownership based rather ludicrously on the assertion that the obelisk texts established a hereditary claim. Salt eventually insisted to the Aga that they would proceed in any case, so, taking physical occupation, the British team camped on Philae and started work on the removal of the granite obelisk and its pedestal. While Belzoni inspected the hazards of the cataracts and devised plans, Bankes liberally distributed presents to the local sheikhs to persuade them to provide labourers and equipment. Some were employed to clear the ground around the ruins and demolish crude brick later additions. This work, subsidiary to the removal of the obelisk, led to the discovery of some new chambers in the Temple of Isis itself, which helped to date it.

The obelisk was rolled on timbers to the water's edge and a boat prepared below to receive it: 'all hands were at work and five minutes more would have sufficed to set it afloat,' Finati recounts. But the wooden pier collapsed under the obelisk's weight and it slid 'majestically' – Belzoni's description – into the river. The Italian strong man with an 'uncommon genius for mechanics' had probably not adequately supervised the building of the pier. His first concern was that the monument might be lost for ever. His next thought was 'the exultation of our opponents'. Bankes stalked off. 'Such things would happen sometimes,' was all he said. But Finati understood that his master was 'disgusted'. He set sail a day or two later, leaving Finati and Belzoni to try again. Eventually, they succeeded in retrieving the obelisk and negotiating its passage through the first cataract and down the Nile, though not without enormous effort, expense and injury to some of the labourers. Months later the obelisk arrived at Rosetta, with other cargo chiefly belonging to Belzoni. There it was loaded on to another boat for the voyage to Alexandria. Several years were to elapse before it was erected in the middle of an English lawn.

Finati was happy to stay behind and supervise the operation as it enabled him to prolong his honeymoon with a young Nubian. And he was excited by the activity of 'the great boat wheeling and swinging round and half filling with water while naked figures were crowding upon all the rocks or wading or swimming between them some shouting and some pulling at the guide ropes . . .' He caught up with Bankes at El-Sebua, where his employer was making small-scale excavations in order to inspect some wall paintings which revealed signs of Christian worship.

On 13 January 1819 the Bankes-Salt party crossed with another party of four Europeans who had travelled up the Nile to the second cataract and were returning downstream. They decided to put ashore and spend a day together. The new group included the young architect Charles Barry, on whom Egypt was to have a great influence, and his patron David Baillie. Barry had already toured France, Italy and Greece when he met Baillie, who was so impressed by the beauty of his drawings that he employed him as his artist.

Barry recorded the Nile meeting in his journal. 'We breakfasted together on the low flat sandy bank. Mr Salt showed me the whole of the sketches that have been made since leaving Philae . . . in pencil and very numerous, the work of himself, Mr Beechey and Linant.' He also looked over Bankes's drawings, plans and sketches 'which on account of their great number, he kept in a basket. They principally relate to detail such as hieroglyphs, ornaments etc and are executed by himself and an Italian doctor in his employ, Ricci'. Barry, impressed, described Bankes as a man of 'brilliancy and talent'.[16] Subsequently there was talk of a joint publication on Egypt, but nothing came of it.

Bankes's team reserved its greatest effort for the month-long work copying all the wall drawings within the great temple at Abu Simbel. Belzoni had cleared the entrance only a few months beforehand. This was important and exciting labour, undertaken semi-naked in steamy, sweaty heat – temperatures were often around 44 degrees centigrade – in uncomfortable positions perched on shaky ladders, lit by up to fifty small wax candles attached to palm branches on poles. Other days, with the help of workmen, Bankes and Salt scrabbled away at the temple façade until they uncovered one of the four colossi there. This, too, was exhilarating activity. The figures were in a remarkable state of preservation and Bankes was eager to continue once he discovered a few Greek letters scratched on the leg of one figure. He took a gamble that the huge legs which were nearer the door would reveal further inscription, and encouraged his fellow workers to continue digging. One difficulty was where to put the mass of excavated sand without expending more time and labour, so part of it re-covered a figure they had just cleared. After three or four more days, they discovered an inscription from the reign of King Psammetichus II, which gave information vital for dating the Temple. Bankes knew from his Greek studies that there had been kings with this name during the 26th dynasty (664–525 BC) and concluded that the Temple's foundation must have predated this period. As he wrote in a footnote in Finati's book, 'The inscription relates to King Psammetichus and is certainly among the very earliest extant in the Greek language.'

Meanwhile they were visited by the Defterdar Bey, son-in-law of Mahommed Ali, who was 'astonished to find so much light burning and so many hands employed in such an atmosphere for purposes which he could not comprehend and which it was in vain to endeavour to explain to him for he always returned to the question of "What treasure have they found?"'

Probably Bankes's greatest achievement during this trip was his discovery at Abydos, in the temple built early in his reign by Rameses II, of an inscribed list of Kings of Egypt. According to Finati, 'nothing that he found seemed to give him more pleasure or to excite more interest'. Cleaning a small inner chamber to take measurements for a building plan, he noticed that one wall was carved with several rows of royal cartouches. This he believed represented the names of many kings in chronological order. He understood immediately he had uncovered a prime historical monument which could contribute important material to the decipherment debate. He set about making a careful copy, which as soon as feasible, he dispatched to Thomas Young, as he did with other inscriptions from Egypt.

Revealingly, Bankes did not attempt to remove this crucial table from the wall. He was aware of conservation issues, unpretentious in his claims to original scholarship and not, for the era, overly acquisitive. Unlike other travellers, he rarely recorded his presence at sites he had excavated. Abu Simbel was an exception and there on the left flank of the southernmost colossus can be read:

Wm Bankes
opened (this) [very faint]
Colossus

A further inscription inside records that Salt and Bankes had opened the temple. A few years after his return to London Bankes was to find himself embroiled in a row which accused him of sending out to Salt implements for the removal to England of a Zodiac 12 feet across by 3 feet thick and weighing about 20 tonnes, considered one of the greatest treasures of ancient Egypt. Bankes strongly refuted this accusation and in a letter to the *Quarterly Review* stated clearly

how he had 'always deprecated, in the strongest manner, any spoli-
ations of existing and entire monuments, such as that temple is'.[17]

Ten years later J.F. Mimaut, French Consul-General, ripped the
King List off its wall with scant regard for the integrity of the text
and took it back to France to form part of his private collection,
which was sold in 1839. The King List, purchased by the British
Museum, where it can now be seen, is considered one of the leading
Egyptian finds of Bankes's generation.

Bankes's longstanding ambition on this trip was to continue south
as far as Dongola or even Meröe. But at Wadi Halfa a 'tedious nego-
tiation' began to obtain the protection of Hussein Cashef. Bankes
supplied cash, Salt lent authority. As they sat down under a canopy
to start the bargaining, it seemed at first that neither presents nor
persuasion could prevail. But eventually the reluctant Cashef agreed
to provide camels and an escort, conceding, 'the duty of a Prince is
to keep his Friends out of danger – I will afford you my protection *so far as I can assure your safety*.'[18]

But in March 1819 Salt fell dangerously ill. His companions, fearing
he was on the point of death, sent him back immediately with Linant.
Bankes continued with the others and a new English companion,
John Hyde; ten strong camels and the promised escort from Hussein
Cashef followed on foot. But 150 miles above Wadi Halfa their protec-
tors abandoned them, taking the camels. Hyde, too, now succumbed
to illness and although Bankes desperately wished to continue, 'and
used both arguments and large offers in order to accomplish it', the
Cashef told them unequivocally they could go no further. If they
persisted, they would find their 'graves already dug for us'.

Hot and weary, 'creeping along like so many beggars', they returned
slowly to Wadi Halfa, Hyde now too weak to walk. Bankes, desperately concerned about Hyde's health, stole some pack animals,
ensuring that there was one camel to carry the sick Englishman.
This part of the expedition, without the protection of the Consul
and with the threat of war in Nubia, was the most hazardous.
Eventually they reached Thebes, then Cairo and during the course
of the next few weeks, dispersed.

Bankes, however, now had another distraction. In June he was shown an advertisement in a Calcutta newspaper announcing the forthcoming publication of *Travels in Palestine* by James Silk Buckingham, his erstwhile travelling companion. Whoever alerted Bankes to this obscure publication while he was at Thebes also ensured he was shown a list of chapters, including two or three that referred to Djerash. Buckingham and Bankes had spent in total less than a week together but the ruins at Djerash were the high point of their joint trip. Bankes was immediately convinced that Buckingham's book, which he did not wait to read, was plagiarising his own travelling notes. Bankes could be both angry and phlegmatic at once. He wrote a furious letter to Buckingham dated Thebes, 12 June 1819:

> Mr Buckingham – After some anecdotes respecting your conduct which you cannot but suspect have come, however late, to my knowledge before this time, you cannot expect that I should address you otherwise than I should the lowest of mankind. It is indeed with reluctance that I stoop to address you at all.
>
> It will require, however, no long preface to acquaint you with the object of this letter, since your own conscience will point it out to you from the moment that you shall recognise a hand-writing which must be familiar to you since you have copied it and are about to turn the transcripts to account . . .
>
> You have hoped that the distance of place would befriend you; you have hoped that I should shrink from proclaiming that I have been imposed upon; it would have been far more politic in you to have shrunk from being proclaimed the man who has imposed.
>
> In that advertisement by which you announce as your own the works of another you have at least spared me the humiliation of being named in the list of your friends.

It was a long letter, in which Bankes maintained that any notes were dictated by him and above all that the plan of the ruins at Djerash 'was constructed and noted with my own hand and that all the assistance that I derived from you even in collecting materials for it was in Your ascertaining for me the relative bearings of some of the buildings with *My* compass.'

He concluded by demanding the return of copies of his papers 'and let all that portion of the work advertised that treats of a journey made at my expense and compiled from my notes be suppressed'.[19] Not content with sending the irate missive to Buckingham himself, still in India, he also sent his father a copy giving him permission to publish in England if he saw fit.

His rage only temporarily assuaged, Bankes returned to Cairo where he once more enjoyed the company of his friend Salt, now recovered, and also met the entertaining Nathaniel Pearce, married to an Abyssinian, whom Salt had appointed to run the Cairo consulate. He was preoccupied too with a final discovery in the days returning from Nubia. At Maharraka he noticed a great granite platform of steps, which he immediately identified as providing the ideal base for his obelisk. Bankes was convinced they had once been the base to another obelisk. The four blocks, the heaviest of which weighed nearly 11 tons, were not finally removed until 1822. Before he left Egypt Bankes charged Linant de Bellefonds with arranging their shipment to England. The obelisk meanwhile still lay at Alexandria and its pedestal had not moved from its sandbank at Philae. Bankes also paid Linant to investigate and copy the inscriptions on the supposed temple of Jupiter Ammon at the oasis of Siwa and then to continue up to Meroe in Nubia, where he himself had so desperately wished to go. He had already dispatched Ricci to copy some primitive paintings in rock tombs at Beni Hasan which Bankes had come across during his 1815 trip, and had immediately understood their importance in explaining contemporary life.

Belzoni also left Egypt in September 1819, not before warning Bankes that Drovetti was persisting in his claim to the obelisk even though he had 'no more right than the governor of Siberia'.[20] When Belzoni arrived in London at the end of March, 1820 he found himself a celebrity in a city avid for first-hand accounts of these dangerous discoveries. Belzoni, despite his poor English, was swiftly commissioned by John Murray to tell his amazing story and for weeks scribbled away in his publisher's little back parlour in Albemarle

Street, refusing any help except for correction of his spelling. 'As I made my discoveries alone, I have been anxious to write my book by myself,' he wrote.

By this time Bankes, too, was on his way home. He had made generous payments to all those who had helped him including ample salaries to Linant and Ricci for further copying, a thousand piastres for Pearce and a parting gift of pair of diamond earrings for Henry Salt's new bride. 'I dare say you are very impatient to see her,' he wrote to Pearce, 'she is very young and very pretty.'[21]

His decision to leave was not taken wholeheartedly. He was tempted to remain and undertake further explorations with his friends Salt and Pearce, Linant and Ricci. 'Of all the parts of the world which I have visited, Egypt and Nubia are those which interested me, beyond all comparison, the most and have made the deepest impression upon my mind,' Bankes was to say much later in life.[22] At the same time he always understood that family obligations would require his eventual return to England. 'I hope to divide next summer between Cornwall, Dorset and Wales, counties where I shall make fewer discoveries and yet find more to delight me than in these,' he wrote tactfully to his father, adding somewhat disingenuously: 'and in Dorsetshire, George's cottage at least will be as new to me as the chamber in the Pyramids.'[23]

Having decided to go home, promising himself he would return in a year or two, he waited impatiently with Beechey at Alexandria for a boat to Trieste. While delayed, he had a chance meeting with Henry Hobhouse, brother of his Trinity acquaintance John Cam Hobhouse, and hearing that he was travelling to the East, was tempted to entrust to him another letter to India, expressing his fury and rage over *Travels in Palestine*.

Hobhouse gave him news of Byron, whom he had not seen for seven years. Learning that Byron's marriage to Annabella had collapsed in disgrace and scandal and that he was living in self-imposed exile in Italy, Bankes decided to linger in Trieste, hoping that Byron might visit him there.

Byron had kept himself well informed of the progress of his former Cambridge circle. 'I am glad that "us youth" have made our due noise in the world . . . William Bankes hath made a stupendous traveller,' he wrote to John Cam Hobhouse.[24] But by November, when he finally replied to Bankes, he had to tell his friend that it was impossible for him to come to Trieste. 'A tertian ague, which has troubled me for some time – and the indisposition of my daughter, have prevented me from replying before to your welcome letter.'[25] He explained how he had been on the point of returning to England himself when the illness of his small child, Allegra – the illegitimate offspring of his brief affair with Mary Shelley's half-sister Claire Clairmont – had kept them in Venice, 'dependent on a Venetian Proto-Medico.' The little girl, not yet two, had fallen ill with the same malarial fever from which her father had just recovered. Travel to England in midwinter was clearly the least sensible option, but he wanted to sort out his tangled financial affairs and to discuss publishing projects with John Murray. The first two cantos of *Don Juan* had been published in July 1819, but he been sent reviews from England which viciously attacked 'this miserable man'[26] for his private life and for writing a 'filthy and impious poem'.

Depressed by this, and unable to decide whether to move to Ravenna with his nineteen-year-old mistress, Countess Teresa Guiccioli, Byron seemed pleased to be in contact again with his college friend Bankes. He wrote warmly telling Bankes how he had been following his progress and discoveries, and warning him of the changes he would find in England, especially among their old College contemporaries. However,

> You may rely upon finding everybody in England eager to reap the fruits (of your labours) – and as you have done more than other men – I hope you will not limit yourself to saying less than may do justice to the talents and time you have bestowed on your perilous researches . . . you have had better fortune than any traveller of equal enterprise – (except Humbolt) in returning safe . . . it is hardly a less surprise than satisfaction to get you back again.[27]

Byron's assurance that if he decided to return home by way of Venice he would receive a warm welcome was irresistible. For a short period in the winter of 1819 he went to stay with Byron in his splendid apartments in the Palazzo Mocenigo, on the Grand Canal just above the Rialto Bridge. Pedestrians entered the trio of sixteenth century palaces by way of the Campo Santo Stefano, through a dark courtyard garden, which leads into an even darker, damp cobble-stoned entrance hall, where the private gondola was docked. After walking up a flight of ornately carved wooden stairs Bankes would have reached the piano nobile to find his old friend living in great style, but temporarily alone, as his new young love was in Ravenna with her sixty-year-old husband, hoping Byron would follow.

Bankes would have admired the view overlooking the canal from the stone balcony outside the elegant drawing room. Byron's study next door, a room of similarly grand proportions, boasted a *Pavimento a la Veneziana* mosaic floor with a central coat of arms of the ancient Mocenigo family, who had once provided the city with so many of its Doges and now the exiled poet with a noble home. One can imagine Byron's enjoyment as he showed his rich friend the beamed ceilings with gold leaf, the painted frieze in the drawing room and the 'gorgeous suite of tapestried halls'[28] for which he was paying the heavy sum of £200 a year.

Physically, both men must have been much changed since their last meeting. Bankes's naturally fair skin was tanned and weather-beaten and his hair grown long. Bankes admitted later that he had found Byron 'greatly altered' and grown 'coarse'.[29] But he was touched by the way his old friend, delighted at the prospect of a visit from Bankes, 'had marked down the pages of different books he had been reading in which Bankes was favourably mentioned.'[30]

There is no record of how long Bankes stayed at the Palazzo Mocenigo, though the 'Nubian explorer' – Byron's term – and the exiled poet must have had much to exchange. When Bankes was not entertaining Byron with his amusing travellers' tales, the pair wandered the coldly beautiful city, in the midst of preparations for its famous carnival, which began just after Christmas.

According to Thomas Moore, Byron's first biographer, while Bankes was roaming around Venice admiring churches and pondering purchases, he met an Englishman, one Mr S[aunders] – dismissed by Byron as 'nothing but a d–d salt-fish seller' – who remarked that *Don Juan* was all 'Grub Street'.[31] Why Bankes, knowing his friend's sensitivity, felt it necessary to pass this on is unclear, but it indicates he had lost none of his old arrogance. Byron, wounded by this disparagement, could not bring himself to write another line of the poem for some time.

At all events, as soon as Allegra had recovered, Byron revived his insistence on travelling to England. But at the last minute – chests packed, servants sent on ahead – he changed his mind. On 24 December he left Venice, the city he now declared he found tedious, and went instead to Teresa and the Palazzo Guiccioli at Ravenna. Bankes decided to follow a few days later.

Byron was happy to introduce his courageous English friend to all the 'Ostrogothic Nobility as well as to the Dama whom I serve'.[32] The two Englishmen threw themselves into local life. According to Byron,

> the Carnival here is less boistrous but we have balls and a theatre – I carried Bankes to both and he carried away, I believe, a much more favourable impression of the society here than that of Venice ... Bankes and I took tickets for [the lottery] – and buffooned together very merrily – he is gone to Firenze.[33]

Three weeks later, Byron was trying to entice Bankes back. He told him in February there was room for him to stay if he wished, though the accommodation was less magnificent than in Venice. Moreover, since tropical heat had been no impediment to Bankes on his travels the Italian snow should not deter him either. Byron then teased his friend with memories of his gondolier Tita, a ferocious-looking giant with a great black beard, but a kind and gentle nature. Byron had hired Tita – Giovanni Battista Falcieri – whose family had long been in the Mocenigos' employ, when he had moved into the Mocenigo Palazzo. The gondolier became devoted to Byron, moved with him

to Ravenna and remained with him throughout the rest of his life.*
'Tita's heart,' wrote Byron teasingly to Bankes in February, 'yearns
for you and mayhap for your silver broad pieces; and your playfellow
the monkey is alone and inconsolable.'[34]

Byron was pressing. 'I forget whether you admire or tolerate red
hair, so that I rather dread showing you all that I have about me
and around me in this city. Come nevertheless,' he urged him. He
would not be much company in the daytime. 'But, then, all your
evenings, and as much as you can give me of your nights, will be
mine.' He also had a small commission for Bankes. There were more
cantos in his drawer '(and be d-d to them) of what courteous reader
Mr S[aunders] calls Grub Street,' to be delivered to his publisher,
'my Maecenas, Murray.'[35]

Bankes, once again dominant in this fifteen-year relationship, was
in Bologna, negotiating the purchase of a major painting, when
Byron wrote again. 'Pulci and I are waiting for you with impa-
tience,'[36] he began. Byron never pretended to be knowledgeable
about art. He once told his publisher that he knew nothing of
painting and actually detested it 'unless it reminds me of something
I have seen or think it possible to see'.[37] In Venice he had done
little to familiarise himself with the works of art tumbling out of
palazzi. But when he did finally visit the great picture collection at
the Palazzo Manfrini he was immensely moved by the 'poetry of
portrait' in the beautiful features of a sensual woman. He described
one such as 'the kind of face to go mad for because it cannot walk
out of its frame'.[38] Yet he knew enough to urge Bankes to buy what
both then thought was a 'Giorgione':

> To me there are none like the Venetian – above all Giorgione. I
> remember well his Judgment of Solomon in the Marescalchi in
> Bologna. The real mother is beautiful, exquisitely beautiful. Buy her,
> by all means, if you can and take her home with you; put her in

---

* After Byron's death he became a servant of Isaac D'Israeli and Benjamin Disraeli
got him various government posts. He lived to seventy-six, enjoying the celebrity
of having been a favourite servant of the poet.

safety; for be assured there are troublous times brewing for Italy . . .
it will be my fate to be head and ears in: but no matter, these are
the stronger reasons for coming to see me soon.[39]

Bankes had already bought the painting from the Marescalchi Palace
in Bologna on 11 January 1820, following his own critical judgment. Fortunate to be in the right place at the right time, he was
aware that the break-up of this once magnificent collection, created
by Ferdinando, Count Marescalchi (1754–1816), former foreign
minister of the Kingdom of Italy, now offered others unique opportunity. According to an entry in Frances Bankes's diary for 8 February:
'A letter from William (who is at Bologna) has horrified his Father,
having drawn five hundred pounds to pay for unfinished pictures
of masters that he does not fancy.'[40]

In fact, he paid 575 scudi for the 'Giorgione'. Based on the biblical
story of King Solomon and the two mothers who claim the same
baby, the *Judgment of Solomon* is an exquisite work painted around
1505–1510, the year of Giorgione's death. But it is neither finished
nor resolved and recent restoration has revealed three superimposed
conceptions of figures and settings on the canvas. In Bankes's day it
was universally attributed to Giorgione and he bought the painting
as such. This would have made it an outstanding purchase as Giorgione
died young leaving few paintings. In fact Giorgione *did* paint a
Judgment of Solomon around 1496, but this was set outdoors and quite
different from the one at Kingston Lacy. Bankes was naturally excited
in believing he had acquired a Renaissance masterpiece and it was
not until 1903 that Bernard Berenson attributed the work to
Sebastiano del Piombo.

Before he returned home, Bankes acquired several other notable
works from this once magnificent collection. The portrait of Cardinal
Camillo Massimi, painted by Diego Velazquez in Rome in 1649–50,
must be considered one of the finest paintings at Kingston Lacy and
his finest Spanish picture, albeit not bought in Spain. Unusually,
Velazquez used ground lapis lazuli as ultramarine in this painting, a
technique rarely used in Spain. The Marescalchi collection also yielded
a fine Titian, now believed to be a portrait of one Nicolo Zen.

Scholars today believe this is one of Titian's 'lost portraits', mentioned by Vasari in 1567 as among his later works. Zen (or Zeno) was a knight, member of the Council of Ten and one-time Ambassador to Charles V. He was also an author and friend of several of the artist's patrons. Bankes bought it believing the subject to be an unknown senator painted by Titian. His other Marescalchi treasure, *Omnia Vanitas*, is in the manner of Titian and, although its author remains unknown, was inspired by Titian's nudes.

Bankes did not return to Ravenna and he and Byron never saw each other again. Bankes continued to write; no replies have survived, though there is no evidence of estrangement. On the contrary, in October 1820 Byron wrote to John Murray that Bankes was one of only three men who had ever 'held out a finger to me – one was yourself – the third a Nobleman long ago dead . . . But of these the first was the only one who offered it while I *really* wanted it – the second from good will – but I was not in need of Bankes' aid, and would not have accepted it if I had (though I love and esteem him).'[41] In 1823, a year before Byron died, suffering pangs of isolation from his long exile, British consul Richard Hoppner wrote to Bankes begging him to use his influence and persuade him to return to England from Genoa. 'I mention this to you recollecting your attachment to him at the same time knowing how capricious he is.'[42] If Bankes acted on this appeal, he was not successful.

In the spring of 1820 William's mother Frances could hardly contain her excitement at the prospect of her son and heir's imminent return. Her diary becomes almost breathless as she records letters from friends or relations giving news of William. In Rome he met his sister Maria, now Mrs Thomas Stapleton, of Grey's Court, Henley on Thames and Mereworth Castle in Kent. Maria, who had married the Hon. Thomas Stapleton, eldest son of Lord le Despencer, on 19 January 1819 while William was travelling, 'announces having the happiness of meeting William after an absence of more than seven years', Frances recorded. William's sister finds him 'altered but conceives he will appear less so when his hair is cut, he has so lately left off his Eastern dress that he has allowed it to grow that it may supply the warmth of the turban and prevent his suffering from cold till he got into a warm atmosphere.' On 23 March, Frances boasts that Lady Bessborough was full of William's talents and that, 'the Duchess of Devonshire has written to say they all regret his leaving Rome, that he has not only seen more than any other traveller in the same time but professes the power of relating what he has seen in a peculiarly lively, agreeable manner.'[43]

Frances often notes with marked lack of interest that either George or Edward dined with her. On 28 February she remarks 'George and Edward came down with us into the country, the one to be re-elected for Corfe the other being mayor as the returning officer.' Her diary records little about Edward's recent engagement to the eligible, well connected and wealthy Miss Frances Jane Scott, youngest daughter of Lord Eldon the Lord Chancellor, or their marriage on 6 April for which William was unable to return. But on 11 April she hears from William in Milan that if he comes across the Simplon pass he will soon reach Paris, though 'the winter still continuing rigorous in those parts, a great deal of snow makes that doubtful'.

Two days later William's letter from Geneva is copied detailing an accident en route. Despite advice to the contrary, the intrepid Bankes tried to negotiate the mountain pass by taking his carriage to pieces and having it conveyed on sledges. 'Although great precautions were taken he was precipitated down the slope into a hole in the snow. He hurt his lip,' his adoring mother wrote, 'and appears to have had a narrow escape of losing his life.' On the 18th a further letter from William announces his arrival in Paris, 'saying we might expect him in the course of a week'.

'William returned after an absence of more than seven years in perfect health,' Frances announces triumphantly on 24 April. To celebrate, there is a small family dinner with Lord and Lady Falmouth, Mr and Mrs Pickard, George and William Woodley and William, of course, who was 'more agreeable than ever and in great spirits . . .

I can settle to nothing and follow Wm like his shadow' Frances wrote the next day. 'He went with me to call upon his sister, Mr Bond, his aunt and Lady Freemantle.'

The following day was a sad one as daughter Maria, long dogged by ill health, miscarried while at Rome. After this, Frances continued on a long round of visits in Dorset and London, where she proudly showed off her son the explorer at Somerset House at a dinner given by the Royal Academy to celebrate the opening of an exhibition. On the last day of the month she wrote:

William from this time occupied all my time and thoughts, which, in addition to the Falmouths coming to town, put an end for the present to this journal.

Her brilliant and beloved son was then aged thirty-four. There was a good chance he would settle in England now, and transform his wealth of notes and drawings into a published work that would establish his pioneering credentials as a traveller.

6

Society

~

'Pining for the Sunshine and the intense Blue Skies of the East'
William Bankes to Byron

THE COMBINATION OF primitivism and danger, art and ancient history that William discovered in Egypt touched him to his core. He responded by undertaking serious work of the highest quality, without knowing how important this would prove for archaeology. Much that he recorded has been subsequently lost or submerged under floodwater. His achievements transformed him from eligible bachelor to much lionised dinner guest in London society fizzing with excitement over Egyptian antiquities and the explorers and adventurers who followed in the wake of the Napoleonic expedition. Although the rediscovery of Egypt had begun in the eighteenth century, interest in this ancient civilisation was now reawakened by its treasures. In April 1821 Belzoni organised a spectacular exhibition at the Egyptian Hall in Piccadilly where the major finds of his four-year stay in Egypt were displayed. At the opening the Italian strongman unwrapped a mummy in front of a gasping audience.

Later that year Bankes published a detailed description of his monument entitled *Geometrical Elevation of an Obelisk from the Island of Philae*. This put him at the heart of the race to interpret hieroglyphics. The illustrations in Bankes's monograph showing both Greek and hieroglyphic inscriptions appeared just when Jean-François Champollion, a French scholar who had learnt Coptic as a teenager, had almost cracked the code. Bankes was in regular contact with the English polymath Thomas Young, who was also close to revealing the mystery, though he failed to make the final breakthrough; and the Egyptian Society, founded by Young for the collection, dissemination and study of hieroglyphic texts, relied much on Bankes's material. Champollion, too, used the hieroglyphs in a cartouche on Bankes's obelisk, believed to stand for Cleopatra, to confirm that his method worked. Bankes himself, although unable to decipher the name in the cartouche, had deduced it correctly by comparison with other inscriptions. Henry Salt in his 1825 essay on Dr Young's and M. Champollion's Phonetic System of Hieroglyphics, described this as a piece of work which would 'impress any researcher who reads it today'. But ultimately it was Champollion, who died in 1832, who proved that hieroglyphs were phonetic and the underlying language was Egyptian, enabling future scholars to reinterpret many ancient inscriptions.

For William, Egypt was one of many interests. Would he now find anything in England that would embrace his spirit in the same way? He talked of completing his abandoned journey to Meroe in Nubia and then going further to investigate the unmapped sources of the Nile, though it is hard to gauge how seriously he contemplated this. He confided to Byron that he found English society 'very dull, very meddling, very silly and very false'. He missed intensely the 'free and vagrant life' which he had enjoyed for the past seven years. 'It is not however so easy, I find, to commence a journey as to protract one and heaven knows whether I shall have the spirit or resolution to plunge again.'[1]

Yet too many salon hostesses praised his joie de vivre to believe he did not derive some amusement from these occasions. William's return to London coincided with the death of King George III and the end of the openly dissolute Regency period. As more sober times began his principal supporter was Mrs Arbuthnot, intimate of the Duke of Wellington, who immediately lionised the famous traveller. Harriet Arbuthnot, daughter of the Hon. Henry Fane MP, granddaughter of the 8th Earl of Westmoreland, sister of a clergyman, married in 1815 to the Rt. Hon. Charles Arbuthnot MP, was a deeply conventional pillar of the Tory party. At the time of the marriage, Charles Arbuthnot was Secretary to the Treasury and Patronage Secretary so she was, through him, a woman of great influence. But the Duke believed that Harriet in her own right was the sort of woman who 'makes the whole world do whatever she pleases'.[2]

Five days before this comment, Mrs Arbuthnot met William Bankes for the first time at a dinner party given in Henry and Frances Bankes's London home to celebrate the safe return of their son. The Arbuthnots reciprocated a month later when William dined with them and their close friend the Duke of Wellington. Harriet Arbuthnot was enchanted by William's 'very delightful and agreeable' conversation and her patronage may be said to have launched, or rather re-launched, the mature William into London society. No longer a second rate MP trailing in his father's shadow, he now reinvented himself as intrepid traveller and raconteur, his stories no doubt embellished in the re-telling.

Mrs Arbuthnot initially considered Bankes to be even wittier than Henry Luttrell, one of Regency London's cleverest wits, and Samuel Rogers, the banker-poet in whose rooms Byron had earlier often been entertained. The novelist Maria Edgeworth found him 'exceedingly entertaining'[3], while Princess Lieven, one of the most influential hostesses in London, describing an evening when Bankes recounted the anecdote of having to pay passage for a donkey along with his prized Raphael, told afterwards how Bankes 'could not open his mouth or move his arms (he makes the quaintest gestures) without my exploding. I laughed for two hours, and spent nine hours of sleeplessness in bed; I had become hysterical with laughing.'[4] Rogers commented that even the legendary wit of Sydney Smith might be 'absolutely overpowered by the superior facetiousness of William Bankes'.[5]

Bankes knew more than simply how to make ladies laugh, as the following account by Stratford Canning, cousin of George, reveals:

I dined at Brompton with Mr Frere. Wood and Mr Bankes were of the party. The latter particularly entertaining – a various reader, an enterprising traveller, with great fluency and liveliness, more memory, I should think, than judgement, more singularity than wit and yet with a sagacity and promptitude that might often pass, and occasionally with reason, for those more valuable qualities – I found him talking on my arrival at a quarter after seven, and it was his voice that concluded the conversation at eleven, his power of utterance unwearied, and his stores of memory to all appearance undiminished. He talked of his travels in the East. Cairo, he says, is visibly wasting away under the effects of the commercial monopoly exercised by the Pasha of Egypt. He being almost the only merchant in his territory, that valuable class cannot exist under his government and their former habitations are consequently deserted and going to decay ... at Jerusalem there is no similar appearance of decay; that city is the great market town to the surrounding country.

Bankes then went on to talk of his impressions of Lady Hester living 'in full persuasion of her being one day called to the assembling of God's chosen people, in the capacity of Queen of Jerusalem. This fancy, Mr B. represents, as having taken full possession of her mind.'[6]

Entertaining though he was, the impression lingers that he was trying too hard, not quite at ease in London society, any more than he had been at ease in Cambridge corridors hoping for admittance to the Speculative Society. In the capital, gaining repute as explorer and entertainer, he was still deeply involved in matters Egyptian. This was partly because of his aspirations for Ricci and Linant de Bellefonds, whom he paid to continue where he left off, aspirations that were only partially fulfilled. Bankes, generous to a fault, could also be demanding about money. 'I was to pay his expenses travelling, but not to keep him for his own wish and pleasure all his life,' he complained of Linant.[7] More complex connections existed, too, between Henry Salt and Bankes. Charles Barry had understood when they met on the Nile that all the drawings made by Salt and his employee, Beechey, belonged to Bankes. Yet whatever the disparity in their wealth the Bankes–Salt relationship was, in some ways, during this trip more equal than that vignette would imply. Salt was a man of achievement and stature when he arrived to take up his position as Consul-General in 1817. He had gone to Egypt intending to collect antiquities – 'the only solace of existence in this place as the society is so wretched'[8] and, with no official pension to rely on, his sole means of providing one. He had been urged by Sir Joseph Banks as President of the Trustees of the British Museum to seek antiquities to enhance the Museum collections.

After Bankes's departure from the region the two men continued in regular correspondence, with Henry Salt effectively acting as Bankes's agent and much involved with directing his affairs in Egypt. Bankes, in return – or so Salt hoped – was doing his best to promote Salt's interests with the British Museum Trustees, one of whom, since 1816, was his father Henry. Henry promoted the Museum's interests in the House and chaired the Parliamentary Select Committee which recommended the purchase of the Elgin Marbles. But in this instance he could do nothing. To make sure of his man, Salt sent William in January 1822 a present of a red granite sarcophagus and cover, originally owned by Amenemopot, chief steward of Thebes, discovered by one of Salt's team. 'It is well covered with hieroglyphics, is very perfect, and will I hope prove an acceptable addition to your Egyptian antiquities. Pray do me the favour to accept it,' Salt wrote.[9]

Salt consistently maintained that most of his collecting was on behalf of the British Museum and that he had risked his own money for his antiquarian speculations. Yet when he asked the Trustees for 'a modest recompense' he found he had unleashed a storm and 'was accused, unheard, of being a dealer, a Jew, a second Lord Elgin'. He was advised to cease his collecting activities forthwith, even at the risk of losing unique monuments which he had discovered. But as Salt explained to Bankes, he had good reason to expect that the British Museum Trustees would purchase his collection of Egyptian antiquities for around £4,000 'or otherwise I shall feel myself aggrieved.'[10]

The Trustees, suddenly unwilling to lay out money on the collections of gentlemen in the Foreign Service, used William Bankes as their go-between, instructing him to write to Salt. Bankes advised he should feel free to seek another purchaser and accept the best offer. Meanwhile negotiations dragged on unpleasantly for months. Eventually the Trustees offered Salt £2,000, half of what he had asked for, for the collection minus an alabaster sarcophagus. Bankes, uncomfortable about the way his friend was being treated, explained to Salt that he found himself in an awkward position: 'All that I could do I have done. I have protested both privately . . . and publicly to every person who has spoken upon it against so inadequate an award and against the principle on which the estimate was made.' Being the son of one of the Trustees made his position doubly hard. 'I make little doubt of being successful in bringing the compensation up to what in common reason and justice it ought to be. But should we fail, it is yourself that you may thank for having missed your opportunity.'[11] It was not the most helpful letter to send to an erstwhile friend. By this time William himself was again a Member of Parliament and Salt mistakenly believed that he would use his influence in the House to get him another thousand pounds.

Salt had more success on Bankes's behalf. The obelisk astonishingly, considering not only the physical difficulties in transporting it but the ongoing rival claims, arrived at Deptford in southern England in the summer of 1821. Bankes took 'an immense party', which included the Duke of Wellington, to welcome it. It lay for a while in the hold of the transport *Dispatch* and was then transferred to the deck of the *Shear Hulk* while some repairs were carried out. The Duke suggested conveying it to Dorset in a gun carriage, where it arrived in August 1822. But the huge platform of steps was still exactly where Bankes had first spotted it at Maharraka. Linant managed to bring down one stone towards the end of 1822 but an unexpected fall of the Nile waters prevented him from moving others. In February 1823 this single stone, weighing 11 tons, languished at Salt's country house, near Bulac, waiting to go to Alexandria. Salt warned that it was so heavy and awkward 'no common merchantman will undertake to carry it'. He tried to persuade Bankes to be satisfied with just this one, which would 'make a sufficiently fine front stone and the rest might be built with other stones'. But William refused to forego any of the steps, which he now considered his. 'It would cost more to make the stones in Scottish granite . . . if you upon the spot and with all the influence of your public situation cannot bring about what to me appears so simple, I am sure that I cannot suggest any action (?) but must sit down content with a disappointment.'[12] Salt never saw the results of his efforts *in situ*, nor was he to meet Bankes again. He died in 1827, aged forty-eight, and was buried with consular honours in a corner of his own garden.

Bankes had by then switched his interest from Egyptian explorations to English country houses. But his life lacked conviction. In 1821 he had been elected to the Society of Dilettanti, an exclusive dining club for gentlemen with an active influence in public taste and the fine arts. The official qualification for membership was having been to Italy; the real one, quipped Horace Walpole, was being drunk. The society was devoted to the pursuit of antiquarian knowledge in a wide variety of fields. When William joined, membership was strictly limited to seventy and a prized social distinction; a number of well-known personalities failed to gain admittance, including Taylor Combe, Keeper of Antiquities at the British Museum. William, indolent in such public matters, took no active role in the Society nor sat on its committees.

In the early 1820s he was frequently travelling around England and Wales, occasionally visiting Paris, making critical notes about the contents of other houses. 'An abundance of pretty knickknacks but fewer good works of art than I had expected,' was a fairly typical comment in a letter to his father.[13] Then in 1821 he received an unexpected present. As he explained to his father:

> A young architect to whom I had been of what use I could when abroad, and to whom I had lately been able to do a pretty essential service in introducing and recommending him to Archdeacon Cambridge, who is one of the most active commissioners for the erection of new churches (his plan, which appears to me a good one is accordingly on the point of being adopted, which in so young a

man is a great point; his name is Barry) has presented me with a
very fine finished drawing of the great temple at Karnak, which was
made and coloured by him on the spot and is both very clever and
very exact.

Bankes had scruples. He felt sure the drawing would not be sold
for less than twenty or thirty guineas in a shop, so perhaps he should
not accept. But since it was not offered, but sent, to decline it would
appear rude. There was also the question of where to hang it. If he
took it to Soughton, where he was spending increasing time, it
would hardly do justice to the young man to take it out of sight.
'He is a very nice architectural draughtsman,' Bankes went on, 'and
when I move to Dorsetshire I will have him down to Kingston Hall
in order to have exact elevations and plans made of these alterations
there, which I have only roughly sketched upon paper.'[14] William is
urging his father on but it seems to have taken another eight years
before Barry and Henry Bankes undertook any serious discussions.

When William first met him Barry was scarcely embarked on a
career. Born in 1795 to a stationer of small means, Charles Barry
grew up in humble surroundings in a house in Bridge Street,
Westminster, a few yards from what was to become his masterpiece,
the Houses of Parliament. He had scant schooling and at fifteen was
articled to Messrs Middleton and Bailey, a firm of architects and
surveyors in Paradise Row, Lambeth. His six-year apprenticeship gave
him a sound training in professional practice and enough time to
complete architectural drawings that were exhibited at the Royal
Academy when he was only seventeen. These years were key to his
future success. 'He diligently learnt the business part of his profession. No one knew better how to prepare measurements and valu-
ations, to calculate dimensions, to estimate prices, to judge the quality
of materials and workmanship, to make out specifications and working
drawings.'[15] Meanwhile his creative aspirations were given free rein
in his attic bedroom studio which he transformed into a grotto with
painted murals. In June 1817, having inherited a small legacy from
his father, he decided to travel 'for the sole purpose of professional
study'. He began and ended in Italy, studying the principles of Italian

architecture, measuring and sketching wherever he went. The Palazzo Farnese in Rome, the Palazzo Strozzi in Florence and several Venetian palazzi all impressed him deeply as worthy of note; his predilection for the Italianate, running counter to the fashionable Greek Revival style, never left him.

In 1820, his inheritance all spent, he returned to England and began his professional life in earnest. His old firm put some surveying work his way. Then, in 1821, he contacted William Bankes. Barry's friend and patron David Baillie had already been in touch. 'If any of Mr Barry's drawings, plans or architectural detail could be of any service to you I should have the greatest pleasure in placing them all at your absolute disposal . . .' he told Bankes, reminding him that Barry was 'the most diligent person as ever I knew, and it is rare to find a person who draws so well and in so many different manners.'[16]

Barry had grasped early the importance of patronage for an ambitious architect and he knew that Bankes, who stood to inherit a great house and already owned a lesser one, admired his work. It was not difficult for Bankes to recommend his young friend, first to the Church Commissioners. A few years later Bankes introduced him to Robert Peel, the reforming Home Secretary and family friend. Bankes told Peel that since his return he had 'been much in the habit of seeing and conversing (with Barry) on subjects unconnected with his profession and pursuits (having a very high opinion both of his natural tastes, talent and of his skill and proficiency)'.[17]

William was deeply frustrated at being unable to set in motion changes to Kingston Hall. A Deed of Settlement in 1821 made him First Tenant in tail of the manors and other hereditaments, which entitled him to receive and take the rents, dues and profits. But although it confirmed his inheritance in due course, at this stage he could do little more than suggest where pictures might be hung and act as irritant to his father to make changes. One small alteration was made around this time a sop to William. With the help of the architect Thomas Cundy Junior, he arranged for modifications to his bedroom apartment upstairs in the north-west corner of Kingston

Hall. This involved dividing the closet and connecting his inner closet and the service stairs.

In matters of art, William knew his own taste very early in life. He wrote to his father,

> I have always preferred, even in the works of the greatest masters, what is legendary to what is purely historical. That is, I mean, such subjects as admit of light, and angels, and concerts in the clouds etc. . . . The best classical subjects are equally out of nature or above it . . . Rubens seems to have been (particularly) sensible of this preference to be given to ideal subjects over plain everyday matters of fact . . . it is my firm belief that a Protestant country will never produce an historical painter of a high class.[18]

He spent much time in Wales where he now owned the old mansion of Dol-y-Moch as well as the rather grander Soughton Hall. Dol-y-Moch, the name deriving from nearby rapids, stood in a sheltered nook on the western side of the beautiful Maentwrog valley, renowned for its biting winds, and featured in records of the Civil War. The Dol-y-Moch estate has medieval origins and features in Welsh folklore as 'a place of virtue . . . a shining meadow . . . a place for feasting'.[19] Wild and isolated, it would have provided William with a wonderful secret retreat. But he preferred staying at nearby Soughton, which offered greater possibilities for alterations. At Soughton he was in control, and in particular was brimming with plans for changing the entrance door from the south to the north side, where it now stands.

Soughton Hall – today a hotel – is an extraordinary house. Set in a hundred and fifty acres of parkland in the remote North Wales countryside, it is approached by an avenue of limes a quarter of a mile long, one of the finest in the country. Creating this impressive entrance involved stopping the lane between Upper and Lower Soughton – 'for which more than an equivalent in land had been given by me to the public'.[20] In a letter to his agent of June 1821 he insists that this was not initially his idea and that 'when I first came into this county it was among my first wishes to have lived amicably and well with my neighbours.' But he was not so naïve as to imagine that the enclosure of his lands – carried out more for privacy than for agricultural efficiency – would be welcomed by his Soughton neighbours. The Miss Lloyds of Upper Soughton were furious and detested William Bankes. He in turn made fun of them. The friction rumbled on for at least ten years over proposed walls, fences, hedges, stiles and gates, ultimately with law suits threatened. When a gate was slung across the Lower Soughton entrance road, Bankes instructed his agent: 'unhang it and take it away early in the morning.'[21] Eventually, the old road was done away with 'as if it had never existed.'[22] 'Of course a good cartway to be made and right of way allowed in the most formal manner by covenant.'[23]

His interior schemes were less controversial and Bankes soon summoned his friend Barry to advise, although this probably meant largely executing Bankes's own ideas since the finished result is 'a dreadful incoherent mish-mash,' according to Barry's biographer.[24] Barry's connection with Soughton was discovered only recently. Its significance to him lay in what it led to. Bankes was a useful patron: within a few years Barry was winning competitions to design churches and commissions to remodel country houses, although not yet major ones.

Bankes himself decided on the mullioned windows, the first-floor drawing and dining room and the Islamic-inspired turrets on the court walls. He designed a canted porch as his new main entrance, rising into a hexagonal Belvedere turret with ogee roof; there was also an unfulfilled plan to surround the courtyard with a cloister. William was already collecting examples of Gothic woodcarving, and Barry's design for the entrance hall and the saloon doors above incorporated some of these. Bankes's interest in antiquarian carvings had became known among dealers and he was offered some oak fittings from a 'convent in Flanders most beautifully carved with some figures as large as life and very richly worked, made for a room eighty feet long . . . now in a stable in Northamptonshire'; there is no trace of these now. 'Everybody that sees what I have done seems well satisfied,' William wrote to his mother[25], 'and I am persuaded that both my father and you will find it a much better job than you have any idea of . . . if I do with it all I think of there will be few prettier in this part of Wales.'

Engrossing though all this was, in the summer of 1822 Bankes found a more amusing and worrying distraction: a romantic entanglement with the 'very young and very handsome' wife of the 5th Earl of Buckinghamshire, formerly George Robert Hobart. The earl was known chiefly for the fact that, shortly after succeeding to the title in 1816, he fought a duel with Sir Thomas Hardy, Nelson's Flag Captain at Trafalgar, as a result of a dispute at Almack's. She, the former Anne Glover, illegitimate daughter of Sir Arthur Pigot, Attorney-General in Grenville's Ministry of all the Talents (1806–7), had been married for three years to 'a man she cannot endure'[26] when she was introduced to William Bankes. George Villiers, later Earl of Clarendon, who found the short-lived romance worthy of gossip, commented that she was 'young, rather particular looking in dress and face, tho' prettyish, and had a strong case of flirtation with him [Bankes] all last year [1822]. I cannot recollect who she was but I have heard that her family traced their descent in a strait line from King Alfred and I believe eat oatcakes in honour of him.'[27]

Neither party was discreet about this love affair. Mrs Arbuthnot, to whom he unburdened himself, was convinced it would end by William 'getting into a scrape' as he was 'very much in love with Lady Buckinghamshire . . . who is still more desperately in love with him'. Harriet Arbuthnot, herself married to a widower twenty-six years her senior, might well have sympathised with the young Countess's plight. By this time she was certainly the chief confidante and comforter of the Duke of Wellington, believed by many to be his mistress. But her passion was for friendship and political intrigue; she was, as even the Duke observed, probably too sensible for romance. Her advice to Bankes was cautious and practical:

> She is about to be separated from her husband, not about Mr Bankes, but because their tempers and tastes do not suit, and she is excessively anxious to induce Mr Bankes to go off with her and to take her with him disguised as a boy into Africa . . . I have entreated and urged and implored him not to listen to a scheme fraught with such

ruin to both and, as he is not so blindly and madly in love as she is, I hope he will resist the temptation. He is endeavouring to prevail on her to return to her husband, but she is very clever and eccentric, which suits him exactly.

As the older experienced woman recognised, Anne clutched at Bankes as an escape from an unhappy marriage. Her offer to disguise herself as a boy might even indicate she was aware of Bankes's sexual preferences. Anne continued to implore Bankes to abscond abroad with her, assuring him that she had separated from Buckinghamshire in the summer of 1822. He demurred, perhaps recognising he had led her on too far, and that the ensuing disgrace would ruin them both.

In August 1822 a far more serious scandal rocked London society. The Foreign Secretary, Lord Castlereagh, a close friend of the Duke and Harriet Arbuthnot, cut his throat after blackmailers accused him of a homosexual affair. Whatever plans Bankes and Lady Buckinghamshire may have had paled in insignificance compared with this.

In autumn 1822, following the death of John Henry Smythe, Bankes was persuaded to stand for Parliament on a vacancy for Cambridge University as an opponent of Catholic Emancipation, still the unresolved burning question of the day. Although the Union of Great Britain and Ireland had come into effect in 1801, Catholics were still prevented from sitting in the Westminster Parliament and excluded from many public offices and only Anglicans were allowed to vote. The Anglican ascendancy in the British Parliament opposed any concessions to Catholics and although a number of Catholic Emancipation Bills were passed by the House of Commons in the 1820s, they were always rejected by the House of Lords.

By November Bankes had pledged himself to 'the most steady and decided opposition to any measures tending to undermine or alter the established church'. The issues at Cambridge reflected those in the rest of the country; the Tories were closely identified with the High Church party, the Whigs with dissenters who, until the later nineteenth century, were still denied full access to the University.

Bankes's two opponents – the Whig lawyer James Scarlett, later First Baron Abinger, who already had three years' parliamentary experience behind him as MP for Peterborough, and a young nobleman, Lord Hervey, who, as the Earl of Bristol's son and Lord Liverpool's nephew by marriage, enjoyed the backing of the Tory Government, much to the disgust of old Henry Bankes – both favoured Catholic relief. All three contestants were graduates of Trinity College, and until two days before the election Bankes was seen as the outsider whose chances were 'ridiculous' according to Lord Colchester. In the event, he won with a wide margin – 419 seats, to Hervey's 281 and Scarlett's 219. How did he pull it off?

In the first place, he made a point of winning over the country clergymen who voted in droves to support 'no popery'. One of the clergymen on William's list was tutor to the Duke of Wellington's sons and therefore particularly easy prey. But elections for university seats were still different from other elections in one sense: they were contests for personal distinction. Bankes's stock was high in 1822 and even his opponents conceded he was an excellent canvasser of residents, achieving 'great things by his good humour and pleasant stories about Africa and the East'. *The Times*, in a long and amusing article written about the election, gave the following account of Bankes's 'irresistible' tactics: 'What could I do, Sir? He got me into the centre of the great pyramid and then turned round and asked me for my vote.'[28] Charles Shore, a potential candidate who had retired, commented on Bankes's 'colloquial facility'. He was 'quite at home in the college hall and combination rooms and capable in an easy, good-humoured way of keeping up the ball of conversation with Whewell, Sedgwick or any other professed talker'. Professor Sedgwick, who had voted for Scarlett rather than Bankes, nonetheless described the winner as 'a very extraordinary man . . . [with] a wonderful fund of entertaining anecdote . . . I don't think we can depend on him as a man of business, though as a literary character, and a man of large fortune, he is a very proper person to represent us in Parliament.'[29]

The large fortune, however, was to arouse complaints that Bankes had – a mere ten years before the Great Reform Act – 'introduced the payment of voters' travelling expenses'. More likely he had refused to agree to the sort of limitations informally arranged between the committees in 1807. While the candidates had, for some years past, paid the expenses of non-resident voters, Bankes had probably spent 'a vast sum', severely antagonising the other candidates. Hiring stagecoaches to bring in the voters was, at £130 a throw, an expensive business. For Bankes, it was an insignificant outlay,[30] legal if increasingly unacceptable.

A few weeks after his unexpected victory, 'the principal news of the day' according to Villiers was that Bankes, 'that wonderfully travelled high churchman (so recently deemed a fit – and the only fit – representative of the extreme high church of Cambridge)'[31] had eloped with Lady Buckinghamshire. On 30 December 1822 the Rt. Hon. Charles Wynn reported 'that the newly-erected pillar of orthodoxy, young Bankes, has to encounter an action for Crim. Con.* from Lord Buckinghamshire, and that Scarlett is retained for the plaintiff'.[32]

Scarlett, almost twenty years older than Bankes and another product of Trinity College, took silk in 1816 and was considered the most successful lawyer at the bar. His domineering and dictatorial attitude was particularly persuasive before a jury and he would have been a formidable opponent. It is not known how Bankes managed to avoid this almost certain humiliation – or even if the elopement actually took place – but the threat apparently evaporated. Possibly money changed hands; more probably, although the husband claimed to have 'perceived improper intimacy between Bankes and Miladi'[33], he was persuaded that he would find no evidence of adultery. By 1823 there was no more mention of the case and Bankes once again settled into the life of a parliamentary backbencher.

For the second time, Bankes was less than a success as an MP, despite Charles Arbuthnot's belief that he could do well. His first speech against Catholic relief was delivered in a low voice and

---

* The abbreviation for Criminal Conversation – the term used to indict alleged seducers.

received with constant heckling. Some described it as 'a total failure, colloquial, flimsy and <u>very</u> <u>bad</u>'.[34] Worse followed. On 14 May he declined 'with infinite reluctance' an invitation from his former Cambridge contemporary, John Cam Hobhouse, to attend a meeting in support of Greek Independence, the cause for which his friend Byron ultimately gave his life and to which he himself insisted he felt warmly: 'The measure itself I highly approve.' But he slithered out in a weaselly four-page letter on the grounds that he approved neither of the chairman named (Lord Milton) nor the venue (the Crown and Anchor).

His parliamentary performance reached a nadir in April 1824. Welcoming the allocation of £500,000 for the erection of new churches, he announced to gales of laughter: 'It certainly ought to be a main object with government to provide for the union of sexes' – he had meant to say sects – and continued, 'That union had been an object much attended to in Ireland. It was an union that it was of the greatest consequence to keep up.' He was stopped by renewed laughter, finally aware of some inadvertent solecism. William Horton described Bankes's 'lapsus' as 'the funniest thing I have heard . . . you never heard children laugh more.' His reputation as a parliamentarian was fatally damaged and he was never again taken seriously. Sedgwick now saw fit to describe him as 'a fool . . . brought in last time by a set of old women . . . who whenever he rises . . . makes the body he represents truly ridiculous.'[35] Such repeatedly dismal performances are hard to explain in one who enjoyed so much natural talent and ability in conversation. At the height of his popularity in London society his reputation for being 'excessively entertaining'[36] won him two entries in a collection of anecdotes entitled '*Gossip Redeemed by the Speakers and the Subjects*' published by the well-connected Frances Williams Wynn. She wrote: 'I have heard this evening a strange wild romantic story from Mr Bankes, almost too improbable for a novel, and yet the leading facts seem established beyond a doubt.' One tale, romantic but apparently true, concerns a mysterious stranger who arrives at the house of the British Consul in Jaffa, tips lavishly and confides that he is the brother of the

Emperor of Austria travelling incognito. The other centres on a meeting between Bankes and Vivant Denon, by then no longer Director of the Louvre, in Paris where Bankes had been invited in May 1821 for the baptism of the Duc de Bordeaux. Bankes wished to visit Roustan, the Mameluke servant of Napoleon in Egypt, who was then keeping a shop. But Denon informed him that such a request was impossible since the servant had abandoned his master and was therefore a traitor.

Bankes was urged by many to do more than *talk* about his travels. Mrs Arbuthnot wrote to him: 'I hope you will perservere with yr. intention to publish Mahomet for I long to see the conclusion of his adventures.'[37] But 'as to publication,' he wrote to Byron, 'I am always thinking of it, and, from a strange mixture of indolence with industry, always deferring it. I hate, and always did, method and arrangement and this is what my materials want.'[38] He might have added that his vast amount of materials also lacked punctuation and were often scarcely legible. While failing to produce his own work, he was widely considered to have been the author of the Oriental and Turkish sections of Lady Caroline Lamb's novel, *Ada Reis*, published anonymously by John Murray in 1823. More seriously, he had to look on as his former friend, James Silk Buckingham, published *Travels in Palestine*, 'a volume so filled with gross blunders and ignorance and ill taste'[39] that he had little desire to lay claim to any part of it, although much of it represented Bankes's work and was made possible by his hospitality. Several other erstwhile travelling companions beat him into print. The two naval captains, Irby and Mangles, produced a joint book in 1823, *Travels in Egypt and Nubia, Syria and Asia Minor during the years 1817 and 1818*, while Thomas Legh's *Petra* appeared in 1819, before Bankes had returned home. 'I abstain from attempting to enter into a more minute account of the wonders of this extraordinary spot,' Legh wrote, since the public would surely soon 'be favoured with a much more detailed and accurate description of them from the pen of Mr Bankes, whose zeal, intelligence and unwearied assiduity in copying inscriptions, delineating remains of antiquity, and ascertaining points of curious classical research, cannot be surpassed.'

Though Bankes continued to mutter about publication for the next ten years or so, the closest he came was in preparing fifty-six lithographic stones of inscriptions collected from his travels in Egypt, Nubia and Syria and Asia Minor, intended for a privately printed edition for which he paid himself, with John Murray as publisher. The stones have been preserved, a sad testament to unfulfilled promise, and are today in the attic at Kingston Lacy. He even offered himself as a reviewer to the *Quarterly Review*, since he had much leisure. In a tactful letter, John Murray declined his offer to write about Mr Pepys' Papers on this occasion – they had already been assigned – but hoped he would favour them with an article in the future.

Perhaps his lacklustre parliamentary performance owed something to two painful losses he suffered at the end of 1823. On 15 October his younger sister Maria, who had married the Hon. Thomas Stapleton and was the mother of one child, Mary Frances Elizabeth, died aged thirty-two at her Oxfordshire home, Grey's Court. Maria had suffered from ill health for much of her short life and her death was probably a result of childbirth. Buried with her baby in the family vault, she was described in *Gentleman's Magazine* as 'amiable in her disposition and exemplary in her conduct . . . possessed of a cultivated understanding, pious without pretence and charitable without ostentation.'[40]* More than three weeks later William was, strangely, still at Soughton, not comforting his bereaved parents in Dorset although his father was recovering from a bladder operation. He explained his absence to the Duke of Wellington on the grounds that his mother, fully occupied looking after her granddaughter, had requested it. 'She fears the shock of the meeting,' he maintained.[41]

The following month, William's adored and adoring mother Frances died, also very suddenly. After her many pregnancies Frances had grown so much in girth that one diarist commented that 'her broad figure occupied a large square' at a royal occasion.[42] But she had been in good health until a few days beforehand when, feeling

---

* Six years later, Thomas Stapleton also died and their surviving daughter, William's niece, became Baroness le Despencer in her own right.

unwell, she had come up with Henry to Old Palace Yard to consult a London doctor. Within days her condition deteriorated dramatically and she died on 22 November aged sixty-two. Her funeral a week later, at St Margaret's Westminster, was a grand affair. In addition to her three sons as chief mourners, the funeral party included the Lord Chancellor, Lord Eldon, the Duke of Wellington, Lord Colchester and Lord Falmouth in their carriages. Twenty-five other carriages of the nobility and gentry followed but Henry, her widower, was absent, apparently grieving so much the doctors considered him in 'too dangerous a state. The knowledge that the funeral was taking place was kept from him.'[43]

Less than four months later, Byron, aged thirty-six, died at Missolonghi, in Western Greece on 19 April 1824 as a result of fever. The news did not reach his friends in England until 14 May when Douglas Kinnaird received a diplomatic package addressed to Hobhouse. Soon all London knew. Within days, the group representing Byron's executors met at John Murray's Albemarle Street offices where it was decided, largely under the influence of Hobhouse, concerned how his friend's posthumous reputation might impact on his own, and jealous that Moore, not he, had been entrusted with the memoir, that Byron's memoirs should be burned. Thomas Moore protested. Bankes, not one of the 'Elect' involved in the decision, apparently told Hobhouse later of his approval. 'Byron's best friends could always recur [sic] to his poetry and conceal his life,' he commented.[44] The funeral was held on Monday, 12 July at the Byron family church in Hucknall Torkard, since the Dean of Westminster had refused permission for the poet to be interred in the Abbey. Although a large procession followed the hearse as it made its way out of London, in general society stayed away or sent empty carriages. Mrs Arbuthnot, who had never approved of Byron, could not resist watching from her window:

> It was nothing very fine. [The opposition] have tried to make a grand funeral for him because he died in Greece; and as it failed to excite public feeling they abuse the govt. and say it is just like them to carry their rancour beyond the grave as if there could be any possible

reason for following the hearse of a man who perverted his splendid talents to the worst of all possible purposes, whose writings are so profligate they are not fit to be read and who was good for nothing in every relation of life.

After this splenetic outpouring she noted that she had often discussed Byron with her friend Mr Bankes, and 'Tho Mr Bankes wd. not have trusted him with his own sister yet that his genius, his enthusiasm and even his caprices rendered him so attractive that, tho he knew him so well, he could not help liking him.' Mrs Arbuthnot also quoted Bankes as saying that 'in the eccentric parts of their characters, they had many points of similarity'.[45]

William was not one of the small party of mourners which included Hanson, Tom Moore, Kinnaird and Francis Burdett who went to Nottingham. Perhaps he watched the London part of the procession. For seven days in early July Byron lay in state in the front parlour of Sir Edward Knatchbull's house at Great George Street; his face, by this time, was unrecognisable. But although no record remains of Bankes's visit, it seems likely that he would have paid his last respects here. And Hobhouse wrote to him in 1824: 'I send you, as promised, a lock of Byron's hair cut from his head after his death. It is, you will see, very gray and is much changed from what it was when I saw him in 1822. But it is his, you may depend upon it.'[46] The hair, a seal of Byron's and the letter were among William's most precious possessions, placed in a special glass cabinet, among the last objects he handled before he himself was finally forced to flee the country. Only the letter, kept in an album at Kingston Lacy compiled by William's sister-in-law, Georgina, can be found today.*

In 1825 William was invited to join Hobhouse's committee to decide upon a public memorial to Byron. The poet had already, in

---

* In a letter to George from WJB dated 26 May 1844 he writes 'Did I mention before that there is also a mourning ring from Ld B containing his hairs sent to me by Hobhouse and also another lock of his hair. And there is a great ugly seal on bloodstone that he gave me. These should be kept together.'

(*Above*) Henry Bankes, William's father, aged 22, painted in Rome by Pompeo Batoni

(*Right*) Frances Woodley, William's mother, aged 22, painted by George Romney in 1780–1, three years before her marriage to Henry Bankes

Kingston Hall in William's childhood after changes made by his father, showing the pergola added to the south front and new basement entrance with Ionic porch to the east front

Drawing by William Bankes, of Wadi Hedid temple, showing a faint
outline of the ruins of Gamli temple on the far bank of the river (*left*).
He was especially fascinated by columns

Soughton Hall, Flintshire, which William inherited in 1815 and later
remodelled with Charles Barry. The Moorish turrets on the court walls,
mullioned windows and new main entrance followed William's ideas

Bankes's designs for embellishing the Obelisk, never carried out,
included a Fleur de Lys (*top right*), the family crest. The four sides are
inscribed with single columns of text in Ptolemaic hieroglyphs

The Holy Family, bought by William in Spain in 1813 as a Raphael, is now described as from the circle of Raphael. The magnificent frame commissioned by William incorporates medallions of the picture's former owners, including Charles I

(*Above left*) *The Judgment of Solomon*, bought by William from the Marescalchi collection in Bologna as a Giorgione, now attributed to Sebastiano del Piombo. The unfinished picture – there is no baby – was later overpainted and has been considerably restored

(*Left*) The Spanish or Golden Room, with its embossed gilded leather walls on which William's collection of Spanish paintings was displayed. He could only enjoy it in his mind's eye

(*Above*) Lord Byron's apartment in the Palazzo Mocenigo, overlooking the Grand Canal in Venice. William visited his Cambridge friend here in 1819

(*Left*) William Bankes by Sir George Hayter, a portrait sketch in oils painted 1833–5, around the time Bankes was acquitted of charges of indecent exposure. The sketch was used for the larger study of the Meeting of the First Reformed Parliament, completed in 1843

May: one of twelve designs by William for the doors to the Spanish Room, each depicting a month. He commissioned an Italian painter to copy his designs which he considered to be his best drawings

The top landing and upper marble staircase at Kingston Lacy display
many of William's commissions to Italian craftsmen, some executed in
a rare two-tone marble. The garlands of birds and fishes, inset on the
staircase pilasters, were carved by Salesio Pegrassi of Verona

1817, at Hobhouse's instigation, sat for his bust to the celebrated Danish sculptor, Bertel Thorwaldsen. But the sittings were not a success; Thorwaldsen was frustrated by Byron's restlessness while Byron complained that the finished work was a poor likeness. However, the Committee now commissioned a further statue from Thorwaldsen, full length and on a plinth, which they hoped would stand in Poets' Corner in Westminster Abbey. But the Abbey refused and it did not find a home until 1845 when it was placed in the Wren Library of Trinity College. William now offered to help Thomas Moore with his biography of Byron – a change of heart from his reported opinion to Hobhouse – and said he had a 'key' to the persons alluded to in *Hours of Idleness*, which Byron had given him. The key still exists and is housed at Kingston Lacy, one of the few Byron relics neither lost nor stolen over the years. However, when Moore needed it Bankes was unable to find it.[47] At the time of his flight this was one of the documents he lamented having hunted for in vain to help Moore, but it could not 'ever be found at all'.[48]

Whatever Bankes might have said to Harriet Arbuthnot about Byron, he longed for posterity to mark the friendship between him and the disgraced poet, friend of his wayward youth. In his last surviving letter to Byron he begged for some lines to engrave upon an embalmed head of a King of Egypt, which he had brought back from Thebes. A glass globe was to be blown around the head to preserve it. The relic no longer exists, presumably Bankes's descendants found it distasteful. 'I think the subject is not unworthy of you,' Bankes wrote to Byron, proud of his find and convinced of its royal nature. Failing that, he reminded his friend that in a stanza of *Don Juan* – which he encouraged Byron to continue in spite of the odium and abuse it was attracting – there was a thought 'which you had told me was transplanted into it out of a letter of mine, but without any note upon it . . .' He concluded pathetically: 'I have sometimes wondered that I should be the last of your early friends to whom you should have thought of dedicating any of your works, or of writing in them. I confess that it would have given me pleasure to see our friendship so recorded and the more had the mention come from yourself.'[49] Byron, consumed with his own troubles, failed to oblige.

In 1825 a new election was required by the dissolution of Parliament and another bitterly contested fight for the two Cambridge seats loomed. As the years of his foreign forays faded, Bankes was no longer viewed as the exciting traveller he had been. Thomas Moore, happy to pick his brain for the Byron biography, nonetheless noted in his diary that he 'talked enough for two parties and who (in spite of all his knowledge) is very disagreeable'.[50] Henry Fox, son of Lord Holland, friend of Byron but never an admirer of Bankes, recalled in his:

the conversation turned on dramatic poetry, which gave Ward and Wm Bankes an opportunity of expressing their heresy about Shakespeare. Ward abuses him with an asperity and violence which would induce a stranger to believe he had suffered some actual wrong from him. William Bankes is unceasing; his voice is painfully unpleasant, but he is full of knowledge and originality.[51]

In Cambridge, too, the tide had turned. The Dean of Ely, former Master of St John's, told Palmerston that his rival Bankes 'had shocked the university by his pursuit of Lady Buckinghamshire' and that 'his moral conduct was causing concern'.[52] Even Bankes's generous gifts to the University of more than twenty ancient and rare books and his donation of 100 guineas towards building an observatory did not help.

In the June 1826 election the principal issue was again Catholic Emancipation, but this time two other candidates were as staunchly anti-Catholic as Bankes: John Singleton Copley, a distinguished lawyer, and Henry Goulburn, later Chancellor of the Exchequer. It was perhaps a measure of Bankes's insensitivity to others' opinions of him that he believed in his own victory until the last. Hobhouse commented: 'He is exactly the same rattling, grinning fellow as ever and he talked at the hall table today the same sort of nonsense as he used when a pupil at college. One of the Fellows, Macfarlane, who was sitting next to him, actually left his place, and coming to me told me he could not endure Bankes's chattering any longer.'[53] In the event, Bankes lost to Palmerston and Copley, who both won seats. Even Mrs Arbuthnot, who in 1822 had been prepared to get herself 'in a great scrape' with her husband by canvassing for Bankes in Cambridge, was now less robust in her defence of him. A few months after the election, at a dinner hosted by Wellington for Sir Walter Scott, then experiencing serious financial difficulties, she commented: 'Mr Bankes, who dined also at the Duke's, provoked us excessively by engrossing as much as possible all the conversation, and talking so loud as quite to drown Sir Walter's conversation. I never saw such bad taste in my life, I almost thought he was drunk.'[54] Scott himself considered that Bankes spoiled the evening by giving 'with unnecessary emphasis and at superfluous length his opinion of a late gambling transaction'.[55]

Perhaps Bankes might be forgiven for this exuberance. Just a month before, 'that swindler Buckingham' had successfully sued him for libel in a case that had been dragging on for seven or so years. Bankes was unlucky to have lost and the episode did him little credit.

Buckingham's handsomely produced book was published in 1821 by Messrs Longman, Hurst, Rees, Orme and Brown; its full title was *Travels in Palestine through the Countries of Bashau and Gilead east of the River Jordan including a visit to the Cities of Geraza and Gamala in the Decapolis*. The frontispiece carried a picture of its author, J.S. Buckingham, Member of the Asiatic Society, Calcutta and of the Literary Societies of Madras and Bombay, resplendent and serious in a magnificent turban, with beard and dagger, 'in the costume of a Turkish Arab'. In the preface, explaining his desire to travel, he referred to 'the elegant poetry of Lord Byron, and though it belongs only to a genius like his to express those feelings well, yet men of humbler talents may and do experience them with equal force'. How Bankes must have fumed at the attempted association with Byron, *his* friend. 'I am preparing for the Review, which I have not yet begun but you shall have it within a very few days,' he promised John Murray from

Soughton.[56] His seventeen-page article in the *Quarterly Review* was scathing.

> It is a distinction reserved, we believe, for the work before us, to display a blunder of the first magnitude upon its title page. The names of TWO ancient cities only (Geraza and Gamala) are there set forth in capitals: and of these two the one is certainly wrong and the other doubtful. We must therefore commence our strictures with assuring the member of the Asiatic society at Calcutta and of the Literary Societies at Madras and Bombay that he, decidedly, was never at Gamala and very possibly not at Geraza in the whole course of his journey.

The unnamed reviewer, widely recognised to be Bankes, proceeded to tear apart Buckingham's pretensions as a traveller and as a writer, listing errors in history and geography: 'Mr Buckingham does not appear to be very scrupulous examining the sense of his extracts since we frequently find him setting down a passage in his note that makes directly against some sagacious conclusion in his text.' He criticises the 'complicated ignorance and absurdity . . . of our accomplished traveller, who sometimes uses gratuitous information and other times takes things for granted.' He accuses Buckingham of employing 'a sneering and irreverent tone' concerning matters connected with sacred history, and is scornful that 'our author would have us believe that he understood and spoke Arabic better than Mr Bankes' interpreter [Finati] who . . . had made the pilgrimage to Mecca and Medina and been resident several years at Cairo.'

The article,[57] which Buckingham saw in India, reprinted in the *Calcutta Journal* on 14 August 1822, fuelled his anger and strengthened his case for libel: this was, however, based on the letter Bankes had sent from Thebes in 1819 which had been widely disseminated. The case was to drag on for years. By the time it reached court, Bankes was an MP of no special distinction and, through his failure to publish, a traveller who had lost his claim to originality. *The Times*, in its June 1825 summary of events, was decidedly biased in favour of Buckingham. According to its report, the two travellers met casually, each had dissimilar objectives and 'while they were together, each paid his share of the expense and was in every respect independent of the other'. Bankes, it surmised, fired by jealousy when he heard of Buckingham's plans to publish a book, wrote instantly to his father asking him to prevent Buckingham from finding a publisher by claiming that the book was constructed from pirated notes. However, as *The Times* pointed out, 'neither he nor his father could possibly know what was in the manuscript as at this time neither had seen it . . . They presumed, because Buckingham had travelled only seven days with Bankes, he was incapable of saying anything on any part of Palestine without the inspiration of Mr Bankes' imaginary notes.' Although the case was still in progress, *The Times* concluded: 'Public opinion has already decided distinctly and completely in favour of Mr Buckingham, whose talents and moral character will not fail to be more highly estimated in proportion to the unjust persecution he has undergone.'[58]

Buckingham, by then returned to England and living in Regents Park, must have savoured this prejudicial account. Meanwhile Bankes had brought Giovanni Finati and Antonio da Costa to England, putting them up at Soughton, to verify his own version of events. Finati, although 'very averse to long voyages by sea', agreed to his old master's request. Linant de Bellefonds, accompanied by an Abyssinian lady, came too and the party provoked much local comment about exotic costumes and imagined habits. Frequent adjournments caused the group to stay much longer than planned and Finati grew attached to the place before he left it.

> The simple manners of the Welsh villagers pleased me much better than the rude behaviour which I met with in some principal cities . . . where my dress attracted not only attention but so many insults from boys and idle people that I found the necessity of taking refuge in a shop.

On 17 December 1825, at the Court of King's Bench, London, Buckingham won his first small victory against William's father, Henry Bankes, on account of the letter he had sent to John Murray asking the publisher to have no transactions with the author. The jury found for the plaintiff. Damages: One Shilling. Buckingham had retained as his counsel the brilliantly abrasive Whig barrister Henry Brougham, who, after successfully defending Queen Caroline in 1820, and retaining her rights as a future Queen Consort, had become something of a popular idol. Brougham, later Lord Chancellor and immortalised by the invention of the single horse carriage named after him, was renowned for his arrogance and eccentricities and would have relished the idea of prosecuting two members of this resolutely Tory family. Ten months later, in the same court, Bankes and Buckingham clashed again. The trial lasted just one day, from nine in the morning until almost seven in the evening, and after a one-and-three-quarter-hour opening speech from Brougham, in excellent form that day, seven witnesses were called, including Finati and da Costa. 'Two foreigners who could scarcely understand the plain questions put to them now and nine years ago pretended to have understood the whole of the conversation between Mr Bankes and Mr Buckingham,' was how Brougham effectively dismissed their evidence. Having listened to Brougham plead the case for his client, the Lord Chief Justice had little choice but to direct the jury that Bankes's plea of justification for writing the letter could not be established. The jury took three quarters of an hour to decide that Buckingham should be awarded £400 damages.

Was Bankes fairly dealt with? When he wrote the libellous letter he had, after all, seen only an advertisement for the book, not the contents. But he already knew that Buckingham 'neither copied a single inscription nor made a simple sketch on the spot . . . you had not a single sheet of paper on which you could have done either'.[59] Brougham, however, was able to demonstrate that since Bankes had fleetingly contemplated writing a book with Buckingham, he could not now claim that the man was 'the most ignorant of impudent pretenders'. Bankes should have worked harder to dig up Buckingham's notorious past, such as his expulsion from India in 1823 for journalistic attacks on the government. But Brougham was brilliant, Bankes's witnesses weak. Even John Murray, according to Thomas

Moore's journal, 'cut (as all the world knows) a very sorry figure'.[60] James Silk Buckingham remained in London, continued to publish and outlived his adversary. It was a sobering introduction to English justice for William Bankes.

7

Arrest

~

'Love, love, clandestine love, was still my dream,
Methought there must yet be some people found
Where Cupid's wings were free, his hands unbound
Where law had no erotic statutes framed,
Nor Gibbets stood to fright the unreclaimed.'[1]

Anon, 'Don Leon'

TEN YEARS AFTER his return from Egypt, Bankes finally set upon ensuring that his own version of his travels was made available to posterity. The stimulus might have been his renewed acquaintance with Finati; the galling success of Buckingham, now regarded in some quarters as a worthy author and explorer; or perhaps the heir-in-waiting's eternal dilemma of how to live a useful life. At all events, he told John Murray in November 1829 that, in spite of delays and deferments, he was taking great pains with the book. 'I think you might be glad to add Mahomet's life to the advertisements for publication [in the Quarterly Review].' He promised delivery '<u>POSITIVELY</u>' by the end of the month 'and flatter myself that both you and the public will be pleased with it when it appears'.[2] William was emphatic that his own name should be added in much smaller characters merely as the *translator and editor* of the book *dictated* by Finati, although, it was generally recognised that he was the author at least of the second volume. Both were eventually published in 1830*; in spite of the rich material Bankes had brought back with him, neither was illustrated. It remained the closest he ever came to publishing; he had allowed the moment of immediacy to evaporate, replaced by the duties of the landed gentry to tenants and the local community, work which would never fire his imagination. He had not given up all pretensions to being a Member of Parliament, but for a man without political ambitions this was scarcely a career of choice. In 1827 he lost for the second time at Cambridge – again beaten by a lawyer, Sir Nicholas Tyndal, the Solicitor General. As he admitted to his family, he had much leisure. Some of this he spent touring the countryside, contemplating other houses and making extensive notes and sketches. His chief project in the late 1820s was the repair and erection of his obelisk, symbolic of all that travelling in the East had meant to him and still lying on the lawns of Kingston Lacy. The obelisk had been damaged during its long journey but repaired with granite from the ruins of Leptis Magna given by George IV, an indication of the extent to which national interest had been aroused.

During 1827 John Barker, British Consul at Aleppo when Bankes first met him, wrote several times, mostly about the transport of his blocks of granite from Maharakka, and money, which Barker lacked. In October Barker used the pretext of Henry Salt's death two days previously to remind William that not only were the stones still unmoved but that twenty-eight years of service made him a strong candidate to succeed Salt. Presumably William helped Barker with cash and patronage, since almost two years later, Barker thanks him for the information that the stones have arrived in England 'where they will be a lasting monument of the literary fame acquired in the beginning of the 19th century by one of the Bankes of Corfe Castle' and expresses his gratitude at obtaining his new post 'through Bankes' exercise of powerful interest in the Foreign Office'.[3] William

---

* *Narrative of the Life and Adventures of Giovanni Finati, native of Ferrara, who, under the assumed name of Mahomet, made the campaigns against the Wahabees for the recovery of Mecca and Medina and since acted as interpreter to European Travellers in some of the parts least visited of Asia and Africa.*

was by now thoroughly familiar with the difficulties for British consuls without private means to earn a living commensurate with their station in life.

By 19 April 1827 Bankes was ready for the Duke of Wellington to come and lay the obelisk's foundation stone. From the moment of William's return from the East, the Duke had taken a particular interest in this antiquity – there was nothing of its kind in England at the time. Cleopatra's Needle, less important to the study of hiero-glyphics, was erected on the Embankment in London only in 1879. Although presented to the British by Mahomet Ali in 1819, this obelisk, made for Tuthmose III and carved with hieroglyphics praising him, acquired its name because it was removed during the Greek Dynasty to Alexandria, the Royal City of Cleopatra, and erected there in 12 BC in the eighteenth year of Augustus Caesar. It proved even more problematic to transport than Bankes's obelisk from Philae, but was eventually moved from Alexandria encased in an iron cylinder, abandoned during a storm in the Bay of Biscay and recovered only after it had claimed the lives of six men involved in its journey. In 1832, in a parliamentary debate on the grant for a purpose-built National Gallery, Bankes disingenuously maintained that it was hardly worthwhile to bring Cleopatra's Needle to England and objected to the removal of an obelisk from the Temple of Sesostris, which would entail virtual destruction of the building. He concluded he would 'never consent to ornament London at the expense of Thebes'.[4]

Although the Duke chose the precise site for the Philae obelisk – at the end of a long wide gravel walk in front of the house – Bankes had already made clear his own views: 'I believe I never can consent to remove so fine a monument out of sight of the house at Kingston Hall.'[5] He had experimented with long poles planted in front of the south windows at different distances to judge the effect. Henry, however, wished that the obelisk had been placed at Soughton,

where there is a small walled court before his principal front, much better adapted to it than my spacious lawn. But I submit to it as a disorder in the Bankes family, which sometimes passes over one generation like madness or gout or the King's evil and breaks out again in the next. My uncle, who passed a long life in this house and was no improver nor builder could not help erecting two Obelisks and thought that he had done enough.[6]

When Henry wrote this letter to his daughter-in-law Georgina, he had in view a large pile of bricks deposited outside his window, waiting to strengthen the foundations. The granite steps had finally arrived in Poole but were still in the vessel. William wrote in October that it had taken nineteen horses a whole day to drag them from the coach road across the green to its place. 'The other three pieces, weighing something less than the total, may be conjectured to be from 35–36 tons – 16 men besides the crew of the vessel were employed four days at Poole in landing them. They have been skilfully put together and I am well satisfied with their appearance.'[7] The completed monument was finally erected in 1839, more than twenty years after he first saw it, giving William a mere two years to enjoy it.

During his stay the Duke also planted a cedar sapling – today a massive tree marked with an engraved stone – a few paces from the obelisk, to commemorate the occasion. It had been grown from one of the seeds Bankes had gathered from the renowned Cedars of Lebanon and carefully propagated in Dorset until large enough to plant out in 1821. But although both obelisk and cedars gave William intense pleasure, he was thinking constantly about changes he wished to make once Kingston Hall became his. He was rather cavalier about his Egyptian antiquities. There was no attempt to arrange them or build a collection. The obelisk stood alone.

As he admitted in his 1836 memorandum, the closest William ever came to a confessional diary that has survived, 'I made plans very early in life.' These plans initially involved an ambitious rebuilding of the ruins of Corfe Castle, such was his emotional attachment to the place where his family had first settled in the county, as well as his recognition of its unrivalled grandeur and singular position. 'Had my Dorsetshire estates devolved to me earlier in life, when from the possibility and even probability of many years in prospect I might have normally anticipated that . . . a 9th part of my income set apart for any purpose annually would have provided a very great sum, it is very probable that I might have seriously undertaken the restoration of Corfe Castle as my principal residence,' he reflected. It was the only estate in that county which he believed would have done justice to his grandiose schemes. In general he considered Dorsetshire a county unsuited to expensive and time-consuming efforts such as he had in mind. 'It consists of landscapes without character and widely spread as my possessions there are and including both suncoast and forest I have not a single spot where, if I had to at random, I should choose to fix one.'

Among Bankes's surviving papers is a heavy tan calf skin folio with a remnant of a label inscribed '*Blan*' – presumably once *Blank Book*. It is undated but the watermark is 1797. The contents date from the early 1820s and include a draft of an 1822 parliamentary speech as well as detailed notes about furniture and oak carvings he had spotted in shops around the country. He records the price asked and his opinion of what the piece is worth. Whether these items are intended for Soughton, Kingston Hall or even a rebuilt Corfe Castle, what is apparent is that he was seriously entertaining grandiose, romantic and not necessarily unrealistic notions for the reconstruction of his ancestral home. Tracings of possible ground plans indicate that he had undertaken detailed research on castles. Either he had access to old family records (which no longer exist) or he spent hours wandering around the ruins measuring, thinking, planning and dreaming.

The book contains jottings about the imagined reconstruction of the castle and several delightful ink and colour wash sketches, occasionally embellished by lines of second-rate poetry. In one drawing he shows the keep on one side and the castle on the other as well as King John's Gloriette (hunting lodge). Another features sleeping dogs in kennels at the entrance, as a carriage rides up the hill to a large Tudor mansion not dissimilar to Hardwicke Hall. In sketches for the interior he has two versions of a great medieval dining hall, one with exposed wooden beams in Tudor style, the other with fan-vaulted ceiling in high Gothick revival style. No indication survives that he took these private sketches any further.

In 1827, William acquired two large canvases by Frans Snyders, the virtuoso painter of game and hunting scenes, from the Altamira Collection. These gory pictures of hounds attacking a bull and wolves a horse had been looted by Napoleon in Madrid and sent to the Gobelins to be copied as tapestries, but after 1815 were returned to the owner who subsequently sold them in London. William intended the canvases for the dining room and thought so highly of them that in his memoranda notebooks of 1836–40 he listed 'making provision for two large Snyders pictures' as one of his thirteen reasons for altering Kingston Lacy. William would have been attracted by their provenance, as well as by their decorative potential and imposing size. The canvases are now on the top floor landing of Kingston Lacy, framed by plaster swags of flowers and fruit; in order to accommodate them here, it was necessary to fold them over at the top by some 29 inches, presumably when the paintings were moved from the dining room in the 1890s.

At the same sale William bought one of his finest Spanish pictures, the full-length portrait of Philip IV by Velazquez.[*] In May 1828, following the death of George Baldwin, an earlier Consul-General in Egypt, he bought a Roman green basalt bust, life-sized, of an unknown man found near Canopus in Egypt around 1780. According to the sale catalogue it was thought to represent Octavius Augustus from the resemblance it bore to coins; later the bust was thought to be of Mark Antony, but this too is no longer thought accurate.

Between these occasional bouts of collecting Bankes did his duty as an MP. In March 1829 he was returned as Member for Marlborough, Lord Ailesbury's pocket borough, specifically to oppose Catholic Emancipation. He was one of the select group which, in

---

[*] This was sold in 1896 and is now in the Isabella Stewart Gardner Museum in Boston.

September 1830, set off in high excitement to celebrate the opening of the great Manchester–Liverpool railway, a potent symbol of the industrial North's revitalisation of the whole country and, to Bankes, 'a work so extraordinary . . . and magnificent in some parts that I can find words neither to describe it nor to express the sensation of surprise that it produced upon me especially the point of view at the mouth of the great descending tunnel which makes for the length of a mile and a quarter under the whole breadth of the town and the viaduct as it is called . . .' Bankes was honoured to be sitting in the principal car, a splendid gilded coach with a scarlet velvet awning, edged with tassels and draped pelmets of gilded wood, with the Duke of Wellington, by then Prime Minister,* 'and we set out very happily with an immense train following at the rate sometimes of 30 mph.' Bankes, it appears, had regained Mrs Arbuthnot's favour as she describes the Duke's party, which in addition to Bankes and the Arbuthnots included (Prince) Esterhazy and Lord Burghersh, as 'particularly agreeable'.[8]

At this speed the Duke could not read the mileposts beside the track but he could see and hear the cheering crowds along the embankment. At about 11.30 a.m. the *Northumbrian* train halted to take in water and have the wheels oiled. 'A particular printed caution had been given to us that none of the company should quit their carriages during this pause,' William wrote later that day to his father. But the warning was ignored by many, and William Huskisson, MP for Liverpool, took advantage of the halt to stand talking in the middle of the other track and to greet the Duke. Before he could do so a loud shout went up: 'Stop the engine! Clear the track!' Too late: Stephenson's prize-winning *Rocket*, which the engineer was parading up and down to check its speed, came dashing towards them on the other line. Most jumped back in to their seats. But the heavily built Huskisson, 'instead of remaining quite where he was, where no harm could have happened to him, endeavoured to scramble around it and in the act of so doing either slipped or was caught

---

* From 9 January 1828 until 16 November 1830.

by the engine which in an instant crushed his left leg all to pieces. The shrieks from the car were dreadful and the groans from the poor sufferer and the confusion indescribable and the spectacle bloody and horrid to the last degree.'[9] William heard Huskisson's utterance 'let me die here,' in fact the wretched man did not die until nine o'clock at night, in great pain.

Plans for the two days of banquets and festivities were abandoned, but the following day Bankes and other members of the original party went for a private drive on the railroad accompanied by 'Mr Stephenson, the engineer' and then visited a plate glass 'manufactory' – a visit not without significance for his future plans for Kingston Lacy.

Bankes's unfalteringly reactionary views led him to make one notable parliamentary speech at this time – yet again against Catholic relief, which eventually became law in 1829 – and another, less notable, during the second reading of the Reform Bill in July.[10] According to Hobhouse, a Reformer who clearly had not softened in his attitude towards his ultra-Tory college contemporary, Bankes was so opposed to reform he 'looked as if his face would burst with blood':

> William Bankes rose and made one of the most extraordinary exhibitions I had ever seen. He whined, clasped his hands, and put himself into attitudes concluding one of his sentences thus: 'The Lord deliver us out of their hands, I say!' To be sure he was in earnest for the Bill annihilated the Corfe Castle Dynasty.

He voted against the Bill the following day. A few days later he made the emotional decision to concede the extinction of his family borough of Corfe Castle, a clear example of the sort of rotten borough the Bill was designed to eradicate. But he denied to the last that it was 'decayed'. In August, still obstructing, he objected to a proposal to sit on Saturdays to speed progress on the bill on the ingenious ground that if Jews were admitted to the House they would thereby be presented with a crisis of conscience.

He must have known he was opposing an unstoppable force, for, by the time he proposed the toast at a dinner at the Kings Arms

Inn at Dorchester in honour of his father Henry's loyal support for the agricultural interests of the county in Parliament over many years, the Reform Bill had passed into law. Dorset had stood out as one of the counties least favourable to reform and the dinner was an occasion for much backslapping, cheering and drinking. At the end of the evening the chairman proposed a toast to William, then MP for Marlborough, who had offered himself as a candidate to represent the county at the next election. 'His principles are before you, he is known to all of you and his ties and connections with this county are equally known . . .'[11] The toast was drunk to deafening cheers, several times over.

The conviviality was brought to a shattering conclusion when a brick was thrown through the window and hit the silver candelabrum presented minutes before to Henry, which toppled to the floor. Guests who went to the broken window were shocked to see an immense crowd outside 'cheering and huzzaing'. There could have been no clearer warning that the old order had come to an end.

On 6 June 1833 Bankes's surviving parliamentary aspirations were shattered as dramatically as the window of the King's Arms when he was arrested on suspicion of 'attempting to commit an unnatural offence'. He had been dining with the Earl of Liverpool and was on his way to the House of Commons when, as he later testified in court, he was struck by the urge to urinate and went to use a small public convenience behind St Margaret's Church. This was (as the prosecution later maintained) a strange decision since his own house at 5 Old Palace Yard was a mere 320 feet from the principal door of the House if he had taken the path across the swept crossing, and even less by the more direct route.

The night watchman, James Smith, who had been doing the same job for eight years, came on duty in plain clothes as usual that night at 9 p.m. and walked from the western gates of the Abbey around by Poets' Corner, through the courtyard to St Margaret's church, where he noticed 'two persons conversing together'. He then saw one of these men (Bankes) in a cloak, enter the convenience 'that afforded accommodation only for one individual', and shortly after, the soldier with whom Bankes had been talking earlier, Thomas Flowers, a private in the Second Company, First Battalion, Coldstream Guards, went into the same enclosure. He recognised the soldier's white trousered legs. His suspicions aroused, he went in search of a police constable. (This was not so easy; just four years after the intro- duction of a metropolitan police force, 'Peelers' were still an amateur group. The Home Office regularly offered rewards for the detection and prosecution of particular criminals; there is no evidence that this happened in Bankes's case but entrapment was not unknown in homosexuality charges.) Eventually Smith found one and ten minutes later the pair, with another witness, apprehended the shocked Bankes and Flowers, both still in the convenience.

They were taken to Tothill Street police station, where a magis- trate was to consider their case. Here the real humiliation began. Both were searched and their clothes examined. Flowers had his front braces undone and the front part of his small clothes and trousers undone. Bankes said he thought he had a sovereign in his purse but this was instead found loose in his pocket. He invented a story about how he was rushing to the House when he met a soldier whom he thought he knew from abroad, by the name of Robertson. It was not the same man, but he asked if the soldier knew Robertson who had been in the same regiment. A few minutes later, when the soldier came over to the convenience while Bankes was there, Bankes maintained he did not recognise him as the man with whom he had just been conversing.

The magistrate took down the two men's stories then locked them up for the night; partly for their own good. Within hours, news of the arrest of a Member of Parliament had spread through the capital. A 2,000 strong crowd, howling for 'justice', gathered outside the police station. Mob violence in homosexuality cases was occasionally horrific and their threatening behaviour made it dangerous and difficult to extract the prisoners from their cells the following morning. Bankes, the main focus of interest, had to be brought up in a hackney coach to the front door. It was only thanks to the 'protection of the constables that he was got unhurt into the office'. The public and press were thrown out of the building, which provoked an angry response. 'It's because he's a rich man,' the crowd yelled.

A secret examination, lasting about two hours, followed with Bankes and Flowers sitting on opposite sides of the room. The magistrate, Mr White, concluded it was his 'painful duty' to have to send the case to sessions. Bankes was required to find two sureties in the region of £3,000 each and himself to enter into his own recognizance in the sum of £6,000. His total bail required was £12,000.

Flowers, however, was returned to a lock-up cell, but only after a sergeant from the Coldstream Guards had come to remove his cap and tear off the lace. Midway through the proceedings, a distressed Henry Bankes arrived. According to one version – difficult to prove without official witnesses – he never once made eye contact with his son. Some press accounts later made out that Henry sat with his back turned on his son, 'thereby conveying the insinuation that even he believed the charge against him'. Later in court, Bankes's defence counsel admitted the father's grief but maintained that Henry was so far convinced of his son's innocence that he had suggested William's underwear 'should be preserved in the state in which it was found' and used as evidence. Once bail had been accepted, father and son left together, escorted by a large body of police and a crowd of voyeurs, and made their way to Birdcage Walk. As soon as they got into the park the constables blocked the gateway while William climbed into his father's carriage, which was already waiting there, and drove off unmolested.[12]

Six excruciating months later the case came to court one cold December day. At Bankes's request, it was heard before the Lord Chief Justice at the Court of King's Bench with a special jury: a well trod path by 'gentlemen' accused of this offence as jurors here were more likely to be taken from a similar social class. Bankes maintained that he would not otherwise have an impartial trial. Lacking the automatic right to counsel who would address the jury on his behalf, which did not become enshrined for another three years, Bankes had to make a formal request which was granted.

Bankes was not the only homosexual to be arrested in London in 1833. In February the MP for Guildford, Baring Wall, was accused of making sexual advances to a policeman in Harley Street and charged with 'attempting to commit an unnatural offence'. But the jury believed Wall rather than his accuser and he was acquitted. On 12 August Captain Henry Nicholls was hanged for sodomy while a companion, similarly charged, committed suicide; also that year Richard Heber, a bibliophile friend of Hobhouse, MP for Oxford who had fled when 'his life was compromised', died in exile. It could well have been the Nicholls hanging compounded by Bankes's arrest which prompted an unknown author to write *Don Leon*, probably in 1833 although not published until 1866. This powerful poem was a passionate protest against the barbarism of executions for sodomy; its attribution as a 'Work by Lord Byron' was clearly incorrect since events that took place after the poet's death were included. The author, never identified, was as well informed about parliamentary business as he seemed to be about Byron's pederastic tastes and may have been George Colman, the dramatist and stage manager friend of the poet. A Royal Commission on Criminal Law had been appointed in 1833; no doubt *Anonymous* hoped to influence it in favour of reforming the laws on homosexuality. William Bankes is described in the poem as one 'rich in Moslem lore/ who roamed like me strange countries to explore/ In Moslem lands, like me, long time he dwelt/ the subtle venom of their customs felt.'

The author might have hoped that the arrest of one of their number might make MPs more sympathetic towards reform. But the poem also contained highly erotic passages – probably added later when all hope of legal reform had been abandoned – whose effect was to ensure that the poem was treated as pornography. Nonetheless it remains one of the first literary documents arguing in favour of justice and humanity for the love that the establishment Commissioners called 'a nameless offence of great enormity we at present exclude from consideration'.[13]

Although not prohibited, William did not take his seat in Parliament while the trial was pending but spent the intervening time with his father, consulting lawyers and chasing worthy character witnesses. It was widely understood that a gentleman who provided the correct testimonials was usually acquitted on his first charge of 'meeting together for unnatural purposes'. Baring Wall had succeeded in this way and as William's counsel – by an irony his old adversary, now his doughty defender – Sir James Scarlett, made plain: 'if upon the evidence brought forward it were possible for a jury of English gentlemen to convict the defendants there was no man whose life or honour were safe.'

The Solicitor General, John Campbell, opened with a lacklustre factual case for the prosecution, after which Scarlett took up the cudgels spiritedly on Bankes's behalf: 'In the course of a long experience in the Courts of Justice,' he declaimed, 'I never knew of a case which was calculated to excite deeper anxiety than the present because it involved not only the safety of an honourable and intelligent gentleman, but the safety of every gentleman in the kingdom.'[14]

The jury was then entertained by much discussion about braces, buttons and flaps. Scarlett, skilfully leading his witnesses, had the police constable report a conversation where he had asked Bankes what state his trousers were in, and whether they were undone in front or whether the flap was down. Apparently the policeman had contended that the flap was down. Bankes pointed out that he had no flap as his trousers buttoned in front. Having elicited this information, Scarlett looked satisfied. Bankes's valet, George Read, called as a witness, testified how the linen he had received from Mr Bankes 'was as free from any mark as when he had put it on in the morning'.[15]

It was rumoured that Barker, a key witness who had stood guard on the night in question while the caretaker went to find a policeman, had mysteriously emigrated to America. Several scurrilous newspaper accounts insinuated that his passage had been paid by Bankes, an accusation strenuously rebutted by Bankes.

Bankes produced a bevy of weighty names to testify to his good character including Samuel Rogers; Dr George Butler, former headmaster of Harrow School; Earl Brownlow; Mr Arbuthnot; and the Duke of Wellington himself, whom Bankes had implored to appear following his lawyer's advice. The Duke commented that he had known Bankes for twenty years, since the latter came out to the army in the Peninsula in 1812, 'and passed a great part of his time at headquarters in my house, in company with my aides de camp and the officers of my staff. I was very intimate with him . . . and should think him utterly incapable of such an offence as he is now charged with.' Most poignantly William's father described his son as a man 'of irreproachable character . . . I have lived with him as with my best friend. We were like brothers.'[16] Arguably the most important testimonial came from William's younger brother, George. George Bankes, former MP for Corfe Castle, married to the heiress Georgina Nugent, father of an ever-expanding family, and since 1830 Secretary of the India Board, was a most respectable figure to speak on William's behalf. This most loyal of brothers revealed how, since their days at Cambridge together, he was aware of difficulties William had in urinating: 'When he went to make water he was much longer than other persons usually are.' William feared the infirmity might indicate kidney stone trouble and had consulted a surgeon in Flintshire about the problem. The surgeon, Mr Hughes, testified that Bankes had been a longtime patient. Did he perjure himself or might Bankes have been telling the truth? The Bankes family had a history of bladder complaints.

At the end of a long day the jury consulted together for a mere ten minutes before the foreman returned to deliver their verdict of not guilty. The evidence, however suspicious, was circumstantial; no prosecution witness had seen physical contact between the two men. The jury foreman added: 'I am further directed by the jury to declare it as their opinion that the defendants leave the court without the least stain on their character from this trial.' The additional comment was important: some of Bankes's supporters had been apprehensive that 'prejudice and something of party ill' might have resulted in a less than total acquittal.

And there it might have ended. Wellington maintained that he still considered Bankes

> as he is described by the verdict: and if I had a party of persons at my house with whom he had been on terms of intimacy I should ask him to meet them. If Bankes is wise, however, he will not expose himself to the world for some time . . . a little patience will set everything right.[17]

But the Duke made a more interesting comment at the trial. Bankes, he said, was always 'of a manly and honourable character'. He recounted that in Madrid Bankes had been robbed of his watch by two men 'and he made so manly a resistance that I gave him one of mine'. Wellington would know that perceptions of masculinity were what would count for Bankes. Had his young friend also been a soldier he might have had an easier time managing and not drawing attention to his homosexual desires. While there are no contemporary references to Bankes dressing or behaving in a noticeably camp manner – oriental dress was more a form of disguise – his interests in aesthetics, painting and design made it harder for him, in an age of hardening sexual stereotypes, to 'cover up'. The nineteenth-century masculine image was not simply 'manly', but authoritative, superior, proud and masterful. Adultery, even debauchery, could be condoned but sexual ambivalence could not be tolerated lest the 'soft' morality from Europe might creep in.

At the time of his trial Bankes was a forty-seven-year-old bachelor, unlikely suddenly to have discovered a new need for casual sexual encounters. Probably a part of his personality had always responded to activities he found both exciting and shameful. The fact that he was attractive to women is also not in doubt and offers further evidence that he was good at maintaining contradictory aspects of his personality. He loved and responded to beautiful things. At the same time he must have been aware from an early age that he had to maintain an impression of conventional sexuality.

Much conspired against homosexuals in early nineteenth century England. Even the term itself, coined in 1868 by a German Hungarian named Hans Benkert, did not enter the language until the late 1890s. Before that time practitioners of 'Greek Love' were referred to as Uranians, Satodists, Inverts and persons of 'contrary sexual instinct'. Hobhouse used the term 'methodism'. In Cambridge circles Horation was the code word for bi-sexual and the classical tradition of male love was well understood and often implied a passion for young boys that could be both violent and pure. The lack of definition is indicative of how little understood the behaviour was. Although it is estimated that in London there were approximately thirty thousand adult male homosexuals and molly houses had been catering to their needs for some time, there was little possibility of solidarity, or meeting openly. Nor was there, irrespective of wealth, any possibility of Bankes enjoying a satisfying or open primary relationship. Until her death in 1823, his mother's apparently unquestioning love may have partially resolved this need. Even if Bankes thrived on risk, he was forced to indulge in furtive relationships, which offered neither affection nor concern, let alone love. The double anguish for nineteenth-century homosexuals was the emphasis on biblical sinfulness aligned with legal criminality; he was both guilty and unfulfilled, neither of which are characteristics readily associated with William Bankes. It is hardly surprising that a man such as Bankes should have difficulty living discreetly with these emotions. He may not have flaunted his sexuality but nor could he overcome his desires.

Bankes's meeting with Private Flowers was almost certainly the result of both seeking a sexual encounter. Certain areas of the Metropolis were known to offer the easiest meeting places for homosexuals and St Margaret's Churchyard was one; Hyde Park, Green Park and St James Park were equally popular rendezvous for soldiers and those who sought their company and often the scene of arrests. It is also apparent, not only from the events of 6 June 1833, that Bankes was a risk taker. Today psychiatrists believe that many homosexuals actively seek multiple relationships or put themselves physically at risk in order to increase excitement. The conclusion to be drawn in Bankes's case is not that he pushed the risk element out of mind, thinking he probably would not get caught, but the reverse:

the element of risk was an important aspect in much that he did, expressed in non-sexual situations as well. Moreover, he knew only too well from his earliest Cambridge days the penalties for sodomy and to what extent they were enforced. When Charles Skinner Matthews wrote to Byron at length lamenting the lack of 'quoits' (i.e. coitus) and the 'enormous increase of παίδεράστιά' he concluded: 'But that which you get for £5 we must risque our necks for'. (In using the Greek word for Pederasty he has enlarged the initial capital 'pi' at the beginning of the word to form a gallows from which a man dangles.)[18]

Sodomy was a capital offence in England until 1861, even though by 1833 Russia, Austria, Prussia and Tuscany had all dropped the death penalty. Late in the eighteenth century France had decriminalised all adult male sexual relationships. But as England moved from Georgian licentiousness to Victorian respectability, fear of French radicalism was partly responsible for enforcing the harsh laws against homosexuality in the country. In 1833 the death penalty was abolished in cases of horse and cattle stealing, letter stealing and sacrilege, forgery, certain cases of attempts to murder and attempts at burglary, robbery and piracy, offences against the Riot Act, rescuing persons going to their execution, seducing soldiers from their allegiance, slave trading and certain forms of smuggling accompanied by violence. In 1841 it was even abolished for rape and abusing girls under ten. But for sodomy, the death penalty stubbornly remained on the statute book. Even after 1861, buggery and gross indecency involving consenting adults remained punishable as criminal activity until the latter part of the twentieth century.

During the first thirty-five years of the nineteenth century more than fifty men were hanged for sodomy in England. In one year, 1806, when Bankes, aged twenty, was at Cambridge, there were more executions for sodomy than for murder. In the first third of the nineteenth century, prosecutions were much more common than they had been in any earlier period. Although executions ceased in 1835, more than 200 homosexuals were sentenced to hang during the next twenty years.

Sir Samuel Romilly, solicitor-general since 1806 who committed suicide in 1818 three days after his wife's death, was one of the most courageous early campaigners against the death penalty for all forms of crime. He told the House of Commons in 1810 that 'there was no country on earth in which there had been so many different offences according to law to be punished with death as in England'. Philosophers such as Jeremy Bentham and the influential Italian Cesare Beccaria had been propounding for years that severely punitive measures – particularly the death penalty – were not only evil and mischievous but also injurious to society. Literary circles favoured abolition. William Thackeray, for example, after being among a crowd of forty thousand which witnessed a public execution, wrote that he 'prayed to Almighty God to cause this disgraceful sin to pass from among us and to clear our land of blood'.[19] But opposing such radical voices was the weight of a fearful society that believed in maintaining the status quo to avoid the revolutions that had rocked the continent. Thousands of soldiers and sailors returned from fighting continental wars to deep concern that their peaceful absorption into society would be made more difficult if stringent punishments were not maintained. In the House of Lords those arguing most strongly to keep the death penalty as currently employed were led by Lord Eldon, Lord Chancellor, and William's brother's father-in-law.

Bankes's public career was irreparably damaged after the trial of 1833. Nine months later, on 16 October 1834, the Houses of Parliament burnt down in a dramatic fire and with the dissolution of Parliament Bankes retired from political life. Twelve months later, on 17 December, 1834 his father Henry Bankes died, two days short of his seventy-eighth birthday, at Tregothnan, the Falmouth family estate. He had been ill for a short time and was exhausted from the strain of the last year. Nonetheless, in his latest will, made in November 1833 after William had been charged, he did not flinch from his intention of making his 'dear son William John sole executor of this my will and heir of all that I possess which is not disposed of in this Will'. William's relationship with his father, a man whose 'public life was marked by firmness in principle, a peculiar disinterestedness and undeviating adherence to conscientiously formed opinions,'[20] was complex. That William aspired to attain the approval of this serious, intellectually accomplished scholar and morally upright man is clear from the long letters he occasionally sent him discussing artistic ideas and historical and decorative schemes. But he also felt frustrated by his father's lack of vision for Kingston Hall.

Henry had specifically requested a private funeral. Though large, it was neither as big nor as fashionable as his wife's had been. The procession on Christmas Eve from Kingston Hall to Wimborne Minster consisted of three mourning coaches following the hearse, and after them eighteen gentlemen's carriages followed by seventy or eighty others on horseback and about twenty on foot. There was a short service in the Minster before Henry's coffin was placed in the family vault.

William Bankes was now master of Kingston Hall.

8

Punishment

~

'Had it passed through my hands intact as it came into them
I might have hesitated long about permitting myself to make
any considerable change'

William Bankes

W E ALL HAVE fantasies, aspirations and dreams. Few of us can render them real. William's aspirations for Kingston Hall were perhaps only part of his dreams, but we know about these fantasies because he translated some into reality. The creation of a monument to past and future Bankes drove him in no small measure. William was too generous a personality to see himself as the centre of this world but he was sufficiently narcissistic to have a clear idea of his role in the family estate's transformation. This made him both determined and difficult to work with, as Charles Barry, his partner in the enterprise, came to know.

In 1829 Barry won the competition to redesign the Travellers' Club in Pall Mall, inspired by the Palazzo Farnese. His subsequent commission for the nearby Reform Club was similarly based on an adaptation of an Italian palazzo. In 1833 he began work on Trentham Hall for the Duke of Sutherland, one of the richest men in England, who had recently succeeded to his vast estates. The London clubs with their simple grandeur were influential buildings which transformed Barry's career and brought him conspicuously to the attention of the British public. But Charles Barry never built a grand country house from foundation to roof; his strength and talent lay in replanning, extending and modernising to the extent that he was to earn the epithet 'Veneerer-in-chief to the Nobility'.[1] Mildly derogatory, the comment has come to be seen as praise for what he did extremely well, and nowhere was this flair better demonstrated than at Kingston Hall.

By 1835, when Bankes was finally ready for his 'help', Barry was preoccupied not only with designing the new front of the College of Surgeons but, more dramatically, with the competition for a new design for the destroyed Houses of Parliament, which prize he was eventually awarded in 1836. He had also undertaken remodelling work at Walton House for the 5th Earl of Tankerville. But Barry employed a small army of assistants in order to take on many projects simultaneously, and, after fourteen years of waiting, was not about to let down his early patron – although Bankes's interfering ways and fixed views may subsequently have made him often wish he had. The relationship was not always easy. Bankes, nine years older, had had a lifetime to ruminate on what he wanted to do with the ancestral home and as he neared fifty, was in a rush to transform them. He continued to view Barry as the charming, eager young draughtsman he had first met in Egypt.

Bankes's overriding inspiration in transforming Kingston Hall was his firm but mistaken belief as to the house's original architect. 'Inigo Jones was dead but the work was commenced and carried on from his drawings by Webb, who inherited his fortune and papers,' wrote William in his blue memorandum book. Entries in this book, written between 1836–40, offer the clearest insight into William's ideas and plans. Behind his purpose in setting this out must have been his desire to defend his vision for future generations. He took his destiny seriously.

> The house had continued to the third generation quite unaltered but the naturally timid disposition of my great uncle, John Bankes, induced him to remove the lantern* altogether and to add some very

---

* The lantern, an architectural term, refers to the domed rooftop structure which lets in daylight.

unnecessary supports in the great gallery, which was near it, and in a cellar in the basement. He also pulled down a banqueting room that stood on the terrace facing the south front. It came into my father's hands with no greater alterations than these and had it passed through his hands intact as it came into them I might have hesitated long about permitting myself to make any considerable change. It would have been interesting as a very complete and handsome specimen of the period and there were features in it that, coupled with the impression that antiquity gives, could not have failed to strike both as in themselves grand or as pictures of the life and manners of other days. The great hall especially with its music gallery and broad staircase . . . would have been some palliative for present incommodiousness, which I thought impossible in an altered house that was neither old or modern in its character but a bad mixture of both.

William justified his plans for making changes partly by criticising the changes his father had made with the architect, Robert Furze Brettingham, 'one of the best of a very bad and flimsy time'.[2] William refers to visits he made with his father to stately homes such as Amesbury, 'built as was Kingston Hall by Webb from the designs of Inigo Jones', and the Grange at Northington, after which he felt 'mortification of hearing him say that the staircase was very like that which he had pulled down at Kingston Hall but that his own was the finer of the two'. William had often vainly tried to persuade his father to employ Barry to oversee changes, so by 1835 the architect was already familiar with some of his client's requirements. In 1829 Barry told Henry Bankes he had considered 'the proposed additions', but his response is concerned solely with the ideal number and arrangement of windows.[3] In fact, Henry commissioned at least six schemes for alterations between 1819 and 1827, most by Thomas Cundy Junior but including one by Wyatville and one by G. A. Underwood, driven by the need for a larger dining room. Finally, in 1833, a bay extension was built on the north west side. But this was demolished by William two years later.

William details a dozen largely practical reasons for undertaking alterations. For example there was no means of entering and going upstairs without crossing the saloon – 'even for persons in the most dirty condition from shooting or hunting' – soiling the carpet and destroying privacy in the central rooms. There was inadequate access to the dining room which was small in size and meagre in proportions, and could also be reached only by passing through the saloon. 'Every other room in the suite was rendered insignificant in appearance by the necessity of having first passed through one of such unusual breadth and height as the saloon.' Both guests and servants entered the dining room at the same end, which he found irksome, and the space from table to fireplace was far too narrow.

The only water closet in the house was in the most public and ostentatious situation which could have been pitched upon, nearly opposite and in full view of the folding doors from the saloon and principal staircase.[*]

William also complained about the lack of an entrance hall; guests entering the front door met only a tiny space before a flight of twenty steps with no landing so the effect was cramped. More practically, there was nowhere to put hats or greatcoats. Furthermore, this entrance was at the end of the building 'and consequently obviously not where the architect could have intended it to be'. The drawing room was too low for its width. Two dressing rooms were 'absolutely useless' since they had no access except through the bedroom, while the south-west bedroom was approached only through a dressing room, which was equally unsatisfactory. The space under the roof was also, according to William, useless. 'This fault was original in the building and the lantern (see p. 162) had been taken down long since on account of the length of the timber bearing and the supposed inadequacy of support.' The warm bath was in the midst of the offices and involved crossing a cold hall 'full of people passing and repassing'. In the saloon, library, best bedchamber and dressing room, William was unhappy with floor length windows

---

[*] Flush lavatories, though rare, had been around since the 1770s and Brettingham installed one at Kingston Hall in 1784 and replaced it with another in 1785, presumably as the first did not function properly. Both were made by Messrs Bramah.

without any guard or balustrade outside to protect people opening them. The corridor to the principal bedroom and dressing room had a dark right-angled turning, only partly remedied by a frame of glass over a dressing room door, that led to its being mistaken for a water closet. He wanted 'a proper situation' for the two grand Snyders, paintings which 'were become a mere incumbrance and were first thrust upon a staircase and since touched both the carpet and cove of the dining room ceiling'. Finally, he objected to the banal view from the principal staircase landing over the kitchen courtyard, and listed multifarious defects and inconveniences that he would wish to see remedied in any general remodelling, including the need for more bedrooms for family or guests.

Evidently William had taken the trouble to study the work of Inigo Jones, especially where the roof and chimney were concerned. Two surviving original elevations by the master obviously meant much to him: he mentioned them more than once when abroad, in a letter to George and another to his steward, insisting to his brother that they were at Kingston Lacy in a stitched folder, labelled in his father's hand, and 'should be taken infinite care of'.[4]

William's belief that Jones was the seventeenth-century architect of Kingston Hall is understandable. Roger Pratt was a great admirer and sincere imitator of Jones and his role at Kingston Lacy was known for certain only when his notes were published in 1928. Referring again to the old lantern taken down by his great uncle, William makes comparisons to Coleshill in Berkshire, Pratt's master-piece, then also thought to be by Inigo Jones. One of Bankes's first directives to Barry, although by this time the most successful and busiest architect in the country, was to go and inspect it more closely. 'Mr Barry, who had just then at my desire and expense, seen Coleshill, (of which I know myself only the front shown in Vertues print) had there fortunately sketched the ceiling of the small saloon.'[5] The dining room ceiling at Kingston Lacy is based on one at Coleshill just as the design for the drawing room ceiling, raised by Barry, was fashioned on one at Lees Court in Kent, another assumed Inigo Jones house visited by Bankes which burned down in 1910. As soon as Bankes had seen at Lees Court 'the very ceiling which I had imagined . . . I induced Mr Barry immediately to follow my steps.' Bankes was convinced that this type of ceiling, 'i.e. where the center is deeper than all the rest and is made to affirm the more so by leaving it quite blank and plain white', was uniquely English. 'At least I saw none on exactly the same principle in Italy or France.'[6] It was not only the ceilings at Coleshill that impressed Bankes. 'The lantern is smaller at Coleshill and leads to the roof. It is there octagonal and probably was so at Kingston Hall but I considered a hexagon to be a form better proportioned to a building which has two shorter and two longer fronts. The principle of the angle chimney is borrowed from Coleshill.'[7]

Chimney stacks, fireplaces and ceilings were all of particular concern to William, and became the subjects of long essays later in his life abroad. For the moment, he searched the works of Inigo Jones to find chimney constructions which rose from the wall of a building or emerged from the slant of a roof similar to those at Coleshill. 'I think they should appear to grow out of the building itself, not seem like something set upon it.' He admired, too, the balustrade on the roof at Coleshill, open at one end to let rainwater drain away. Lamenting that the one at Kingston Hall had been removed by his great uncle, he determined to have it restored.

By 1836, if not before, detailed work was under way at Kingston Hall. Teams of local stonemasons and carpenters were carrying out Barry's plans, after approval by William. Outside, the house was to be encased entirely in Chilmark stone with a new balustrade, cupola and dormers for the roof as well as the tall chimney stacks William admired at Coleshill. Replacing the old brickwork with stone would have vastly altered the exterior appearance of the house. Such was William's enormous attention to detail that in order to achieve a break forward on the south elevation he had the original brickwork cut back at both ends by one brick thick. But the major work was moving the entrance back to the north front and excavating eight feet on this side of the house in order to accommodate a *porte-cochère* below ground level. Guests arriving by carriage could avoid the rain and enter the house through a new basement entrance hall, more impressive since the floor had been lowered and the height of the room increased. Kingston Hall was now a three, not a two and a half storey house. On the south side, Brettingham's pretty pergola was removed and a majestic balustraded terrace built along the length of the house at principal-floor level. This idea was based on a similar one at the Queen's House, Greenwich, another Inigo Jones construction on Bankes's list of admired buildings.* It provided a more elegant entry point to the garden, while also masking the servants' outlook.

Inside, the main structural work consisted of replacing the old stone stairs with a staircase of Carrara marble, which linked the entrance hall in the basement with the bedroom floor. An impressive staircase was key to William's aspirations at Kingston Lacy. This, too, he had already been cogitating:

> My recollections of Rome gave the Ruspoli staircase a preference over all the other staircases I had seen, and this I had so strongly in my mind when I described what I wished mine to be to Mr Barry that I sent to Rome for a measured plan and location of it which did not reach me till all those prepared for Kingston Hall were on paper, and I was grateful and surprised to see how strongly all the available points of resemblance were preserved. No variation was accordingly made in consequence of obtaining these details.[8]

Measurements were sent to Italy for the individual treads and risers, which were then shipped to Poole, cut locally and assembled piece by piece.

The Palazzo Ruspoli in the Via del Corso, built in the mid-sixteenth century by the Jacobilli, is one of the most beautiful Renaissance buildings in Rome. Its many impressive interior features include a grand gallery, frescoed by Jacopo Zucchi, representing the Genealogy of the Gods, one of the masterpieces of Florentine

---

* Bankes also copied a ceiling cornice for one of his lady's dressing rooms from the Queen's House, 'an exact copy . . . from the suite of Henrietta Maria in a little room one angle of which is cut off, as here'. (memo book DRO)

mannerism in Rome. Its fine marble staircase, by the seventeenth-century church architect Martino Longhi the Younger, considered one of the wonders of this many-splendoured city, was probably constructed around 1629 when the palazzo became the property of Cardinal Luigi Caetani.

Bankes always considered his staircase one of his most important contributions to the remodelling of the house. Its sense of space and grandeur was achieved by clever use of perspective and he was particularly proud that the return of the third flight, not over either of the two first but over the intermediate space, was entirely his own idea and invention. The aim was 'principally to face in to the saloon door, which would have a striking effect in the directing of company to their bed chamber and also in facing directly towards the eating room door in the morning for breakfast.' The east-facing mezzanine Loggia, with its niches that now house the Marochetti sculptures, was, however, Barry's idea. This half-landing would, during William's lifetime, have overlooked Pratt's stables. Barry, who had plans to turn it into a garden which was eventually laid out after the new stables were built at the west end in the 1880s, proposed glazing bars for the windows here, but Bankes who had seen a plate glass manufactory the day after Huskisson's untimely death on the new railway, hoped that the view could be uninterrupted. Beyond the stables was the park with cedars planted by him in 1835 as part of a projected 'green drive', now grassed over, which would lead to Pamphill Village. But all this was still unresolved at the time of his flight.

Two years after work began he wrote to his brother George:

> I am astonished at the rate of progress of the works, and more than ever pleased with them. The lantern is everything that I could wish and so is the drawing room ceiling, that is to say their effect is exactly what was upon paper – but the staircase turns out far beyond it (if staircase it may be called that stairs has none). It is now formed and roughed out in almost every part, all the openings clear and all the ceiling shaped so that proportions and perspectives and distribution and lighting can all be judged of quite as well as can ever be and I must pronounce (though it cannot be said impartially) that so far as

my judgment goes there is no staircase in England equal to it in effect, not even Wardour, and not many that surpass it in Italy. I delight in the rich Eastern external loggia which is finished, but I do nothing but walk up and down the inclined planes of the Staircase.[9]

Other internal changes were more structural than decorative. The old eating room, still referred to as the North Drawing Room, was eventually prepared as William's Spanish Room and, adjacent to it, Barry was creating a new, larger dining room by removing an internal spinewall and using the space from the Brettingham family staircase. Between the two new rooms, under the servants' stairs, he cleverly created a small gem of a square room, not big enough to sit in, almost an internal folly. What William now called the coffee loggia, was, he conceded, 'originally a suggestion of Mr Barry's and a great improvement' on what was there before. Probably intended as a kind of servery, where the gentleman could pick up their after-dinner coffee on the way to the Golden Room while the ladies progressed to the drawing room, it has a vaulted ceiling at the crown of which an alabaster ceiling boss contained an oil lamp which needed to be lowered in order to replenish the oil and trim the wick. Initially, lack of oxygen prevented this from working, a fault corrected by making ventilation holes in the cupboard doors. In the daytime natural light, which came through the alabaster niche, was increased by mirror glass. Again, it was unfinished when William fled.

On the first floor William did little to the saloon, 'a room of noble and inspiring effect', and left the library alone. 'It were to be wished that the library could accommodate a greater number of books but the fine family portraits are admirably placed in it and I should be at a loss to dispense them elsewhere.'[10]

What were William's other preoccupations during his brief seven years of stewardship? The rebuilding work consumed most of his energy and he was constantly inspecting the rate of progress. Living in the house 'when all without is wet clammy chalk and all within noise and cold draughts',[11] was a matter of extreme discomfort; so he used Old Palace Yard instead. Kingston Lacy never became a real home. Meanwhile, although Barry as architect made the major structural decisions, he was never allowed to give his imagination free rein. Bankes sought to be involved at every stage. He dashed off letters and sketches which made lengthy and exhausting work for Barry, who was juggling many other projects at the same time. It also led to occasional confusion as his Clerk of Works often found to his consternation. 'Mr Barry's finished plans to $\frac{1}{4}$ inch scale is not correct in the balustrade – I have taken it from different drawings and reduced it to $\frac{1}{2}$ inch scale.'[12] If Bankes wished to have a particular cornice copied he would find the best London artist to make and mould a precise duplicate and his standards were always exacting. On 17 May he noted: 'On this day I have given the order to execute the roof ballusters (in one piece) in pottery to be baked hard but white. I have ordered 266 at 3/6 each.' This was not, however, the end of the story. Forty were broken and forty-six discoloured from excessive heat in baking, as he noted again some days later. He oversaw the cutting, squaring, sanding and polishing of four table tops cut from one piece of fine Egyptian red granite already in his possession. His personal involvement in architectural and interior decorative schemes was outstanding even in an era when amateurism held sway.

As William's own memorandum book shows, he and his architect did not always see eye to eye. 'I gave way perhaps too readily to Mr Barry's disapprobation of a proposition that I submitted to him,' William comments, or, 'The dressing to the house doors should have been broader and golden; I urged this in vain upon Mr Barry.'[13]

Less social than he had been before his 1833 court case, he nonetheless maintained contacts with the Duke of Wellington and other old friends. He also seems to have had a tolerable relationship with his brother George. He told him in December, 1837 how he had just spent 'one of the most interesting days that I have passed in my life'. Invited at noon to meet the former King of Spain and Naples, Joseph Bonaparte, and to see *objects d'art*, he found him 'not a clever but a very communicative man'. The objects engaged his attention so much 'that I remained with him till after dark'. He then went to dine with the Duke at half past six and, catching the Exeter Mail at Apsley House at half past eight and 'choosing the Blandford Road that I might see my whole avenue',[14] was back in Kingston Lacy in time to change quickly for a meeting at 10 a.m. in Wimborne. The avenue, leading past Badbury rings, was the beech avenue planted in 1835 in memory of his mother. Planting had been a favourite activity William had shared with Frances Bankes, sparing her the heavy work as it is 'an occupation which I by no means dislike'.[15] By 1838 quantities of oak, ash, scotch fir, hazel and thorn saplings were also being raised in a nursery on the estate. There could be no greater evidence of William's concern to link past and future generations than his dedication to tree planting.

In addition to these occasional forays to town there were visits to Soughton. From 1829–30 William was Sheriff of Merioneth, a largely honorific appointment that required little action other than his appearance in the County. But his overriding concern was Kingston Hall, which now became Kingston Lacy, the change of name to reflect a time when the medieval tenants of the Kingston Estate were the de Lacys, the Earls of Lincoln. The house boasted very little good quality old furniture compared with other equivalent establishments. William may have been giving some thought to furnishings in the late 1830s, as evidenced by surviving receipts. He bought a marquetry commode at a public sale for £21, and paid John Webb, upholsterer and cabinet maker, £10 and 18 shillings for three pieces, presumably restoration work. Roger Nixon, an upholsterer and cabinet maker, sent a bill for a marquetry table with twisted pillars, ebony, ivory and brass. William ordered books as well as a collection of damask table linen, ornamented with fleur de lys, from Ireland. But most of the bills were for gilding, restoring, cleaning and repairing with the heftiest – running into several hundreds of pounds – for marble masonry. How to fill the new rooms with furniture other than marble busts and blocks of alabaster was a problem William had not yet fully addressed.

On 28 March 1839, he bought for £100 from Town & Emanuel of 103 New Bond Street 'a Venetian ceiling', to be installed in his new Spanish picture room, dreamt of since his travels in Spain. This lavish gilt and coffered ceiling came from one of the Contarini palaces in Venice, probably the Palazzo Contarini degli Scrigni as the contents of that magnificent building, with its two *piani nobili* added by Vincenzo Scamozzi to the old Palazzo Contarini Corfu on the Grand Canal in 1609, were being dispersed around this time.[*] William wrote:

> This ceiling had been purchased on speculation by some Jews in London upon the faith of a very beautiful and accurate drawing sent over to them from Venice which is now in my possession.
>
> I never saw it in its original situation nor have had any means of ascertaining since at what height it was elevated from the floor. Generally speaking, it is a defect in the proportion of Venetian interiors that they are too low, which is strikingly the case with most of the gorgeous compartmented ceilings on which Paul Veronese and his contemporaries worked in oils at the Ducal Palace ... If it be true, however, as I was assured by the importers, that the series of enriched oval frames still retained as a sort of extra or sub frieze did constitute part of the decoration of the same apartment we must infer that the elevation not only has surpassed the usual Venetian pitch but must have been rather even in excess ...

Bankes did not use these oval cartouches immediately; they were stored while he worked out the rest of his decorative scheme for the room. He did, however, set about trying to fit the ceiling, which required modifications to make the dimensions conform. Although the ceiling was uniformly attributed to Sansovino, William suspected that some of the minutiae were sketched in under his eye 'though not actually chizzled by his hand'. It remains a magnificent piece of work, dominating the Spanish Room and dictating its character. William had but a few months to enjoy it.

In 1840 he also bought two important pictures from Genoa, both by Rubens, his last major purchases. Both were thought to be

---

[*] Professor A.L. Rowse thought, improbably, the ceiling came from the Ca d'Oro and there have been other claims that it was from the Palazzo Contarini delle Figure, once owned by the Guiccioli family, as an original ceiling was sold out of the house at around this time.

portraits of ladies of the Grimaldi family, although when first referred to in Ratti's *Guide to Genoa* of 1780, a copy of which William owned and annotated and is now in the library at Kingston Lacy, their identity was not certain. According to William, 'There is a slight Venetian tone of brown on the flesh in these pictures, which I have observed in some other of Rubens' early performances in Italy and particularly in the great circumcision altar piece in the Church of Gesu. Some of the Vandyke Genoese portraits have the same peculiarity, which both these great painters discontinued afterward.' William had the page with his own reflections inserted in the rebound book and the new binding was marked: 'Authentication of the two portraits by Rubens at Kingston Lacy.' Experts today consider the first is of Maria Serra, the wife of Niccolo Pallavicino, banker and host to Rubens' employer Duke Vincenzo I Gonzaga of Mantua. In 1606 the Duke gave a sumptuous banquet where the Marchesa Pallavicino might have worn the wondrous dress portrayed. The second is of the Marchesa Maria Grimaldi, daughter of the Marchese Carlo Grimaldi, who put his villa at Sampadiema at the disposal of Rubens and his employer Duke Vincenzo of Mantua in 1607.

In January, 1840 Bankes received a letter from Barry, initially discussing William's proposal for niches in the saloon. Barry then told him:

> I am scraping together just now a sum of money for the purchase of a little property that is offered to me upon advantageous terms. May I therefore request the favour of your assistance with £500 on account of my professional services and expenses in respect of the works at Kingston Lacy?[16]

Three days later Barry wrote from his London house to thank Bankes effusively for his 'prompt compliance with my request and the kind expressions which accompany it'.[17] He explained that he was going to the country that afternoon, returning to town on Saturday evening, and offered to be at Bankes's service any day the following week to discuss saloon niches or anything else. Bankes's instant generous response to his architect is important since John

Lewis Wolfe, Barry's lifelong friend and adviser who always disapproved of Bankes, later put it about that Barry was never paid by him. Perhaps this misunderstanding – or mischief – arose from negotiations conducted by George once William had left the country. A letter from George to William mentions, among other matters, 'Bill of Mr Barry for the balance of his account on which he declined making any deduction. £488.'[18] William was a munificent patron of the arts, not only towards Barry, and his brother's attempts at economy at a time of family uncertainty might have been the seed for Wolfe's accusation.

In September 1840 William wrote to the Duke of Wellington that he was 'longing to have the opportunity next year (which you have kindly promised shall not be wanting) of showing you what has been done. The house is not yet in a state fit for reception, but the few of those who knew it before who have looked it over seem to admire it extremely and to think that it will combine much comfort with a sufficiency of splendour.'[19]

The next few months must have seen a frenzy of activity. As the spring of 1841 came to a close William, perhaps remembering how his parents celebrated their rebuilding in 1791, decided to throw what Hobhouse derided mildly as 'a great ball to all the women of fashion in London'.[20] W. Stinton, a catering firm in Duke Street, charged £80 for organising the evening and providing food, decorations, waiters, cooks and four musicians. A naturally gregarious personality, William, it appears, had plans to use Kingston Lacy for many such parties. In a poignant essay written a few years later about the ideal country house, he makes several references to its uses. 'Upon some rare occasions of festivity such as the coming of age of a proprietor or an heir . . . when at the very least some further illumination of the entrance hall might be desirable . . .'[21]

By June 1841, Bankes's reputation as an arbiter of fine taste was such that he was invited to give his opinions to the Select Committee on the Fine Arts for the new Houses of Parliament. He used the opportunity to champion bronze sculpture in Britain, such as he had admired in Munich and Paris, and expound on his belief in artistic internationalism: in art, he stated, 'true patriotism consisted only in feeling a fervent desire to improve it and bring it to perfection.'[22] His confidence in recommending a German muralist to supervise the decoration of the Palace of Westminster did not win him friends in every quarter; some saw it as an attempt to humiliate British artists.

Asked if he thought it desirable that Cornelius or some other eminent artist who had studied the art of fresco painting, should be brought over to direct the work, Bankes replied: 'Yes I was so much of that opinion that I had invited Cornelius and had engaged him to execute a ceiling or two for myself. I thought it not improbable that he might get employed for the public and I believe he thought so too; but the King of Prussia stepped in and has appointed him the Head of the Academy, and I am obliged to submit to the disappointment.'[23]

Just when his opinion was being sought on artistic matters of national importance, William was arrested for a second time.

By now fifty-five, the master of Kingston Lacy, 'being a person of wicked, lewd, filthy and unnatural mind and disposition', was caught in the act of indecently exposing himself to a soldier of the Foot Guards in Green Park on 30 August 1841. Constable William Bennett of 88A Division took him to Bow Street Station where in his first flush of fear he gave a false identity. He described himself as John Harris, a servant. According to Constable Bennett, one of the newly created Metropolitan Officers, Bankes had been spotted at about 12.30 a.m., in the moonlight, talking with a soldier on Constitution Hill. The two men went over to the palings in Green Park and, observed by Bennett, crossed to the centre of the park, stopping at the far side near a clump of trees. Green Park was notorious as a favourite place for nocturnal assignations and was also regularly patrolled by the police. Just the other side was Wellington Barracks and young soldiers, short of cash, often strolled through on the lookout.

The rest, according to *The Times*, which reported the story on 3 September, mentioning Bankes by name, was unfit for publication.

But not apparently unfit for recording in the subsequent indictment. This document, which the Bankes family conceded must be preserved among family papers, spared few details of how Bankes and the unnamed soldier had behaved together. Bankes was indicted on five counts, the last being the cruellest. It accused him of making an assault against the said person unknown 'and there did beat wound and illtreat him . . . to the great damage of the said person unknown'. For the soldier, seeing the policeman approach, had succeeded in sprinting away. The middle-aged Bankes tried to run, but managed only a dozen or so yards before being apprehended 'with his small clothes still unbuttoned . . . he begged and pressed of me to let him go and took out his purse several times and said he would give me anything if I would, and would reward me afterwards. He said he would then give me all the money he had.'[24]

Bankes panicked. Soon after the arrest, he changed his story about being an unemployed servant and, admitting that he was 'a gentleman of fortune', begged that if his name could be suppressed he would retire to his country seat and could be bailed by the name of Harris. This proposal did not help his case. The soldier, removing himself from the scene of the crime, mirrored his friends' reactions. The reformed Hobhouse, whose perception of Bankes's recklessness had already made him wary of him at Cambridge, wrote: 'Gibson Craig . . . told me that W Bankes had been again caught with a soldier!!! Monstrous madness. I had thought myself obliged to refuse appearing as a witness to his character on the former occasion because I could say nothing which could be of service to him, but he has since been as much in society as if nothing had happened.'[25]

Released by the magistrate on bail of £200 with two sureties of £100 each, Bankes lost no time in consulting the family solicitor, J. S Gregory. John Swarbeck Gregory was among the most eminent lawyers of his day and his partnership, then Adlington, Gregory and Faulkner, one of the largest and most profitable in London. Two senior partners had been members of the Royal Commission on Law Reform set up by Peel and their clients included major aristocratic and landowning families such as Pitt, Cornwallis, Romney,

Falmouth and, of course, Bankes. The firm orginated in 1784 and in 1807 moved to No 1, Bedford Row, where it practises today under the name Gregory, Rowcliffe, Milner. Little has changed about the building, where the same gas lamp still hovers over three low stone steps leading to the front door which William entered in 1841.

John Gregory came from middle-class stock with a highly moral bent. He was the son of Reverend Dr Gregory, Rector of West Ham, who in 1801 became a Governor of Thomas Coram's Foundling Hospital in Coram Fields, Bloomsbury. The son was educated at Eton and, after serving his articles, became an attorney and solicitor in 1811, shortly before becoming a partner in the firm. From then on his life was so entirely focused that his obituarist lamented there was nothing other than his devotion to the law, the esteem in which his brethren held him, and his Presidency of the Law Society in 1851, that had marked his life.[26] His firm specialised in non-litigious work and in general did not accept commercial clients or criminal work other than exceptional cases where private clients were involved.

William John Bankes was one such exception, and surviving correspondence between him and Gregory shows how inexperienced Gregory was in cases of indecent assault – this was probably the first such case he had agreed to defend. Nor could he anticipate how heavily the hand of the law would fall on his client. In advising Bankes to flee before the trial he was well aware that sodomy was still a capital offence for which a man had been hanged as recently as six years earlier. In 1840 yet another parliamentary debate on the abolition of the death penalty had been lost with 161 against abolition, 90 in favour. However, since it was almost impossible to prove that the crime had actually been committed, indictments for assault with intent were open to very flexible interpretations. Although some might be punished with two years' hard labour, even following the Offences Against the Person Act, 1861, a ten-year prison sentence was the norm. Gregory was also aware of the unlikely possibility that if Bankes did not stand trial, the Treasury could take steps to declare him an outlaw, with the result that all the property he possessed in Britain could be forfeit to the Crown.

I have discussed Bankes's case with legal historians who have expressed surprise that a mid-nineteenth century government would still resort to the archaic process of outlawry. Clearly this would be an exceptional step. No one became an outlaw automatically by absconding; by the 1840s criminal outlawry was pretty much a dead letter and it is striking that Bankes's own legal adviser did not know what the procedure was for outlawry. Contemporary legal texts confirm that outlawry was not in widespread use and neither the main textbook on criminal law nor one of the earliest critical and evaluative accounts of the criminal law* has an index entry for it.

Why was Bankes treated so harshly? Literally, the effect of being declared an outlaw was to be put beyond the protection of the law 'so that [the offender] is incapable of taking the benefit of it in any respect'. The punishment was forfeiture of goods and chattels. Gregory, however great his inexperience, correctly advised his client to flee the country quickly and also to convey and assign the freehold and leasehold of his estates, chattels and other personal effects to his brothers George and Edward, and his nephew George Henry Lord Boscawen, 'for their sole and absolute benefit and as Joint Tenants both at law and in equity'. This sad document, which must have been prepared under extreme pressure for its date of 13 September 1841, establishes that from that day William John Bankes retained no interest, legal or equitable, in Kingston Lacy, the house to which he had devoted his adult life, nor in Soughton, the country house that had offered him youthful pleasure and refuge. He was determined that his trustees should be chosen from both his mother and father's side and also wanted a young life included, hence the inclusion of Boscawen. According to a note on the front signed by E. L. Rowcliffe, a later partner in the firm, the original of this deed was preserved at Kingston Lacy, in the muniment room.

---

* Sir William Oldnall Russell, *A Treatise on Crimes* (third edition 1843); James Fitzjames Stephen, *A General View of the Criminal Law of England* (1863).

During the two-and-a-half weeks following the night of 30 August, the family – in particular Falmouth – fielded a number of unpleasant callers and letters. They tried to shield William's sister Anne from learning the lurid details by scouring newspapers likely to carry accounts and preventing delivery of potentially unpleasant papers. '*The Standard* is not, I think, to be feared as upon principle. It is silent upon all such subjects. But the *John Bull* may require inspection,'[27] Falmouth worried. They were lucky: it too avoided mention of the Bankes case. An anonymous letter on 14 September threatened that 'it would be an advantage to you at the present moment to make some compensation to a lady you were once attached to and whose unfortunate affection blighted her whole life. Your strange, and allow me to say culpable, neglect of her for many years has been a matter of surprise to me. . . .'[28] This presumably referred to Anne Buckinghamshire; there is no known reply.*

As well as resolving his legal affairs, William set about packing a few essentials and making domestic arrangements. One activity that preoccupied him in the hours before flight was sorting out the documents which rooted the family mythology in reality. These included papers authenticating paintings he had bought, but he treasured most the letters and documents referring to the defence of Corfe Castle, the tale that had so inspired him in his youth; Sir Ralph's correspondence with his neighbour, Sir Walter Erle, accused of taking the timber from Corfe Castle for his own home, as well as his ancestor's relations with Col. Bingham and documents describing the Bankes's fortunes at the Restoration. Much had already been moved to 5, Old Palace Yard during the building works in Dorset, but who was to say if that would not be confiscated?

In the still unfinished house, searching for papers that must be preserved, he found a cache of correspondence from the Duke of Wellington and Lord Byron, including their covers. 'One cover from Lord Byron I found only the last day I was in England and there

---

* Her husband the Earl died only in 1849 and in 1854 his widow re-married finally, David Wilson of Brook Street.

is in it a line about the supposed recovery of great property in Rochdale, which I had hunted in vain for Moore's work.'[29] He had not yet accepted that the rest of his life would be in exile. Gregory sent him explicit instructions to tell his bankers so that stock could be transferred and powers of attorney sent to Old Palace Yard. Bankes, preoccupied and uncertain, dithered and delayed until the last. On 18 September he was conveyed by carriage to Southampton en route to Le Havre.

> I can't say but it is an awkward sight
> to see one's native land receding through
> the growing waters – it unmans one quite;
> especially when life is rather new:
> I recollect Great Britain's coast looks white,
> but almost every other country's blue . . .

How loudly did Byron's words from Canto 11 of *Don Juan* echo in his ears?

His family's support seems never to have wavered. The tragedy may have been no surprise to them. His brother-in-law and friend, Lord Falmouth, immediately arranged to talk to anyone of influence who might be able to help. He was shocked by the cool response he encountered.

There does indeed appear to exist an undercurrent of persecution which may frustrate all our efforts to steer the deplorable subject of our late association down the stream of social opinion into the depths of oblivion . . . let us only hope that the kind, judicious and influential channel in which I placed it on Thursday will afford a timely check to such cruel immoral and impolitic proceedings,

he wrote to Gregory a month after the arrest.[30]

Waiting anxiously in Honfleur, William considered returning to England to face trial. But Falmouth could ascertain no guarantee among his 'friends of high influence' that the outcome would be favourable, in fact he felt he had failed in his attempt to 'counteract the zeal of mischief of hostile partisans in the Home Office'. The strength of feeling against William was too strong, he told Gregory.[31] William must remain where he was.

For the next fifteen years until his death, Bankes's movements and places of residence were deliberately obscured. Gregory, perhaps fearing that an attempt might be made to bring him back, advised he should never give his address, and henceforth wherever he travelled letters were addressed to Poste Restante, with a few minor exceptions when a location slipped through. This was before the days of formal extradition – the first Extradition Acts were not passed until 1870 and 1873. But Gregory knew that extradition treaties were under discussion and one was made with the United States of America in 1842, another with France in 1843.* These were wholly ineffective but since the case was proceeding in a way, in his view, 'totally inconsistent with the interests of either morality or society,' there were still procedures a vindictive government might take . . .'

In his first days of exile Bankes had no clear picture of his future. He instructs Gregory that he has a few commissions for his servant, William Prince, 'but otherwise I have no wish to be written to unless there is a necessity.' He asks Gregory to forward a letter to Thomas Robson, his steward, informing him of his absence from London as he does not want letters to arrive in Old Palace Yard: but as the London servants think he is in Dorset he also wants to stop letters going to Kingston Lacy. He was soon obliged to give Robson the unpleasant task of discharging most of the servants. He asks whether Childs, his bankers, can authorise the transfer of his stock as well as the dividends upon it and, if not, can the power of attorney be provided forthwith? Gregory chides him for not having arranged this in person while he was still in London. A few days later he emphasises that he wants stock transferred urgently, accusing Gregory of not advising him earlier that power of attorney would be needed. But he has no desire to see Gregory himself; better for his servant to come over with a power of attorney as well as the

---

* Between 1843 and 1865 the French obtained the extradition of one person only although they made upwards of twenty demands.

remainder of his clothes. Torn off the top of the page is a draft for
£300 for Childs. Similar drafts at regular intervals continued
throughout his fifteen years abroad. Since Bankes seems to have had
no difficulty in receiving modest amounts of money, the terms of
the outlawry decree must have been narrow enough that William
remained entitled to anything other than land, goods or chattels, in
other words shares or stock were excluded as was his interest in the
black lead mines of Cumbria. The fact that such a reputable banking
house as Childs was prepared to send regular remittances to an
outlaw indicates that this was not illegal and reinforces the notion
that outlawry was intended as a disability for the individual named
rather than for those he dealt with. But there is also evidence of a
side letter to the conveyance of the estates, which Gregory himself
retained according to which 'the whole usufruct of everything is
reserved to myself during my lifetime and consequently all that accu-
mulates is subject (in honour) to any disposal which I may think
proper to direct during my lifetime or at the time of my death.'[32]
While he no longer owned the property theoretically he retained
the right of temporary enjoyment of it.

Events moved fast. The prosecution indictment, couched in
language redolent of biblical retribution and Victorian morality,
made clear that John S. Gregory had understood immediately the
dangers for his client. Bankes faced five counts of the utmost seri-
ousness and was charged not only as 'a man lost to all sense of
decency, morality and religion who tried to corrupt the morals of
others ... who endeavoured to persuade a person unknown to
commit and perpetrate that detestable and abominable crime (among
Christians not to be named) called Buggery', but also with indecent
assault.

On Friday, 24 September at the Central Criminal Court, the
Home Office made an application to seize Bankes's bail money.
When the judges heard that the defendant was not forthcoming to
meet the charges, they ordered that this surety, already doubled to
a total of £800 but still 'a very trifling sum considering his rank
and property'[33] be paid over, that he should enter into further pledges

of £5,000 himself with two sureties of £2,500, and set in motion the outlawry procedure. 'Government have resolved that offenders of this description shall not be allowed to set the law at defiance as they have hitherto done,' was the official explanation.[34] His defence lawyer on this occasion, Mr Bodkin, weakly argued that he expected his client to be in town before the termination of the sessions and therefore any further action against him was premature. But Mr Phillips, for the Home Office, was having none of it; the departure abroad of Mr Bankes under the circumstances was very suspicious. The judges concluded that since the defendant was a person of station in society and of large property the sum of £5,000 must be forfeit. The defendant was then called, according to ancient tradition, three times in the court and three times outside but, not answering, the money already pledged was ordered to be seized.

Falmouth had hoped that the Government would see 'that forfeiture of recognizances and exile of the accused for life amounted to a far greater punishment than could have been awarded upon conviction of the charge.' But in early October he received a letter from Lord Ripon 'which did NOT convey any intention to pursue the accused beyond the season [nor of] adopting other extreme measures, but certainly leaves an opening for that or any other course of persecution. I have therefore written to him again to point out the unnecessary and to society injurious, violence and notoriety of any such steps.'[35]

Falmouth's enlightened sympathy had little effect on the government law officers. Why Bankes's case had aroused such vengefulness in Government was as hard to fathom then as now. The decent Gregory was both

> grieved and surprised at the course taken, or rather threatened, by the Home Office. Because I think it either shows a subservience to an official whose masters they ought to be or a desire to tremble and bend to public clamour for the sake of gaining ... short lived popularity among the lower grades of society by affecting to deal out equal justice to the great and the little. But it does appear to me that even this spurious claim is being carried much too far on the

present occasion and to an extent which savours of oppression not of justice.

Gregory admitted that he was doing his best to make certain that there was no precedent of 'Government taking upon itself the office of public persecutor in a case of misdemeanor, and where the accused did not appear, going beyond the forfeiture of the recognizance'. But he was not yet able to give his client clear-cut advice as to what options remained open to a Government that appeared to be acting in such a vindictive way.

He swiftly recognised the possibility that Bankes would be declared an outlaw. Nonetheless, 'before I trouble Lord Ripon I am desirous of making myself well acquainted with what are the extreme powers of government in this respect and as to what has been the usage and practice in any similar cases. We must be fully prepared to meet all the difficulties before meeting Lord Ripon.'

Meanwhile Gregory admitted he was 'much disturbed at the nature of Lord Ripon's communication'.[36] Was Lord Ripon, who as a moderate Tory MP since 1806 must have known Bankes, the enemy in the Home Office directing the case? In 1827, as Viscount Goderich, he had briefly been Prime Minister but as Bankes had not been an MP during his seven-month administration there was no obvious source of friction.

Nine months later, when it was clear that William Bankes was living abroad and not about to return, *The Times* renewed its attack, thundering that

> offenders like him would not in future be allowed to set the law at defiance, as they have hitherto done, by paying the trifling amount in which magistrates have thought it their duty to hold them to bail. Mr Maule, the Solicitor to the Treasury, has already taken the necessary steps to outlaw Mr Bankes and on Thursday a writ of *distringas* was levied on him at Old Palace Yard . . . if the defendant does not return to this country and take his trial he will be declared an outlaw and all the property he possesses here be forfeited to the Crown.[37]

It was a very real threat and would not have been the first time that Bankes lands had been sequestered by the Government.

However, it was too late. William Bankes had flown. The property had been safely settled in the hands of his brothers. The Government, possibly informed that it had already been conveyed by the time they embarked on the outlawry procedure, never made any attempt to wrench it away.

9

Venice

~

'I can only fiddle with little details about the body of the House'
William Bankes to George Bankes

IN A REAL sense, Venice claimed William Bankes. The majestic buildings rising out of the water enchanted him with their magic,
beauty and history just as they had countless other travellers. William's
dilemma was that the love of his life was his house and England.
Yet he flourished when he was travelling far from home. Arguably
his arrest in 1841 destroyed him. But in stripping away a layer of
superficial respectability, it also allowed him in Venice to reinvent
himself. He was able to do so partly because of the differences
between London and Venetian society of the time. Though London
considered itself modern, industrial, democratic, Venice offered a
degree of cultural sophistication and tolerance that London could
never hope to reach. As Byron wryly remarked a few years earlier
about his own exile, if rumours which forced him to leave England
were true he was unfit for England, if false England unfit for him.[1]

When Byron came first to Venice he maintained he did not intend
writing there. Yet his romantic imagination was captured by the past
and his perception of the city's decline and decay, especially because
it mirrored his own moral and physical condition. His exile was to
provide him with the stimulus for one of his greatest works, *Don
Juan*. Bankes had a similar, if slower, metamorphosis.

Bankes spent the first winter of his banishment in France. But a
host of reasons urged him to move further south. He spoke Italian

fluently, relished the warm climate and attitude towards art and culture, and nurtured memories of visiting Byron there twenty years earlier during the poet's self-exile. Perhaps he also remembered Byron's description of the Italian attitude towards a sodomite, 'a character by no means so much respected as it should be: but they laugh instead of burning – and the women talk of it as a pity in a man of talent.'[2] Based in Venice, Bankes realised, he could continue work on his unfinished, deeply cherished house.

He probably also had darker fears about staying in France. The French, keen to win the return of criminals lurking in England, might take an unsympathetic view should the British Government request his return. A foreigner needed a rudimentary form of passport, although this could usually be obtained en route. French officials could stop a traveller on the highway, enter the hotel dining room or even a bedroom to demand sight of 'the precious document'. Bankes, as a fugitive from justice, could hardly expect to be granted such a document.

Many writers and artists contributed to the myth of Venice as a city of beauty and vice, pleasure and corruption, of the assassin's dagger and the sculptor's chisel. In the nineteenth century it was still a city where one could live relatively inexpensively, with a strong sense of the past, of licentiousness and decay. The carnival masks – prohibited during the Republic of 1848–9 – were a metaphor for much that was hidden from view by the opulent exteriors of gilded palazzi. Behind them lay the slums and beggars, *gransieri* or crab catchers as they were known to Venetians. The mystery and secrecy surrounded by aspects of exquisite beauty would have a powerful appeal for Bankes. But Venice was also the city which produced incomparable art as Bankes would be the first to appreciate: the home of Giorgione, Titian, Tintoretto and Veronese. Their gorgeous frescoes had once ornamented the façades of the palazzi, now worn and peeling after centuries of frosts and storms. Pleasure-giving Venice was also, since 1637, the home of opera – Monteverdi, Vivaldi, Scarlatti and Handel all conducted operas there and the opera house was the cultural epitome of Italian social life.

Venice had long attracted highly educated British and American travellers who felt passionately about its treasures and its history. But whereas in the previous century Rome and Naples had been the key attractions for young and wealthy grand tourists, vide Henry Bankes, now Venice rivalled them. The city attracted 112,644 tourists in 1843, the year the city was first lit by gas, making an enormous difference to the safety of the dark narrow alleyways. By this time eleven large hotels and numerous *pensioni* catered to foreigners' needs as well as seven theatres, open every night, including the renowned La Fenice, and a number of opera houses.

The British public's images of Venice in the early nineteenth century derived from many sources: Byron, the poems of Thomas Moore and Samuel Rogers, Shakespeare's *Othello* and *The Merchant of Venice*. Ann Radcliffe's Gothic romances described a sixteenth century Venice that she had never visited, full of mystery and terror. The heroine of *The Mysteries of Udolpho* (1794) visits Venice 'with its palaces and towers rising out of the sea . . . as if they had been called up from the Ocean by the wand of an enchanter, rather than reared by mortal hands'.[3] Fanny Trollope, mother of the novelist Anthony, arriving in the autumn of 1841, just as Bankes was leaving England, was concerned that she was already too well prepared for what she would find there by the many paintings of Canaletto and Turner. But she still found 'a freshness of wonder that attends every part of the progress through this floating world . . . a piquant novelty, an untasted pleasure, that can only be described by comparing it with what we may presume might be the effect of magic, if some great enchanter took possession of us and carried us through a world of unknown and unimagined loveliness, taking care to show us nothing that we had ever seen before.'[4]

The Republic of Venice lasted for eleven hundred years from 697, when the first Doge was elected, until 1797 when Napoleon's armies seized control. The Doge abdicated and Napoleon, already stretched, handed control to his Austrian allies. Venice and the Veneto became part of the Hapsburg Empire and were ruled from Vienna. The bureaucratic and occasionally authoritarian rule now imposed on the city fed the *Risorgimento*, the movement towards the unification of Italy. Though probably not as harsh as once thought – arguably, Venice suffered less under Hapsburg rule than it would have done under French – its Austrian occupiers did use police and censorship to reinforce their rule and much time was spent banning subversive literature. Police spies lurked in Venetian cafés and opened correspondence, giving an impression of permanent surveillance, and the image persists, fostered by legends of Italian patriotism, of the Austrians as brutal aggressors.

William Bankes could remain aloof from Italian politics but would soon learn which of the two cafés in St Mark's Square he wished to patronise: Florian's, the older of the two, was the Italian favourite, Quadri's the Austrian, where the Austrian military band tried to soften the opposition by playing Italian operatic music. There were a number of irksome regulations for foreigners, in addition to the secret police in cafés. Foreign newspapers were restricted – although French journals could usually be read at Florian's and English ones at the reading room of the Procuratie Vecchie just off St Mark's Square – and moving freely around the rest of Italy was difficult. That the middle-aged Bankes managed to do so indicates either that he cultivated important friends or was not considered a risk.

Bankes's direct knowledge of Venice derived from at least one earlier stay (at the Palazzo Mocenigo) as well as an understanding of art history that led him to base his image of Venice on its Renaissance heyday. Bankes would suffer crises of identity prompted by loneliness and painful isolation during his exile. Yet ultimately his displacement also fuelled his creative spirit, sometimes to the point of obsession, with the desire to perfect and add permanency to his ancestral home. This, I believe, is the incentive which gave him a robustness enabling him to endure his fifteen years away from Kingston Lacy.

Venice in the 1840s offered a safe haven to an eccentric circle of expatriates. More a port of call for those en route to India than a place of retirement, it did however attract from many nations 'the world of privilege and power on vacation or in exile',[5] which lent the city its unique quality of secrecy and curious social texture. Among the exiles were deposed royalty, political outcasts and social misfits. Perhaps the grandest of Venice's ex-Royalists was the Comte de Chambord, grandson of Charles X, who laid claim to be Henri V of France. His widowed mother, the Duchesse de Berry, remarried to an impoverished Italian count, bought the Palazzo Vendramini Calergi in 1844 and lived there until her death in 1870. The Comte de Montmoulin, pretender to the Spanish throne, lived in similarly opulent style in the Palazzo Loredan at San Vio. These fallen princes would bow courteously to those who recognised them in the squares or streets. German was the most commonly spoken language and William, by his looks, was occasionally taken to be German. Sir George Hayter's portrait of *c.* 1833* shows a fair-skinned man with blue eyes whose once golden locks are now greying and thinning around the temples.

Only a handful of other Englishmen, the most notable of whom was Rawdon Brown, lived there. Rawdon Lubbock Brown, part art collector and dealer, was a scholar who originally set out to scour the Venetian archives for the origins of the Venetian allusions in Shakespeare's plays. Subsequently his search broadened into a study of the letters of Venetian diplomats abroad and he edited the despatches of Sebastian Giustinian during his period as Venetian Ambassador to the court of Henry VIII from 1515 to 1519. In the event he stayed for fifty years and nurtured vain hopes that he might be made Consul in Venice, partly to supplement his meagre income. But his picture-dealing activities brought in some money and he negotiated the purchase of a codex of drawings by Jacopo Bellini on behalf of the British Museum. He was eventually given a government commission in 1862 to study and index the Venetian State papers which might have a bearing on English affairs. Unlike most visitors, he did not seek to escape Venice's cold winters or hot summers. He was helpful to other scholars visiting Venice and was

---

* An individual oil sketch was used as a study for the massive group portrait of 375 members of the first Reformed House of Commons completed in 1843. The studies, mostly done between 1833 and 1835, were offered to the sitters for 10 guineas each.

renowned for his introductions of people and places. When the 6th Duke of Devonshire, a few years older than Bankes and similarly smitten with his magnificent family home, Chatsworth, went to Venice in 1838, he met Brown and they discussed painting and sculpture in Italy.

In such a small city Brown, who arrived in 1833 aged twenty-seven, would almost certainly have known Bankes, particularly since John Murray was an old school friend from Charterhouse with whom Brown kept in touch. Murray effected the introduction between Brown and John and Effie Ruskin in 1849. Other factors, too, tended to force the company of one Englishman upon another. Venetian nobility was notoriously impenetrable to all foreigners, as Fanny Trollope commented. Even Byron, with all his fame and glamour, 'never was admitted to that small select knot of Venetian aristocracy which holds itself precious, apart and unapproachable'.[6] Italian dealers, too, knowing when important collections were to be broken up, would often offer Italian masterpieces only to Italian collectors to ensure they remained in the country. English collectors were offered more modest works by provincial masters. Although Bankes appears to have done his own scouting and avoided agents, the likelihood that disadvantaged foreigners interested in art and treasures would meet by chance or by choice was high. But Brown left strict instructions that his personal papers were to be destroyed after his death in 1883 – only his public papers survive, in the Public Record Office at Kew – and there is no record of Bankes and Brown ever having met.

When Effie Ruskin met Brown in Venice she described him as 'a most agreeable, clever, literary person and yet not at all grave. He knows and has seen everybody worth seeing of English and has lived in a beautiful Palace [Businello] on the Grand Canal for the last fifteen years. . . . He has much influence here.'[7] Effie maintained in her letters home between 1849 and 1852 that there were only two resident Englishmen in Venice at this time: Brown and Colonel Edward Cheney. The latter was one of three brothers, none of whom married and whose other home was Badger Hall in Shropshire. In

Venice, Cheney lived in the Palazzo Soranzo-Piovene on the Grand Canal, a magnificent residence which he visited once a year. The rest of the time it was empty bar servants. Effie was wrong, of course, about there being only two English inhabitants: in addition to William Bankes, there were a few English businessmen. Edward Leeves, an even more shadowy figure than Brown, was a wealthy bachelor 'formerly of Tortington in the county of Sussex' (according to his will) about whom history would probably be ignorant had he not bequeathed a small diary to a friend. The diary, discovered relatively recently, covers a short period from 6 April 1849 until 31 July 1850, when Leeves was mostly in Venice, at the end, pining for a love lost in England. He was probably a little younger than Bankes, of ample means and refined taste, homosexual and well connected both in England and Italy. He maintained a comfortable establishment at Palazzo Molin in Venice, where he was looked after by a manservant and cook and led a busy social life.

Leeves and Bankes must have been, at the very least, acquaintances with friends in common. Leeves names the executors of his will as 'his valued friends' the English brothers, John S. and Alexander Malcolm. The latter, a noted banker and businessman, who owned the Palazzo Benzon and a timber business at Longarone, was honorary Vice-Consul in Venice from 1852 to 1855, based at the Fondo Barberigo near St Mark's Square. It was Malcolm who was to sort out Bankes's affairs after his death and to whom Leeves left his gold repeating watch and chain.

The role of British Consul had developed haphazardly from the idea that merchants overseas should band together and appoint a spokesman to conduct affairs of common interest. But although the role gave them both status and opportunity – Messrs Malcolm Bros of Venice are frequently mentioned in Foreign Office memoranda as winning contracts to supply this or that commodity – they were not assigned any rank by the Foreign Office in London, which exploited their usefulness while trying not to pay them. Bankes had first-hand experience of this through Consuls Barker and Salt in Alexandria, and knew how most had to live off private means.

Alexander Malcolm was no exception. Privately, he traded in antiquities. Publicly, Her Majesty's Vice Consul for the Austrian Territories on the Adriatic Sea was required to transmit returns of Births and Marriages of British Subjects within the district of the British Consulate, and was empowered to grant passports to British individuals claiming British protection. It seems inconceivable that he and Bankes did not come to a quiet private arrangement which left William free to travel when he wanted.

Expatriates such as Rawdon Brown and Edward Leeves may have been comfortable with their own kind. But William John was not one who flourished in a group. His disinclination to create links among the tiny and gossipy expatriate community was probably deliberate. Instead, his passion to embellish Kingston Lacy became his *raison d'être*. He would seek out the very best raw materials as well as the most talented local Italian craftsmen, experts in marble and stone cutting, gilding, woodcarving and other crafts, not just in Venice but further afield in Ferrara, Padua, Verona, Lucca, Perugia or Siena. Artisan crafts of all sorts flourished in Venice and William Bankes developed close links with this community, particularly marble carvers and gilders – the use of gold had always been lavish in Venetian decoration. He made it his daily task to observe, draw, paint, sketch and finally commission, usually copies. It took several years before he was ready to ship anything home.

During his early years in the city Bankes was absorbing, sketching, discovering, observing. With time and Murray's *Handbook for Northern Italy* in his grasp, he would have had little difficulty finding a stonemason's yard. A good restaurant was harder. 'There are none good at Venice,' the *Handbook* stated baldly. 'The best, in the Campo Gallo, a small piazza close behind the Procuratie Vecchie, is both bad and dirty.' The cafés were frankly better. It also listed apothecaries, physicians, shops for English goods and much other useful advice. The first edition of Murray's *Handbook*, mostly written by Sir Francis Palgrave, appeared in 1842 and preceded Baedeker by a year. Bankes would probably have purchased his at the bookshop of Herman Munster – 'a very obliging man who speaks English and is well supplied with maps, handbooks, guide-books etc.'[8] It was full of crucial information such as hotel prices and times of trains. The railway bridge into Venice, inaugurated in January 1846, would have made a huge difference to anyone wishing to travel in and out of Venice, as William did regularly. By 1847 three trains left Venice daily for Padua, Vicenza, Verona and Brescia as well as daily diligences to Milan and Trieste.

Bankes moved constantly, from one month to the next. This nomadic existence, picking up his mail from the Poste Restante, not only suited him, it was what he craved. Occasionally he lived in expensive hotels for an extended period – the Due Torre, a converted palace in the Piazza S. Anastasia once home to the Scaligeri family, seems to have been a fairly regular stop in Verona. In Paris, the Hotel Choiseul, and in Venice, the Europa – not the Danieli where the Ruskins stayed – were his hotels of choice. The Europa, housed in the late fifteenth century Palazzo Giustinian Morosini, stood at the mouth of the Grand Canal; Turner had also lived there, making many drawings and paintings of the views from his bedroom window. Occasionally Bankes's receipts for rents on apartments and bills for servants (Bernardo) and household expenses indicate a different way of life. Living on the Grand Canal, the most sought after location, was no longer as cheap as it had been* but Bankes could easily have found other reasonably priced lodgings. Mary Shelley, in 1842, commented that it was almost impossible to spend much money in Venice as even an apartment filled with antique furniture could be had for a modest cost.

In high season William escaped Venice. He told his sister in September 1847 that he had taken refuge briefly in Padua

> from the great crowd and bustle which the meeting of the learned
> from all parts and quarters of Italy has brought upon Venice. Their

---

* According to an anonymous article in the *Quarterly Review* (1850) The Grassi Palace on the Grand Canal was sold for 70,000 livres (£2,300) ten years previously but had changed hands several times since then each time at greatly increased prices until the sum of 400,000 livres (£13,500) was unhesitatingly rejected.

coming, however, into these parts is the occasion of two spectacles at which I gladly put myself out of the way to be present avoiding all the rest. One of these took place last night in Vicenza (a distance of only one hour from hence by railroad). It was the representation of the tragedy of King Oedipus translated into Italian from the Greek of Sophocles . . . and set to music by Pacini, who was present himself to direct the Orchestra. What added beyond measure to the interest of the representation (and what no other city in the world could have supplied) this antique play was performed in the theatre built by Palladio, two centuries and a half ago, in the exact imitation of those of the ancients.

It was a buoyantly happy letter. 'I am delighted to have had the opportunity of being present at so singular an exhibition,' he wrote, before telling Anne that he was shortly returning to Venice to attend the regatta 'which in that floating city must be a most beautiful as well as most appropriate show'.[9]

William's fifteen years in and around Venice coincided with a period of enormous change. In 1849 after the Siege, roughly seven years after his arrival, the city took on aspects of a military garrison with some palazzi requisitioned as barracks; the city and its people suffered terrible privations. William's final half-dozen years in the city were more sombre; even at its best Venice was often cold, damp and smelly. By his death in mid-century the Byronic ideal of Venice was, as Ruskin observed, '. . . a thing of yesterday, a mere efflorescence of decay, a stage-dream which the first ray of daylight must dissipate into dust'.[10]

10

Family

~

'For the sake of those that come after me'
William Bankes to George Bankes

UNCERTAINTY ABOUT WILLIAM'S future persisted for months after he left England. Blackmail was a common threat and surviving correspondence includes several attempts at intimidation. One stranger wrote 'offering my services', another suggested he 'could assist in the late unpleasant affair' if allowed to meet William, and several were delivered from a 'persevering foreigner' whom Falmouth tried to deflect. William's determination never to give his address was sensible. There are no surviving letters from erstwhile friends offering him comfort or support or suggesting that he was being harshly targeted.

The family may have wished that if William lay low for a while, he might eventually be able to return home. Gregory wrote to his client two months after his flight that he rather hoped by not drawing attention again to the case, 'that it may escape further notice and be suffered to fall down in the stream of time . . . the more especially because the officer whose acrimony we had most reason to fear has retired and it is not very probable that the Solicitor to the Treasury will take up the business.'[1]

He also suggested that his client might plead without making a personal appearance, 'a procedure which is by no means impossible'.[2] But the family suffered a devastating blow in the final days of 1841. William's brother-in-law, friend and adviser, Edward Falmouth, died suddenly, aged fifty-four, on 29 December. The Falmouths had just one surviving child, George Henry Boscawen, who now, aged thirty, became fifth Viscount and second Earl of Falmouth and, as soon as could be arranged, third 'trustee', or more precisely beneficial owner, of William's former possessions. William, who had few close friends, was profoundly shocked by the premature death of his closest, to whom he owed 'eternal obligations' and was deeply grateful 'for the kind part he took and good advice he gave me at a moment when I was incapable of making sensible decisions about the disposal of my property'.[3] Falmouth, who had greatly admired what had been done at Kingston Lacy, had helped him to protect his own rights in two ways:

> I should not place myself or my concerns too exclusively in the hands of any one person, secondly that I shouldn't give any pledge or promise myself that I would <u>not</u> return to England or that I would <u>Not</u> marry should such be my pleasure. Though no such promise on my part ever would or will be given still, if the treatment which I received were satisfactory, a return to England is just the last thing that I should ever have dreamed of.[4]

Falmouth's death threw him more than ever upon the good-will of his brother George, with whom relations had not always been easy. Although he fully accepted that George and his descendants would be the ultimate beneficiaries of his estates, he nonetheless encountered both aesthetic and financial difficulties in dealing with his brother. Matters apparently progressed without major incident until the final illness and death of the resident steward, Thomas Robson. Until 1843 William corresponded weekly with Robson

> and had the satisfaction of punctual assurances that my instructions were understood and attended to. His sudden incapacity was a heavy blow and communications on such subjects were made more difficult by my brother being utterly incapable as not so much as understanding the terms which it is necessary to employ ... when you contemplate his masterpieces at Studland and East Sheen you may

easily conceive also what I <u>must</u> think of his taste and judgment in such matters.[5]

William's accusations may be a little harsh. For George, his younger brother by less than two years, lacked neither family sentiment nor intellect. He had obligingly stepped in to become MP for Corfe Castle in 1815 when William declined to return home from his travels. At the time, George was a recently qualified barrister practising on the Western Circuit. He unexpectedly joined his father in representing the ancient family seat when John Bond, co-patron of the Borough, offered it gratuitously in the recess of 1815 to Henry for either of his sons. Almost as soon as he was elected he obtained leave of absence to go to the Circuit. His father had already procured for him the 'sinecure place' of Commissioner of Appeals. On resuming his seat he made a habit of voting with ministers and was as reactionary in his views as he was long-winded in his speeches. He feared change and his parliamentary record indicates scant sympathy for those less fortunate than himself. He supported a bill amending the Game Laws which made poaching a felony, punishable by transportation for seven years, voted against Catholic relief and against Brougham's motion for an inquiry into the education of the poor in 1818. George Bankes represented Corfe until just before the Great Reform Act, which he opposed, and was then Member for Dorset from 1841 until 1845 as well as three times Mayor of Corfe Castle and Recorder at Weymouth from 1823 until his death. He held other minor government positions, including an appointment as Cursitor Baron of the Exchequer from 1824 until his death, when the post was abolished. He was appointed a Treasury Lord from April to November 1830, Privy Councillor in February 1852 and Judge Advocate-General from February–December 1852.

The holder of such importantly insignificant positions is easy prey to caricature. George, the uxurious patriarch and typical Tory county squire who found contentment and satisfaction through his wife and eleven surviving children, or else by dining at the Athenaeum, easily fits our notion of the self-satisfied Victorian. William and George differed widely in temperament and artistic sensibilities. Yet William, the aesthete, was no liberal in parliamentary affairs and George was an honourable man who loyally fulfilled the difficult task of managing his brother's estates for fourteen years. He simply lacked imagination.

Nowhere was this more clearly demonstrated than by his decision to remove his second son, Henry Hyde Nugent, from Eton after three years, 'finding it expedient to limit the cost of his further education in some degree'. As he explained to William in a letter thanking him 'for his kind recollections of expenses in respect of my children, which has come at a time that is particularly opportune . . . he has now got the manner of an Etonian.' This, George considered at a time when there was no other school of equivalent reputation, was all that counted.[6]

George had married the tall and beautiful Georgina Charlotte Nugent in 1822, when he was thirty-five. Officially the daughter and heiress of Admiral Sir Charles Edmund Nugent, Georgina was believed to be the illegitimate offspring of Ernest Augustus, Duke of Cumberland and brother to George IV. At first George and his rapidly growing family lived mainly at East Sheen, on the edge of Richmond Park outside London. They apparently stopped living there in the watershed year of 1844 and rented it out, increasingly using the Bankes home at 5 Old Palace Yard as their London residence.* But from about 1825, holidays were spent on the Isle of Purbeck where George built the Manor House at Studland Bay. Today a hotel with the same splendid clifftop view over the bay that George and his family adored, the Manor House was a seaside residence; continually enlarged until George's death in 1856, it has a rambling, asymmetrical look. The house is thought to have incorporated parts of an earlier medieval building but some of the carvings, dated 1636, probably came from the Old Palace of Westminster and may have been acquired for George through Charles Barry

---

* In George's will, Old Palace Yard was passed to Georgina who lived there after her second marriage as Mrs Manningham Buller. The house was demolished in 1937 to clear a space for the King George Memorial.

when he was working at Kingston Lacy. Barry may even have had a hand in small aspects of the Manor House, such as the Gothic shafts on the first floor landing which support plaster ceiling vaults. Built into the cliff immediately below the house was a boathouse, which probably sheltered the boat used by William when he made his brief return from exile. When George, Georgina and their children were not in residence at Old Palace Yard, they preferred to live at Studland, using Kingston Lacy only for short holidays and occasional visits. Given the continuous alterations throughout William's exile, the more palatial house can hardly have been comfortable or cosy. Visiting the ancestral home was a chore for George, who also had his house at Sheen, now rented, to administer.

Robson's death brought matters to a head. Until then, William believed he had spared George all the trouble of correspondence about house decoration by transmitting written instructions addressed to his Clerk of Works, as he still perceived the position. 'I little did expect that [George] could have taken it upon himself to obstruct . . . I am not a man of complaints and you have therefore never heard of this before. But your mother, my dear, dear sister knows about the frustration,' William protested to his young nephew. 'There are limits to endurance. It is now a matter of extreme urgency. Capricious behaviour cannot be tolerated.'

William does not specify in the surviving letter what George has done to incur his wrath. But his brother's attitude to the treasures he was starting to send home had clearly angered him. George, whose artistic tastes were always at variance with William's, regarded them as an extravagance. To William they were his life's work, 'not as mere accessories or afterthought ornaments, but as integral parts or essential members of a fine work undertaken and left incomplete'.[7] Living in exile in Italy, William believed he could have remained contented and, 'with a naturally cheerful disposition, almost happy'. But matters were more complicated, and seem to have hinged upon whether or not money accumulated in rents was being spent on the Kingston Lacy Estate in the way he had instructed, or sent out to William. William explained that he was now approaching his nephew Henry reluctantly on a matter of such importance that George should be shown this letter and made to shoulder 'the blame for the crisis which he had knowingly produced . . . my spirit has been too much broken for me to cherish resentments though not enough for me to endure to be trampled upon. Should therefore a satisfactory paper be sent I can not only pardon but I can endeavour to forget the past.'[8]

To his lawyer, William was more specific and entered into a discussion about wills. It is easy to recognise how after three years abroad an exile might feel excluded, inflate petty grievances and worry that his life's work was being thrown away by others who stood to gain from his suffering. More émigré than refugee, dispossessed and occasionally homesick, he was an outsider gazing inwards, with neither bitterness nor guilt. Yet his ability to admire and absorb the new culture without losing hold of his own cultural identity is evidence of a certain vigour and adaptability. If he lamented his destiny he did so for the most part privately. But even if he was not in conflict with himself, the fate of so many exiles through the ages, he could still suffer and brood.

From Rome William wrote to Gregory that he felt 'the whole course of his life' now depended on the answer he could give him. 'I shall be grieved indeed if I shall have wronged (in thought only) a brother to whom I was always affectionately attached by even a shadow of suspicion.' George's strangely systematic reserve unnerved William and made him suspicious that something had been done 'which it was wished to keep from my knowledge'.[9] So disturbed was William by unjust acts he could only guess at that he even offered to write to the Secretary of State that

> sufficient period having now elapsed for the subsiding of prejudice I am ready to surrender and to take my trial. I am quite aware that this course will not restore me to my property but it will at least do away at once with the outlawry and I shall be competent if I so please to contract a lawful marriage in England or elsewhere and then would be seen the gross injustice . . .

> It has not escaped me, that upon my surrendering I shall have to

live in prison like the time of trial, not being able to produce bail in my own person to the amount required, but no consideration whatever will weigh with me against the fixed determination which I have taken should my fears be realised.

In fact I had rather lie in prison for life than submit to be trampled upon and by those whom I have constantly benefited.

If on the other hand (which God in His mercy grant) I have taken alarm without reason and all is only done according to my instructions, great will be my joy at learning it and I hope you will not lose a post in quieting my apprehensions.[10]

This Gregory tried to do. But even if he sent his reply by the next post, William would have remained in unresolved anguish for at least a week. By early October, William was able to write that his mind was at rest. His desperation and sense of isolation are understandable.

You lawyers do not easily conceive how completely ignorant we laymen are upon many such points. When I urged cross wills [between William, George and the other two joint tenants] I had no idea at all but that in the case of any one of the three dying intestate his next heir would have been entitled to that share. But from the moment I became better informed I came round to the opinion, which I gather to be yours and my brother's, that it was unnecessary and better left to the law without any testamentary disposition at all.

The 1844 exchange of letters seems to have cleared the air sufficiently to set the tone for William's remaining eleven years. In the rush to convey the estates, Falmouth had advised 'that I should so order matters that there should be NO accumulation whatsoever but that all the income should be annually spent on the spot where the bulk of it is derived ... and that I should keep up a large establishment abroad.' William felt from the start this was going beyond his views or intentions; there is every indication that he lived very simply, even frugally. He wrote to George later that year thanking him for a letter 'so kind and affectionate in its tone and purport that it does my very heart good to read and acknowledge it; the natural effect of reverse of fortune and of living habitually so entirely alone, is to make the spirit rather more irritable and susceptible and any impression, however lightly taken, gets the more quickly hold and is the more apt to dwell and predominate.'[11]

But in return William, deprived of his inheritance, expected George to recognise his sacrifices, especially in favouring George's family over their next brother, Edward; the very least George could do was to implement William's instructions for finishing the house. In another undated memorandum to George from around this time William set out from memory the value of the various properties and an inventory of possessions once owned by him amounting to a total value of at least £347,000 (approximately £15 million today).

> You will observe that the amount contingently destined for you and yours is larger than that destined for Edward and his and it was my intention that it should be so. The confidence that I have shown and felt is unbounded for during three weeks I could, if I had wished it, have conveyed abroad all that was most precious in the moveables, and, by a mere stroke of the pen, have converted the stock into foreign funds where naturalisation (which is very easy) would have placed it under my immediate control in spite of all the outlawries in the world.[12]

William did not do so largely for fear that he might not be able to make it pass by will afterwards in England. He was to die intestate and denied himself the cushion of extra income during his lifetime, leaving it as part of the Estate for the benefit of his heirs. But he wished his family to know that in doing so he was 'quite aware that if I should legally have any provision to make for a wife it can only be from the proceeds or principle of that money.'

William goes on to advise George as to the recompense he should take for administering the estates since, he insists, it is far from his intention that George should be out of pocket. William's intention – 'had poor Mr Robson remained efficient' – had been to treat the estates exactly as during a well conducted and affluent minority, by improving and maintaining roads, draining and planting lands and above all repairing and improving farm buildings, which were in poor condition both in Dorset and in Wales. This would have benefited the local labourers as well as increasing the value of the property 'far above any that can arise from accumulation'. But William recognised that such work could only have been done by a resident steward who understood and cared about the Estate.

> I had contemplated also carrying out gradually with his superinten-
> dence all the plans for the house and appendages indoors and out
> so that little or nothing of the income would then have been laid
> by for many years. The late Lord Falmouth had recommended this
> and I think it was excellent advice.
>
> As it is, I can only fiddle with little details about the body of the
> house which however as far as it goes still furnishes a resonance to
> me and which I am as well able to direct from a great distance as I
> before was used to do from London since in point of fact I was but
> very seldom on the spot when the works were actually going on.[13]

This poignant letter laid out the ground rules for George. A careful, measured sort of man, George was a lawyer and bankruptcy commissioner more in his father's mould than William. He cared about the family inheritance sufficiently to write his book about the history of Corfe Castle (1853). But he minded, too, about money going out of the estate that could have been spent on general upkeep; his brother's extravagance might even have jeopardised Kingston Lacy. Yet in general George, like the rest of the family, colluded with his absent brother. He even tolerated being accused of blunders in artistic matters by William and was prepared to discuss matters of flooring and ceiling with his new steward, Peter Osborne. His fulfilment in life came not from the house which he stood to inherit, but from his family based at Studland or his parliamentary work in London.

None of the three remaining siblings actually chose to live at unfinished Kingston Lacy, where only two bedrooms were habitable at the time of William's flight – according to an 1841 inventory these were the south bedroom and Mr Bankes's bedroom, the south east suite. The state rooms were stripped bare and the remaining bedrooms used as storage areas. The two census returns for 1841 and 1851 show only staff living in the house on the two nights in question: in 1841, John Lovelace, gamekeeper, and his family; by 1851, Peter Osborne, carpenter, and his family. George came regularly for short inspection visits, sometimes accompanied by his son-in-law John Floyer, a Dorset MP. The widowed Anne Falmouth may have been encouraged to spend time at Kingston Lacy and, according to the diaries of George's daughter Octavia, seems to have come for a few days at a time with her dog Muff, when the other families were staying there or at Studland, and thoroughly spoiled her nieces. But she too preferred her London residence at 10 New Street, Spring Gardens, where she was not subjected to constant building works, and the Bankes girls liked to visit her there.

Edward and his family also stayed at Kingston Lacy occasionally but from then on his branch of the family weakened its links with the Dorset Bankes and on William's death in 1855 became the Welsh, or Soughton Bankes. Edward, Henry and Frances's fourth son, had been educated like his brothers at Westminster and Cambridge (Trinity Hall) where he gained a Bachelor of Law degree, but otherwise seems as unlike William as he could be. He pursued a career in the Church and numbered among his appointments Rector of Corfe Castle from 1818 (the year he was ordained) until 1854, rising to Canon of Bristol Cathedral from 1832 to 1867, which brought him £800 a year (approximately £34,000 today) and a residence, and finally Chaplain-in-Ordinary to King William IV and Queen Victoria. Within a year of his first wife, Lord Eldon's daughter, dying in 1838 after bearing him four children, he married Maria, daughter of the Hon. and Very Rev. Edward Rice, Dean of Gloucester, brother of Lord Dynevor. They had a further four children. According to a granddaughter descended from this second family, Edward's first wife was 'a very undesirable spouse except in pocket; when she died he married to please himself.'[14] Even the staid Annals of Bristol[15] saw fit to record that

> The Rev Edward Bankes . . . having married a daughter of the Lord Chancellor had more than the usual share of favours extended to the Great Lawyer's connections . . . Although he became enormously rich on the death of his father-in-law (Lord Eldon 1838) Mr Bankes

continued to hold his preferments for some years after he was incapable of performing the duties attached to them. This was, however, natural enough, seeing that he had rendered very perfunctory service when in his vigour.

Both William's brothers had made excellent marriages, according to their mother's lights. Neither lacked for any of life's luxuries. Had William been of a jealous nature his occasional wistful references to marriage when he was approaching his sixties might be seen as bitter reflections of comforts denied him, which they both enjoyed. More likely, making provision for a wife was something William considered in the context simply of defining his rights to his brothers at a time when, in reality, he had none.

Having made his point, that he might have taken more money abroad had he chosen to do so, William tried to adopt a less hectoring, more cajoling tone in letters home. But his fussy taste and demanding personality were two aspects of the same personality. 'I am grieved to be obliged to give you trouble, but having lost poor Mr Robson what can I do?' he asks George. 'If the shallow bookcases made by my father for the Saloon will be of any use in your new room at Studland . . . pray let them be taken if they cannot accord in character with anything at Kingston Lacy.'

Osborne, 'an intelligent and sensible workman but a <u>Very Poor</u> draughtsman', according to William, was the new man on whom he depended to carry out his instructions and measurements so that he could send over fixtures and fittings from Italy. 'I do what I can to assist him in what I want by sending a paper enclosed where there will be nothing to do but to put the figures,'[16] he told George, and then asked him to give further commissions to two of the London staff, Cooper and Lipscombe. The latter, however, died in 1844.

Now that poor Lipscomb's annuity is at an end, I would fain do something to help my poor old servant George Read if he is still out of place and not in a way of gaining a livelihood for himself and helping his family. £100 would probably enable him to set up in some business and, if given now, would be much more likely to be of real use than later in life. If you see, therefore, no objection pray let him have it, without withdrawing for the present (till he may seem able to shift for himself) any weekly or monthly allowance that he may have had, if such has been extended to him till now. If I cannot be happy myself I would fain at least make those so who have been dependent upon me.[17]

Forced to rely on George, he occasionally came dangerously close to treating his younger brother as staff. Had Knott of Wimborne ever completed the sawing of the oriental red granite into slab? he enquired.

If so, at some time, a pair of them should be sent up to London to be polished at the steam marble works in Holywell Street, Westminster. They are very fine and are intended to stand to the centre of the East and West wall of the entrance Hall. They should be set one inch lower than the usual height of pier tables to increase the apparent height of the hall. They are intended to be supported on griffons or other animals of stone or marble but perhaps the great gilt eagles might be temporarily so applied and, if the effect be not amiss, a wash of stone colour with water so it might be got off afterwards might be painted over them. But this of course when you and Edward are on the spot and have nothing better to do. I only mention things as they chance to occur to me . . .[18]

It was typical of the stream of requests George faced over fourteen years besides ensuring that his brother did not run short of funds.

'I still have a good deal of money left,' William wrote from Perugia in 1845, 'but, never liking to run matters too close by too much dependence upon the post office, therefore send £300 in circular notes,'* he instructed.[19]

A conciliatory tone was often too much for William, who was back to his usual exigencies by May 1844. In a letter from Lucca in high summer with 'the night air quite alive with fireflies', he berated his brother when something went wrong 'which an adherence to the plans or a simple reference to me would have saved. Is

---

* A letter of credit addressed by a banker to several other bankers in favour of a person named therein.

it conceivable that anybody <u>could</u> have supposed that the main door-ways of entrance could be intended to be four inches narrower and two inches lower than all the others that is to say that those which go only from room to room. Such a blunder would be enough to disgrace any architect or any building.' To William's deep chagrin, there was no architect in charge any longer.

For all his concern to help his family avoid the shame of associ-ation Bankes was, it seems, insensitive to potential problems Barry might experience in associating with an outlawed homosexual. He wrote to Osborne:

> Next time you hear of Mr Barry at Canford, go over and inquire of him whether he still has the semi-good opinion which he had of the galvanic process for gilding and whether it comes pretty reasonable? Whether he would in short recommend it for the great dining room ceiling whenever the gilding of that is to be proceeded with.[20]

Wistfully, William suggested:

> Should he happen to call again at Kingston Lacy show him the four bronze figures . . . which are to lie on the marble pedestals in the drawing room and get him to place them in the proper position on the blocks . . . and show them to Mr Barry that he may instruct you if they want any change, for it is rather a nice job [a favourite William coaxing mechanism]. Ultimately those pattern blocks will either be sent out to me or I shall give you instructions to be worked on at home, the two male figures should have a metal leafing provided to fit about the loins with, of course, no other fastening than the binding round.[21]

There are other such notes. 'Should Mr Barry come over let him see the model up and take his opinion and advice.'[22] But Mr Barry never did call. In the biography which appeared in 1867, written by his son, the Rev. Alfred Barry and published by John Murray, his collaboration with William Bankes at Kingston Lacy has all but vanished.

To George he ranted, 'It is cruel, too, to have spoiled that glorious pair of doors between the two great rooms by putting the handles in the wrong place and where no handles ever are in Italian doors and of all things in the world, oak knobs in a room where there is gilding!!'[23] He then issued a list of further commissions for his brother. William's main concern was that all the precious items from Old Palace Yard should be sent down to Kingston Lacy, the most precious of these being several miniatures by Henry Bone, the most valuable of which he believed was one of Lord Byron. He was worried, too, about the whereabouts of the Duke of Wellington's watch, a present to him for his manliness responding to robbers, and reminded George of the two Caraccis from the Cambiaro Palace at Genoa, which he considered the finest things in his possession (excepting the Raphael, the Bercham and the Titian). He suggested sending these to Kingston Lacy where they would be safer and away from dirt. But he allowed George to decide whether they and the Gobelins tapestries should be ultimately transferred to Soughton, where the room was built for them. The walls of the Saloon, although prepared for them, were now filled with oil paintings.

William rarely lost an opportunity to criticise his father for diminishing the value of various prints 'by cutting the margin and pasting . . . There were also in the garret at Kingston Lacy Sadeler's prints of the Emperor and Empress. My mother cut these separate and I inquired of them of my father but never could find them and am half afraid that in the last years, when he did so much mischief, he may have destroyed them. If found I had half intended to have intrusted the cleaning of them to Colnaghi.[24] Simultaneously, he tries to encourage George to try out the effect of various works of art in different positions. After all, he reminds his brother with a flourish: 'Whoever could say of the arts with more truth than I can "Res secundas ornant in adversis solatium et per fugum praebent,"* a beautiful passage which I remember, I think, in Cicero's letters.'[25]

---

* Art is the ornament of good times and consolation in bad times; slightly misquoted from Cicero pro Archia 7:16.

While constantly chivvying George about the treasures of Kingston Lacy, William was also apprehensive about the future of Old Palace Yard, where many items had been sent during the renovations. An urgent tone enters his letters as he tries to recall where everything was stored before he fled and where it should be placed for posterity. His deep attachment to family history demanded that objects be traced: papers respecting Hampden's trial, letters from the great Lord Strafford and parliamentary speeches by Sir Peter Wentworth, for example. His belief in the continuity of the Bankes family gave William his sense of purpose during his fifteen-year exile. But he recognised he could achieve nothing without George's cooperation. In 1844 he was also motivated by a real fear that, under the terms of the outlawry, his London house was at risk of seizure. 'Mr Barry told me that ultimately the government must have my house, he and they believing the freehold in me, and of course I did not undeceive him,'[26] he warned his brother, showing he had communicated with Barry since September '41.

A few months later, this time from Rome, William had to ask his brother again to try the effect while he and Edward and their families were at Kingston Lacy, 'of placing the two Italian wooden pedestals (with fauns and bacchantes carved upon them) upon the marble landing half way to the bedroom storey'. William suggested 'one facing exactly to the saloon door, and the other to the centre of the top flight, one of the oval bronze vases with the small handles to be placed on each of them; between them, corresponding to the little narrow sunk panel, one of the white wooden pedestals which were always in the house, the vases to stand each with a different face towards you. Should the effect be successful, Osborne can find a carver to repair the husks on the pedestals in soft wood, they should be continued white.'[27]

This relatively straightforward request – others were not – encapsulates the relationship between the exiled William and the landed George. Apparently George did not carry out his brother's suggestion.* There was a more complicated proposal for George in the event of wet weather: 'here is another experiment which I had been on the point of trying myself.' One can imagine the horrified reaction of George or Georgina to the following:

> In that fatal pasteboard box to fit which my father cut the margins of all the finest prints that he possessed, you will find near the top the print, (in two sheets), from that noble great Rubens which I purchased (The Triumph of Charity). With the print are two cut papers which, laid over it, leave nothing visible but the great oval of angels now that is precisely the part of the picture which I intended for the centre of the dining room ceiling. The nature of this ceiling will not admit of the vast picture being raised against it, but I had intended to have lifted it 20ft 4 inches (which is the true height) from the floor in the Saloon, blanking temporarily the upper windows – and there to cover with the thinnest India paper or linen (exactly according to the cut pattern on the print) such parts as are not intended for the ceiling and thus to judge at once whether the scale and effect would be good and well proportioned to the space and height, it is a nice and difficult job, but Osborne's forte is a certain ingenuity and great care and precaution in experiments of this nature and if it is well explained to him what is wanted, I feel quite satisfied that he can do it; a few strings across the picture at that great height would not much infuse its effect but should thin paper be

* In an intriguing aside, Daphne Bankes, unmarried elder sister of Viola and the last owner, Ralph, who rummaged through the family papers in 1932 re-typing some letters, removing others and arranging a selection of what she considered the most interesting (but least revelatory) in approximately chronological order, commented about this: 'Strange to say it was my mother, Henrietta Jane Bankes, who in 1905 placed these pedestals on the staircase where they now stand, quite oblivious of the fact that William John Bankes wrote all this (for she had never seen these letters of his until I found them nearly thirty years later). The two pedestals were separated and in different places but with her unerring instinct and artistic sense my Mother placed them together here in just the exact positions William John had originally intended for them.' (p. 75 of her notes) Daphne was writing at a time when the Bankes Art Collection was considered a wonderful but secret treasure trove that only a select few were able to view personally. Both she and Viola inherited William's desire to show their family collection as of the highest quality.

employed for the covering the least gum in the world just upon the extremity could be softened afterward with hot water and would not hurt the picture. It is so very large that if it be too troublesome an operation while you are in the house he could be instructed to do it at another time just before yours and Edward's coming so that you could find it in place and judge of it on your arrival. I believe you never saw the picture: it is an extremely fine one but colossal . . . it occurs to me as not unlikely that a great Paul Veronese (fresco transferred to canvas) may have been rolled up with the Rubens. If so do not be uneasy at its being damaged. It was so when I bought it but is of the highest class of merit in that kind. If left in London it had better be set to rights.[28]

William's relationship with Anne was always warmer, though occasionally he seems to have assumed that she too existed in order to execute his detailed plans for Kingston Lacy. Having made a painstakingly accurate model of an ideal country house inspired by his own, nearly finished by 1845, he is now arranging to have this sent with drawings and details to England to be placed opposite the top flight of the great stairs. He entrusts it 'to dear Anne – who needs little commissions and little nothings to do for me . . . to offer momentary relief from fretting and moping even if for a single day or hour.'[29]

Four years into his exile William started to feel more at ease with the task he had set himself. Many of the sketches he sent home are on blue Bath paper, torn from a notebook made to slip into the side pocket of a loose-fitting artist's jacket, perhaps worn by William with a matching floppy hat. He would pay a visit to Antonio Sanquirico, the dealer whose emporium of fantastic treasures and curiosities filled the huge Scuole Grande di San Teodoro in Campo San Salvatore,* or stop to sketch something that caught his eye. He would not hesitate to take a tape into a church or the Accademia

* It was Sanquirico who disposed of the Grimani Marbles and of a canvas by Mantegna bought by the English collector George Vivian, now in the National Gallery.

and measure a balustrade, dado rail, plinth or sculpture in order to make a template to send home with copying instructions. In Florence he must have scrabbled on his knees in the Duomo to tell his man at home the exact size of the base of the candelabra lighting the choir. He must have stood outside doorways for hours, copying the shape of an arch or some fine carving. He excelled at observing detail, a skill honed during his Egyptian travels, and still loved to transcribe Latin inscriptions. He made hundreds of small sketches and wrote essays on architectural minutiae in every city and town he visited. He had long since abandoned ideas of publication. These essays and observations helped sharpen his memory of the one house in the world he truly loved. His drawings and diagrams show delicacy and freedom as well as precision and although he was never good at figurative drawing he could turn his hand to almost anything, from pedestal bases to the bronze studs and nail heads over the Pantheon door.

After five years, he was ready for the first cargo of finished work – there would be a dozen or so altogether – to be crated up and sent home. Exporting art treasures was a common enough activity at the time and William would have learnt from Murray's *Hand-book*, if he did not already know, that Messrs J. and R. McCracken, 'by Appointment to the Royal Academy and National Gallery', were recommended as agents for the reception and shipment of works of art, baggage etc. from and to all parts of the world. William's first shipment set sail from Venice on 5 December 1846 and contained seven crates of marble, each marked with a different letter of the alphabet and accompanied with precise instructions upon opening as to where each section should go and how they should fit together. Another four shipments in 1847 mostly took several months to arrive in the Port of London, whence they moved on to Kingston Lacy by road. These cargo ships, which often plied their way from Belfast to Liverpool and then Venice and further east before coming home more than a year later, attracted a motley crew. William was right to venture down to the port himself to see that his crates were properly nailed up before being loaded. Although the crew were required to be 'orderly, faithful, honest, careful and sober',[30] pilfering was not unknown.

Once a reliable means of sending his treasures home had been established, William's passion was limitless. He had had some marble stacked up at Verona for months while he investigated the safest method to get it back. He need delay no longer. Wherever possible he tried to deal directly with Osborne, instructing him how to draw to scale and constantly reminding him 'not to lose a single post'. Give me the dimensions of this, he suggests, or draw the other to scale. He arranges for Osborne to hire another pair of hands, Seymour, who proves reliable. Seymour had been lured away from a London employer with an offer of six months' certain work at high wages. After the trial period, Bankes told Osborne that if Seymour were to continue he must make a fresh agreement 'at a fair and full rate of wages but still not exorbitant since other sculptors can be found for what work will remain'. Luckily, Seymour stayed. But his labours at Kingston Lacy, for an employer no less exacting for being absent, gave him no opportunity for slack. Often the measurements were just out and pieces of marble or stone perhaps a quarter of an inch short. 'What an error the men in Italy has made,' was a typical refrain from poor Seymour, who was ultimately required to turn William's dreams into reality. He would then be sent to find additional matching pieces, or obtain prices for the finest Portland stone or panels of gilt or, most importantly, veneers for the Spanish Room doors. 'This rough sketch is to no scale whatever, it is for you to understand what an error the men has made in Italy in back jointing the consoles,' he wrote in frustration to William. 'Of course, the two centre consoles to each table are intended to stand central to show there are margins on red marble bases. But I am sorry to say it is not so.' On occasions like this William could do nothing: 'I must leave it to your discretion and you will make the best job of it you can . . .'

How relieved Seymour must have been when he wrote of the 'Flower de Luce' (fleur de lys): 'In my opinion they looks very well and also in the opinion of many others who've seen them.'[31]

II

Memory

~

'The Best Kind of Englishman'
Foglio di Verona

CONSIDER HOW VENICE was created from nothing out of the water, and it is hardly surprising that the craftsman's talent reached its peak there. Strict delineation between major and minor arts did not exist here and fine artists readily turned craftsmen. Jacopo Sansovino, architect extraordinary, was also a designer of stuccoes and perhaps of tapestries and fireplaces. Titian, Tintoretto and Veronese, all painters of the first rank, designed mosaics and tapestries, while the artist Giambattista Tiepolo was not averse to undertaking occasional excavation and stucco work. The furnishing of Venetian palazzi encouraged many crafts to flourish, notably using wrought-iron and marble but also glass making, ceramics, embroidery and tapestry. From eastern imports Venetians learned to work in stone, wood, iron, gold or silk. From the twelfth century the search for quality became paramount. In response to this and the need to protect the craftsmen's interests a variety of guilds flourished. Many of the magnificent halls belonging to the scuole, mostly founded in the thirteenth century, can still be seen today – evidence of the successful role of the guilds in Venetian life.

Strict rules applied to guild apprentices, and membership was a matter of great pride. Certain guilds were invited to furnish an altar or chapel, while religious or civic festivals and processions provided opportunities for the opulent display of guild banners. The

Stonemasons' Guild was the most important of all, the masons having created not only the magnificent building façades but bridges and balconies, capitals and columns and the well heads that fascinated Bankes. Inlay work was also part of this guild and magnificent effects were achieved with inlaid surfaces of rare marble and semi-precious stone, the *pietra dura* which William admired. Eventually, after nine years in Venice, he commissioned a large cabinet with beautiful *pietra dura* panels from the two Buoninsegni brothers, for his Spanish Room.

William had little interest in textiles, glass or ceramics. Although he visited the island of Murano, where the glassmakers stoked their furnaces away from the mainland because of the danger from fire to wooden buildings, he did not succumb to the gaudy baubles of a coloured glass chandelier. Besides marble and gilt, the local speciality which appealed to him most was leather – leather wall coverings, tanned and embossed or engraved, printed, painted or gilded, were often used as decorative wall coverings in the finest Venetian palazzi. They were more suited than tapestries to the humid climate and by the fifteenth century there was a vast production of wall panels. Although tanning and decorating techniques changed, those that survived were often mentioned in seventeenth century inventories. By the late eighteenth century, leather wall-covering workshops left in the city were reduced to four, with eleven master craftsmen still active but no apprentices. Among the finest gilded leathers that remain today in Venice are those in the private apartments of the Doge and in the six frontals of the side altars in the Church of the Redentore, dated around 1747 and attributed to Francesco Guardi, landscape artist and flower painter.

'I do not know whether my works in sculpture (I call them mine for they are not only executed altogether from my drawings but not a stroke of the chizel is given excepting under my direction) will excite as much admiration at home as . . . they have done here in Verona,' William wrote to his sister.[1] The craftsmen must have dreaded his visits, but by 1847 William was negotiating a steady stream of orders and bills. 'Your estimate is far higher than what I have paid in this city for any other pieces in marble,' he scolded Guiseppe Petrelli of Padua, who was sculpting two lions in Veronese red marble based on those at the Campidoglio in Rome. He even persuaded him to pay the transport from Padua to Venice and by March 1848 had induced Michelangelo Montresor, a marble mason from Verona, to give him a discount as a valued client. But he could be generous too.

Francesco Vason records payment of ten Napoleons 'and two more from the goodness of his heart'.[2] When sickness struck Vason, William sent him twenty-five lire 'as a small witness to my esteem and for the disquiet I feel when I see an artist kept from working because of illness'.[3]

He travelled to various northern Italian cities: Verona, Padua, Perugia, Ferrara, as well as Paris and Rome if he heard of a good craftsmen or important sale. He was lured to Florence, haunt of the English travellers William did his best to avoid, by a tailor he found to his liking.[4]

William told his sister about his idea for producing a Grinling Gibbons design in stone. In Verona he found the sculptor Salesio Pegrassi, whom William considered 'really a great genius. He never can have seen in his life anything of the nature of [Grinling] Gibbons' carving, for it is a branch of art which we got from Flanders, and a description of ornament never naturalised in Italy . . . the success of the dead woodcock and dove suspended with masses of foliage has far exceeded my expectations and in looseness and truth and even delicacy are not much inferior to Gibbons's work'. Pegrassi would make a matching partner 'and the two will be substituted for the two pieces of drapery that were worked in a hurry for want of anything better and resemble too much two towels hung up on the pilasters at the top of the marble staircase.'[5] It is to William's credit that he inspired the Italian craftsman to produce work that he would never have achieved without William's patronage and his knowledge of Grinling Gibbons.

He informed his beloved sister this was not even half of what he had commissioned for the interior of Kingston Lacy.

There are two large, stone baskets for the windows of the entrance

hall, all the five door frames for the drawing room of the richest
yellow marble sculptured and polished and above all two sorts of
pedestal pieces of furniture for lights, to stand one on each side of
the great doors under the pictures of the king and queen sculptured
in the same and with tablets of real serpentine let into them. These
last are not of my design, but are copied from some by the Florentine
Ammanati, the most celebrated among the immediate scholars of
Michael Angelo.

So much work, though there are many hands employed, requires
time and the progress is slow.

Entering his sixtieth year, he was still full of energy but frustrated
by an increasing awareness of the sands of time. Every month more
receipts for work in wood, plaster, stone and especially marble
flooded in.

His employment of 'many hands' was a source of satisfaction to
Italians who marked him out as the best kind of 'British patron who
combines perfect good taste with an exquisite intelligence for decoration of his London palace'.[6] To the local paper, the *Foglio di Verona*,
which wrote about Bankes's support of Pegrassi in 1846 and 1849,
he was 'a liberal Englishman who, instead of trafficking in the immortal
old works of art of Italy, ultimately impoverishing it of its antique
masterpieces, he trains, encourages and commissions rising artists'.[7]

Many British travellers to Venice, although quick to criticise
Napoleon for looting the city, were not above grabbing art treasures themselves once the Austrians were in control. Some pieces
were clearly fake, but several dealers willingly sold off the Venetian
artistic heritage. As Disraeli wrote in 1837:

> Palaces are now daily broken-up like old ships and their colossal
> spoils consigned to Hanway Yard and Bond Street whence, reburnished
> and vamped up, their Titanic proportions in time figure in the boudoirs
> of Mayfair and the miniature saloons of St James's. Many a fine lady
> now sits in a Doge's chair and many a dandy listens to his doom
> from a couch that has already witnessed the less inexorable decrees
> in the Council of Ten.[8]

Ancient well heads were highly prized by British collectors as garden ornaments. William's neighbour, George Cavendish Bentinck, the Duke of Portland's scholar grandson, spread a score of them around the grounds of his home on Banksea Island in Poole Harbour. But William had most of his copied by Italian craftsmen for the lawns and terraces of Kingston Lacy, ensuring his popularity with those who recognised how fast Venice was being stripped of its treasures. Of 5,000 well heads in Venice in 1814, only 2,000 remained by 1856. By the beginning of the twentieth century only seventeen of the Byzantine type could be accounted for and half of those were reckoned to be in the hands of dealers. William's yearning for well heads is also evidence of his concern to give shape and structure to the lawns and his awareness that the relationship between garden and house mattered. Some of his most obsessive instructions to Seymour concerned planting.

> The tubs, you are aware, are to be like wells filled with earth but must be protected as far as possible from the actual contact with the constant damp and moisture internally so that a space may intervene between the mounts and the marble. If long sawings of slate could be had these would answer the purpose best . . . if not oak trimmings hardened by fire and driven in as piles so as to touch one another may serve very well and then the soil which should be selected of rather a dry and porous quality but yet such as bay trees will thrive in, can be poured in afterwards.[9]

In another note around this time he insisted in the border below the terrace nothing but violets should be cultivated. 'Any flower that rises higher above the ground will disturb the architecture . . .'[10]

William did succumb to two original well heads: one from the courtyard of Palazzo la Bernardo (for which he paid 500 Austrian lire plus 100 for a replacement), the other from Palazzo Breganza in Venice, which cost him 1,200 Austrian lire. A further six on the Kingston Lacy lawns were carved for him in Verona between 1847 and 1851. A red marble one was copied at Verona full size from one in the court of a palace of the Bevilacqua family by the Montresor workshop. Another William designed himself and had carved by Angelo Giordani.

While William was sensitive to preserving the Italian heritage, only by copying could he afford otherwise unobtainable treasures. Exile has many faces. William responded with an obsessional burst of creativity. Victor Hugo called exile 'a long dream of home' and so it was for William. With distance, the past became an ever more sharply defined dream. Distance gave him the chance to reflect on who he was and to feed on his inner resources. He existed by living through the past, yet determined to link this to the future; a memory exile.

By 1846, with several key projects in hand, he allowed his imagination to be captured by whatever he happened to encounter. The longstanding ideas included the marble niches in the Saloon — always an important feature of the room designed by Barry in 1840 according to sketches made by William, based on shell-shaped alcoves he had seen in Montpellier and Narbonne; plate glass windows for the Loggia and life-sized bronzes to stand within, painted doors and leather wall hangings for the Spanish Room and ceilings for several other rooms.

For years Bankes had been concerned with the windows for the Loggia, but was constrained in organising this from Venice. Barry had proposed glazing bars but Bankes wanted an unimpeded view. He wrote to Seymour about the framing of the great plate glasses on the staircase, insisting that his only concern was that the frames should be barely noticeable. He suggested Seymour went to London to observe the new showroom windows fitted with a single pane — William knew this was possible from his visit to the plate glass factory the day after Huskisson's death on the railway. He had, even before his exile, been preoccupied about the view from the landing where the statues were to be. He wanted maximum interior light so that everything else 'may have their full effect'.

The price of plate glass is, 'I believe, diminished since I had the estimate. Therefore let me know what will be the ready money price to have these up next season . . . The estimate was, I think, about £70 each but would probably now, owing to the taking off of glass duties, be considerably less.'[11] He was right. Excise duty on glass had been removed in 1845. This meant factory prices were cut by more than half and manufacture on the Tyne collapsed in the face of competition from Lancashire companies exploiting the tax change.

William had not completely abandoned his desire to collect paintings. But his instinct had almost always been to see them as part of a decorative scheme or to buy opportunistically, rather than build a collection of one artist or genre. Most of his acquisitions during his exile were intended as ceiling decoration, in the hope that the fragments, which he trusted his Venetian painter, Francesco Vason, could restore, would somehow fit together.

One reason he could buy cheaply was that, for a year and a half, Venice's inhabitants suffered horrific privations during a revolutionary siege, as Italians in many cities tried to liberate themselves from Hapsburg rule. Bankes was a spectator in one of Europe's most passionate revolts. The *Risorgimento* had been long brewing, and in the winter of 1847 the Fenice theatre became openly embroiled in the political situation when Verdi's *Macbeth* was performed there. Night after night, in Act Four when the chorus reached the words 'The fatherland has been betrayed and implores our aid: brothers we must hasten to save it,' the house was in uproar as harassed police sought to discover from which boxes red, white and green bouquets were thrown on stage.

In March 1848 Daniele Manin, a middle-class patriot and republican just released from prison and still in his dirty prison garb, spoke to the excited crowd, and the new tricolour of an independent Italy was unfurled in St Mark's. The city was electrified. After leading Venetians to capture the Arsenal, the fleet and the Piazza, Manin declared the re-establishment of the Republic. But excitement changed to fear when Austrian troops fired into the crowd, killing five Venetians. For the next seventeen months, Venice was isolated by a blockade which caused enormous hardship to its citizens. They suffered destitution and disease, bombardment and blockade, famine and pestilence until Austrian rule was re-established.

For more than a year Venetians endured attacks from mortars and howitzers that started at dawn and continued until dusk. 24 May was among the worst: 'the whole city was roused from sleep by the ceaseless and deafening roar and her towers and roofs were soon crowded with anxious gazers on the spectacle.'[12] In July, when Austrian projectiles crashed through roofs for days at a time, and several palazzi on the Grand Canal were hit by cannon balls, many Venetians abandoned the city. By August food was scarce, cholera had taken hold and a permanent sulphurous gloom dominated the sky.

Just two years after it had been built, the great railway bridge across the lagoon into Venice was put out of action when forty of its arches were destroyed. It was a hazardous if exciting time to live in Venice; those who stayed found common cause in helping each other. Yet Bankes's notebooks are about art, architecture and details of chimneys and fireplaces. Of daily dangers and political happenings they are oblivious. Meanwhile the British Consul, Clinton Dawkins, was trying to ensure the safety of his country's citizens abroad; evacuation was the safest route. Edward Leeves was easy to persuade and his attitude throws Bankes's stoicism into sharp relief. 'I am starved and frozen,' he wrote in his diary for 15 April 1848. Wood for fuel was almost as scarce as food, and sometimes no foreign newspapers or letters were delivered. The difficulties made him feel 'very unwell . . . when will this end?'[13] Still he dithered: 'So here we are in a fix – to fly and leave all my little all – the collection of so many years – or to stay, exposed to the dangers of an assault, internal as well as external.'[14] On 9 June Leeves accepted passage on a small boat to Trieste and eventually England. It was a tortuous journey 'but I am so worn out with this kind of existence . . . that I could not refuse the first opportunity of escape from Purgatory.' Perhaps Consul Dawkins wished he had left the city the night a 40lb Austrian cannonball landed on his bed in August 1849 without causing damage. The Dawkins family still owns it.

Bankes, without the option of returning home, might have moved to France, but he chose to remain in the city he had made home, decamping to the Europa Hotel. It suited him as a convenient base from which he continued to deal with the craftsmen he had been nurturing. If he was suffering he did not convey his fears. Venice eventually capitulated to famine; it had lasted longer than other European cities in revolt that year. By August 1849 the Austrians were back. Biding his time, William made some shrewd acquisitions. 'I purchased today a pair of oil pictures on canvas by Bonifacio from the ceiling of a drawing room in the Palazzo Capello a San Felice (the next house upon the Grand Canal to the Ca' d'Oro) a palace Gothic in the exterior and said to be of great antiquity but modernised for the most part within from the style of the compartments.* I feel very little doubt that the ceiling in question is designed by Sansovino, the oval and square panels are tinted lead colour the rest is white,' he wrote.[15] Gustav Waagen noted in 1857 that these two pictures were hung with the Tintoretto, above the fireplace in the dining room, 'destined to ornament the ceiling of the library'. 'Where are they now???? DB,' Daphne Bankes asked in 1932.[16]

William must have been a bystander at the notorious case of Venetian vandalism perpetrated on the Ca' d'Oro, adjoining the house from which he did make a purchase. This Palazzo is still today the finest example of Gothic architecture in the city, although little remains of its fifteenth-century interior finery or its gold exterior. In 1846 the Russian prince Alexander Troubetskoi bought it as a present for the ballet dancer Marie Taglioni. Taglioni, aged forty-five, married to a French husband 'who behaved so cruelly to her that after enduring for many years she was obliged to separate from him,'[17] had recently performed in St Petersburg; while there she had pleaded the case of a Russian prince exiled to Siberia, who was subsequently released. Troubetskoi, thirty-two-year-old son of the released prince serving in the Austrian army, fell in love with Taglioni and gave her the semi-derelict Palazzo in gratitude, declaring that he would live with her there. But Taglioni, renowned for extravagance, proceeded to rip out the

---

* The house no longer exists.

glorious interior staircase, considered one of the city's most important Gothic monuments, which was sold with a fifteenth-century well head as 'waste' marble. Was William tempted to buy a piece of the Ca' d'Oro for Kingston Lacy?

In 1851 William wrote to both Anne and George about another ceiling purchase . . .

> I also enclose the stamped certificate by which you will see that the ceiling picture by Giorgione was valued in the year 1843 at 800 Napoleons. It was originally painted in 1510 for one of the principal rooms in the celebrated palace of Grimani, Patriarch of Aquileia, a joint production of Giorgione and his then scholar, John of Udine . . . I purchased the entire ceiling. It is architectural in the distribution with arabesques of figures and foliage by John of Udine in the panels, unfortunately, however not executed in oils but sketched in some sort of distemper and in a very bad state. Parts will be adapted to ceilings in the dining room and library at Kingston Lacy.[18]

As he told Anne: 'I am not surprised at the great admiration which you express for the ceiling picture by Giorgione . . . nothing but the distress produced by the Siege of Venice could have brought it within a sum that I was willing to give . . .' Bankes believed that Giorgione painted the boys only and John of Udine the birds and foliage. 'In its present state of freshness it seems hardly credible that it should have been painted 340 years ago.'[19]

Today the picture can be seen on the top landing ceiling at Kingston Lacy, but as the catalogue points out: 'Giovanni da Udine was indeed briefly Giorgione's pupil but he did not work in the Palazzo Grimani for Patriarch Giovanni Grimani until his return from Rome in 1537.' Other panels William acquired from the Palazzo Grimani during the siege in 1849 and associated with the Giorgione and John of Udine were, he knew, in a very bad state. Vason was employed to restore and complete them so that the ceiling painting in the state bedroom is largely Vason's work. But William's activity during the seventeen-month siege hardly merits putting him into the category of speculator. The gorgeous palaces were already being dismantled by their poverty-stricken proprietors and William Bankes took little part in the process begun forty years earlier.

12

Pride

~

'Where will there be in any private house in England a family monument of equal magnificence?'

William Bankes to Anne Falmouth

FROM VENICE, WILLIAM was able to indulge the deep seated and often insatiable desire of collectors through the ages to acquire beautiful objects. Collecting is not a mere matter of accumulation. It can spring from a motive as simple as a desire to embellish a family tradition; William certainly experienced strong elements of that urge. But the competitive element, in William's case the desire to prove himself especially to his father, a man of high principles, can also be a factor – hence all the memoranda justifying why he was undertaking changes at all and his angry letters to George about his father's cavalier treatment of prints.

It is tempting to interpret William's increasingly frenzied activities as a collector from 1841 onwards in the light of his need for emotional support in an unfriendly world. Even critics of such Freudian interpretations nonetheless admit that such yearning for comfort plays a role and that sometimes the urge is hard to control. Others fiercely reject what has become known as 'the cliché of the homosexual art collector . . . bound up with this dubious model of art as sublimation. In reducing art to a symptom or a cure it fails to integrate the social with the psychological impulse to collect, let alone account for the type of object collected.'[1] Michael Camille emphasises the importance of context – seeing a collector in 'passionate display' amidst the things he collected – 'how they, as subjects, seem subject to the objects of their desire, joined, contained, might one even say imprisoned by them.' Though this could not apply literally to Bankes, in one sense he was imprisoned by his obsession, in that his exile from the one place he would have chosen to live forced him into an obsession with creating and collecting objects for that place. Towards the end of his life he was fascinated by the beginnings of photography and one can easily imagine that a photograph of him say, standing on the half loggia next to the bronzes of his ancestors, would have filled him with intense pleasure – just as one sees Gertrude Stein framed by her Picassos, Peggy Guggenheim among her Cubist and Surrealist art in Venice or even Elton John drowning in shoes.

Among his contemporaries, the collector William most closely parallels is the owner of Chatsworth, often referred to as The Bachelor Duke. Yet there are also striking contrasts since the 6th Duke of Devonshire (1790–1858) had several homes in London and the country and an enormous income, of which £100,000 came from land. Above all he inherited in 1811 at the age of twenty-one and had forty-seven years to indulge his 'unashamed love of splendour and sense of what befitted a great territorial magnate in a modern age of enhanced prosperity'.[2] His aims were to entertain in style at Chatsworth and to provide a worthy setting for the works of art he was amassing. Like William, he had a mania for marble, and both men loved their ancestral home with a passion; however the Duke had an agent working on his behalf in Italy and the incalculable help of Joseph Paxton, who came to the Estate aged twenty-three, as head gardener and quickly became the Duke's friend, confidant and garden designer.

Even when the obvious motives for collecting have been explored, William's inability to see the fruits of his collection, wander among them, touch his sculptures or admire the layout of his garden so carefully planned in his finely drawn maps, the denial of his right to ascend his completed staircase or to arrive home and enjoy his new entrance, make him an unusual case. Instead of these forbidden pleasures, he had to remind himself that George's heirs were Bankes too, the reason he was devoting his every breath to his life's work. He had to rely on a still formidable memory and enjoy his creation in his mind. Buying and commissioning whatever he could, receiving regular reports of the minutiae of changes, helped nourish his hope that one day he would be able to see what he had achieved.

William's dealings and commissions became increasingly urgent during his last few years in Venice. 'Do not lose a single post' is the most common refrain, 'I desire to be informed immediately,' another. By around 1850 he was writing daily instructions about the exact shade of a wood stain or the smooth functioning of door hinges. 'Let me know at once how it looks,' he asks, or 'I recommend starting this immediately.'

It is possible that by 1850 William suspected he was no longer in good health. In September 1853 he refers to a prescription for medicine with details of when to take it, 'This was prescribed to quiet the stomach in case the purgative lemonade should not have set it to rights. I did not require it.' In Paris that autumn he saw a doctor who gave him 'advice on medicines to be taken'. There were doctors in Venice and an excellent English dispensary near the post office in the Campo san Luca, which was in correspondence with Savory and Son, London. In his last letter to Anne, William encloses a prescription for cough medicine for his sister-in-law Georgina: 'I hope it may do the same wonders as it does with me. A cough never resisting this remedy above two or three days. Let it be remembered that it must be had fresh . . .'[3] William himself was taken ill a week after writing this. But there is no evidence that he believed himself to be suffering from a terminal illness, simply that he was fast approaching seventy. 'Do not fancy that I am forgetful enough of my age not to think it very probable that I may be removed [in two years],' he wrote to Anne.[4] Hardly surprising then that he was in a rush to complete all he had set his heart upon collecting for his house: doors, dado rails, well heads, balustrades, beds, windows, wall coverings and ceilings, ceilings . . . and ceilings.

And there was his special creation, the Golden Room, as he chiefly referred to it.

Most of the embossed and gilded leather which William coveted for the Spanish Room walls he had bought in 1849 from the Palazzo Contarini (allo Scrigni) near SS Apostoli. But 'restoring to a good condition those pieces which are broken or holed, silvering them all over again and with a special varnish, restoring the original design' took months. And there was not quite enough. Antonio Caldera was instructed in 1852 to provide additional skins, but not before William had scoured all possible outlets for more. He was tempted by leather he had seen at the premises of Moise and David Rietti, Jewish textile merchants at the edge of the Ghetto Nuovo, just over the bridge. William wrote on the back of their card: 'This Jew has a large quantity of gilt leather hangings, all one pattern, rather coarse and the gilding coppery.' Eventually he decided that Caldera could provide whatever else was needed. The whole lot was finally shipped in the brig *Marco Polo* in January 1853, together with a small bottle of varnish and copious instructions for its use. William, having studied what was needed, became obsessed about the correct sort of varnish and glue. The bottle he sent was 'to be applied wherever the original varnish shall have scaled off by adhering to the paper let it be applied as soon as possible that the silver may not turn black by exposure to the air. If the varnish be not sufficient liquid add a little spirit of turpentine to it and lay it on with a fine brush . . .' There was a similar page of yet more instructions, in his trademark tiny handwriting, about how to join the skins together.[5]

Meanwhile, William devoted considerable time and energy to 'a work which has been in hand upwards of three years done entirely from my designs and under my eye and direction and in parts touched by my own hand,' as he proudly told his sister. 'The artist, who had no celebrity before, is thought to have done himself great credit and has in consequence now as many orders as he can execute and I see every reason to be satisfied with him.'[6]

William was referring to the exquisite doors to the Spanish Room, whose twelve finely detailed painted panels on pear wood, representing the months – 'six upon gold as the summer months and six upon bronze are the winter' – were, he maintained, 'my best and certainly my largest work in drawing and have at least the merit such as it is of being entirely my own invention.' William sent back with the panels his original watercolours, blurred and dirtied after being used as working copies, which he touchingly asked Anne to preserve as they 'will have some interest at least for you'.[7]

He had also conceived 'one of the large vases, on which I have endeavoured to represent by boys the four seasons. The idea is my own and it is my most considerable design in figures. That which represents Autumn I, from lazyness, left to the artist and I am vain enough to think that it has less grace and spirit than the other three – I am proud of my little Winter boy, who is crying and blowing upon numbed and empty hands to warm them . . .'[8]

In some respects William Bankes cannot fairly be compared with great collectors of his own or recent times. He was more of an acquisitor, even a shopper with a good eye for a bargain. But despite his more narrowly defined vision and smaller purse he was imbued with the dynamic collector's spirit. To me, his great understanding of the creative process marks him out from other collectors and must have given him a far greater appreciation of his acquisitions. For many collectors, part of the pleasure lies in being able to sort, arrange or catalogue items; to announce to visitors 'these are my tastes in life'. Bankes could not do this; he could never be united with the objects he had amassed. Yet for him there was an additional pleasure derived from being part of the process which had given life to many of his objects.

The project that most forcibly revealed William's motives as a collector was his longstanding desire to immortalise his Corfe Castle ancestors at Kingston Lacy. This, above all, was the task which reassured William of the continuity of his family line and confirmed his sense of place. It also enabled this most conservative of outlaws to reaffirm his personal loyalty to the Crown.

In 1844 William told his brother that he was contemplating moving to France in order to establish himself close to the Italian-born sculptor Carlo Marochetti, whose home at Vaux-sur-Seine was about fourteen miles from Paris. Marochetti was a large, imposing man and a self-consciously romantic sculptor who, from 1831, when he began to win important royal commissions, had demonstrated his ability to make powerful historical statements. In 1837, following the successful unveiling of his bronze equestrian statue of Emanuele Filiberto, Duke of Savoy, he was created Baron. William considered this 'the finest of all modern equestrian statues (I might perhaps have included the ancient also)' when it was shown at the Court of the Louvre, before its removal to Turin, Marochetti's birthplace. 'I happened to be in Paris when it was first exposed to view and can never forget the impression that it made upon me, as well as upon everybody else who flocked to see it.'[9]

It is easy to understand why Marochetti's work appealed so strongly to Bankes. It was bold and dramatic, enabling him to envisage an unashamed statement of pride in his ancestors. Soon he began planning life-sized effigies of Brave Dame Mary and her husband Sir John, Lord Chief Justice of the Common Pleas, as well as of King Charles I. According to a letter of 31 May 1839, when Marochetti was in London for four days, the pair probably first met in Paris where he remembered 'the goodwill Bankes had shown him there'. They remained in regular communication until Bankes's flight in 1841, when contact apparently ceased. But in 1844 William was asking George to renew the contact if the opportunity arose 'since [Marochetti] still has the pictures of the Chief Justice and his Lady in his hands'.[10] If George were able to persuade Marochetti to start work on the Corfe Castle statues the following year, William was tempted to have a building constructed in canvas, of the exact form and size of the Loggia at Kingston Lacy, 'to judge the more correctly of the scale and effect of the bronzes. It would furnish a great amusement and resource to me, and,' he confidently asserted, echoing his advice to the 1841 Parliamentary Select Committee, 'be the means probably of introducing a fine example of modern art into my country.'

Despite his flight and ensuing legal difficulties, Bankes never lost sight of this major project. Exile imbued the idea with greater urgency. 'I made a sketch for the female figure some time since which pleased me so well as to the position and arrangement that, if I have leisure and eyes to duplicate it, I will enclose it to you,' he told George. Then he read in a French paper that Marochetti's statue of the Duke of Wellington for Glasgow – a commission which Bankes had been instrumental in winning him – had just (October 1844) been delivered and unveiled. His longing for gossip was almost tangible. 'Any account of it, or criticisms upon it, I should be glad to know,'[11] he begged his brother.

Glasgow was one of four British cities which, by the late 1830s, was looking to erect an equestrian statue of the now ailing Duke of Wellington. By April 1840 a sub-committee had drawn up a short-list of distinguished British and foreign sculptors. In considering Carlo Marochetti – at the outset none of the sub-committee had heard of him, while the Duke of Hamilton's first choice was the Danish sculptor of the ill-fated Byron head, Bertel Thorwaldsen – the Glasgow worthies had to consider whether or not the sculptor for a memorial to this national hero should be British. Marochetti had already faced this problem in France, where the journal *La France* maintained that as a foreigner he had less right than French artists to state commissions. Ironically, although born in Turin he became a French citizen who, by the end of the decade, lived in England. The controversy was compounded by the fact that Marochetti was currently working on an equestrian statue of Wellington's arch-enemy Napoleon and the sub-committee questioned whether they could stomach this cultural internationalism.

The committee was divided for weeks. In the midst of these delicate deliberations, Williams Bankes, acting as intermediary between sculptor and committee partly because of his friendship with the Duke of Wellington, wrote to the Duke pressing the claims of the Italian. 'I confess that there is something in the very idea that pleases me of a statue of the greatest living hero of our age proceeding from the same hand as the tomb of the greatest dead one.' Bankes did all he could to promote, encourage and advise Marochetti: he organised an interview with the Duke at his house in Hampshire and offered Wellington some fine tall horse chestnut trees from the Kingston Lacy estate. But the jury made its own decision almost by default at the end of November 1841, when the other main contender for the prize, Francis Chantrey, died. By this time Bankes had begun his banishment.

It appears George did not make contact with Marochetti in 1844 and Bankes did not go to live near Vaux. There is a nine-year gap in the surviving correspondence by which time Marochetti had settled in London. Was the hiatus a result of Bankes's delicacy in the circumstances, lack of approval from his family for such an expensive undertaking or because Marochetti was greatly in demand? In 1851 a powerful bronze of Richard Coeur de Lion, temporarily exhibited in front of the Crystal Palace during the Great Exhibition and later moved to Westminster, immediately opposite the Bankes's house in Old Palace Yard, brought him considerable fame in his newly adopted country. By 1853 Marochetti had reached such a pinnacle that Queen Victoria came to visit his studio, recording that 'nearly twenty workmen' were employed there. In May that year the correspondence with Bankes started up again. Marochetti assured Bankes of his old affection and told him he was prepared to do anything the latter demanded of him for Kingston Lacy. Nonetheless, he regretted that his new-found fame required him to ask a higher payment than originally agreed. Surely Bankes's heirs would not object to being bequeathed £500 less and three Marochetti statues more, given the current value of his work?

A meeting in the ensuing few months was much discussed – Marochetti always suggesting France – yet it seems that they never did meet, and the commission was eventually completed through intermediaries, bolstered by regular suggestions and drawings from Bankes. His interventions do not appear to have irked Marochetti unduly – once he even complimented Bankes on his sketches. While William was considering the possibility of rebuilding Corfe Castle he had immersed himself in painstaking research of the period. To ensure that a bas-relief illustrating the siege of Corfe was historically accurate, he had copied examples of seventeenth century costume, armour, helmets, shields and decorations; these he sent to Marochetti. Once however, before the main work got under way, Marochetti begged his patron to be allowed to work according to his own style rather than imitate some other artist. At the time he was making two bronze medallions for the entrance hall at Kingston Lacy based on (but not copied from) Jean Goujon's medallion adorning the entrance to the Hotel Carnavelet in Paris. One medallion shows Kingston Hall in its original state and Pratt's plan for the main floor.

Yet the two men clearly had difficulty reaching an agreement on the main commission without meeting face to face. As Marochetti recognised: 'We have each been thinking along different lines.' By October they agreed that Bankes wanted three statues, three pedestals and reliefs and accessories in bronze, but they were haggling over the price. Marochetti said he would charge anyone else £2,500, plus the price of pedestals and accessories, but for his friend and supporter William Bankes he offered to make a reduction of £1,000 and do the whole job for £3,000. When Bankes baulked at this, Marochetti countered by telling him again it was an investment for his heirs. Casting the work himself might cost more than having it done by professional founders but would ensure a faithful reproduction.

Negotiations continued throughout the autumn but Marochetti started in any case. Seymour was instructed to take measurements of the niches on the loggia landing which the statues were to occupy and to make casts of them. Finally, when Bankes was in Paris in November 1853, Marochetti agreed to accept £2,500 but hoped that when Bankes saw the finished work he would pay the extra £500. Probably, had he lived, he would have, but his heirs did not react as Marochetti had predicted. An incredibly precise six-page contract – of dubious legal validity owing to Bankes's outlawry – was finally signed between artist and patron on 18 November 1853. Had Bankes personally overseen the statues it is doubtful that he would have entered into such detailed written specifications. None of his other commissions required a similar contract. He was some-times specific to the point of pedantry but at least had the grace to add here and there 'should Baron Marochetti choose' or 'there is no obligation'. King Charles I was to have 'the George about his neck and the garter about his knee, his gloves in his right hand'. But William's real concern was for his own ancestors. In order to have the correct costume for Sir John Bankes in his robes as Lord Chief Justice, he had long since supplied a print to be copied, but also suggested Marochetti might visit tombs of contemporaries in Westminster Abbey or Winchester Cathedral to copy shoes correctly and acquire an accurate historical feel. By coincidence, a nephew, John Scott Bankes, the eldest son of his brother Edward, had married Annie, daughter of Chief Justice Jervis, and this nephew was able to borrow his father-in-law's robes for a few days for Marochetti to copy. The likeness for Lady Bankes was to be modelled from a Bone enamel of her as well as from a Hoskyns miniature and a statue of Anne of Austria by Simon Guillain in the Louvre. All this was stipulated in the contract.

Once the work was under way, the only details over which William argued with Marochetti were the size of the keys in his heroine's hand. Bankes wanted them large 'for I told him that smaller keys in a woman's hand could denote nothing but a housekeeper!!'[12] The original keys today hang over the fireplace in the library at Kingston Lacy.

The contract also stipulated that a full-sized model of the loggia be set up in Marochetti's London studio and 'the whole, if possible, lighted from the same side as at Kingston Lacy'. The entire work was to be completed in two years. William knew he ran a risk of never seeing this. Should Mr Bankes die before completion, his heir in possession of Kingston Lacy at the time of his death would make good any outstanding payment.

Marochetti began work immediately, telling Bankes he hoped to visit him in Italy that winter. But although he went to Genoa and Rome, puzzlingly they never met. Possibly Marochetti had pressing work to complete rather than reluctance to associate with a known homosexual. In April the Baron was back in London at 34 Onslow Square and reported that work was progressing so well that as soon as casts had been made, he would have photographs taken. Marochetti was one of the earliest artists to make use in his work of daguerrotypes – the process of creating images on silver-plated copper was invented by Louis Daguerre in 1839. Although Bankes never saw the trio finished, a few weeks before he died he was most impressed with a photograph which, as he told his sister, was 'a reduced representation produced mechanically on paper and therefore exact to the utmost degree'[13] of the bas-relief Marochetti had made representing the Siege of Corfe. Some of William's ideas can be identified on this plaque and he wrote immodestly to his sister: 'Never, no never was, in my opinion anything so admirably rendered combining as it does delicacy and sharpness and finish with the utmost freedom and spirit. I am more than satisfied, I am charmed with it . . .' He begs Anne to tell Marochetti this herself 'since I could almost fear that some little criticisms I had made might seem drawbacks on my general admiration (which they are not but only attempts to render so exquisite a work of art absolutely perfect). If the execution of the statues be conformable to this high standard of excellence (as no doubt it will be) where will there be in any private house in England a family monument of equal magnificence?'[14]

William had another reason for urging his sister to visit Marochetti's London studio: 'I am anxious to a degree about the likeness of Lady Bankes' head.' He wants to ensure 'that the lips are strongly pressed together to give the face a character of firmness and determination which it is very desirable to preserve.' He asks this favour of Anne since 'George is but a poor judge in art and has but an indifferent eye.'[15]

Marochetti's connection with the disgraced Bankes might have been thought to have compromised a courtier with work in hand both of and for Queen Victoria. But this does not appear to have been the case. In fact, in 1854 he began work on a statue of Princess Elizabeth, Charles I's daughter who died aged fourteen in Carisbrooke Castle, commissioned by the Queen and Prince Albert for St Thomas Church, Newport. This, too, was a life-sized figure, though recumbent, to be placed in a niche. Philip Ward-Jackson maintains that the connection between these two commissions of Marochetti's may well have been William's youngest brother, Edward, who was during these years one of the Queen's Chaplains in Ordinary. Edward, like his brothers, ingested family tales of Corfe Castle with his first milk, and as Rector of Corfe Castle retained a strong interest in the Civil War period. His son had brought the official robes to help with the statue of Sir John. At all events, the Queen was delighted with Marochetti's monument, 'which is really beautiful,' she wrote in her journal on 12 December 1856.[16]

During their negotiations the Bankes were struck by a family tragedy when Anne's only son, George Henry, the fifth Viscount, second and last Earl of Falmouth and third of William John's Trustees, died unmarried aged forty, on 29 August 1852. He was a brilliant man who took a first class honours degree at Oxford in 1832 and was one of the finest amateur violinists of his day; in 1848 he played at a concert with Frederick Chopin in London. William, devastated on his sister's behalf, and desperate to be of help, was touched when Anne asked him to design a memorial window for the small Cornish Church of St Michael Penkivel, where her son was buried. William threw himself into this project and sent Anne some typically vibrant preliminary ideas which included a choir of eight life-sized angels, each playing an instrument and the epitaph: 'Till angels wake thee with a note like thine.' At the end of November he was in Florence, still anxiously awaiting Anne's verdict on this 'and am in fact detained here only to receive [it], which is now putting me to inconvenience, since I am wishing to get back to Venice and not to pass through the mountains quite in the depth of winter.'[17] The East Window in this beautiful thirteenth-century church was indeed eventually erected as a memorial to the second Earl Falmouth but does not incorporate William's ideas.

William was starting to get edgy about money, too. He wrote to George of his concern about some money borrowed 'in aid of your unlucky son ... and any collision with your son during my lifetime is what I should dread and abhor beyond all possible events.' Yet he told George frankly: 'I look all the more narrowly and exactly to things because next year (when I shall probably be in France, should I live) my expenses will be so greatly increased that it is not unlikely that I may require and spend my whole income, there being the bronzes to execute . . . the finishing of the great drawing room and above all the whole rebuilding of the offices and stables.' The latter projects were unfinished at his death.

'In money matters, I always like to know where I am,' he reminded his brother. All this preyed on his mind to such an extent that he told Gregory he was contemplating returning home 'that I should submit to what may be necessary to recover my civil rights and return to England. Of course in that case the first preliminary will be to surrender myself and to submit to my trial and to whatever consequences may result from it.'[18]

He asked his lawyer to find out if the only witness was still serving in the police force: any inquiries he made must be conducted with the utmost secrecy 'since I feel desirous of sparing members of my family all pain and inquietude. It is my wish and determination that until my mind shall be made up one way or another no member of it nor anyone else should even think that such a point is at all in cogitation.'[19]

Gregory responded speedily and coolly. Since the witness against William was alive and, twelve years on, still attached to the police force, Gregory felt bound to advise his client: 'It appears to me therefore that in the event of a trial a conviction would be the inevitable result.' He told Bankes he had been thinking about how he could ever get a trial; 'the outlawry would be a bar to this unless reversed.' According to Gregory, Bankes's only hope here was if he could show some error, either of law or fact of law, in order to prove that the case was one in which the process of outlawry was not applicable. Or else he needed to show some irregularity in the proceedings.

> But as those proceedings in the present instance were taken under the personal superintendence of the Solicitor to the Treasury it is not very probable that any such exist and no examination could be made into them without full publicity as of record . . . If the outlawry were reversed, the accused might then gain and take his trial and the

course in that case would, as it appears to me, be to give notice to the Solicitor to the Treasury of such intention and arrangements might then be made with him for the surrender of the party . . . If a writ is brought, it would be argued before the Court of Queen's Bench, at which Lord Campbell, who was I think Attorney General at the time of your former trial, is now the Chief Justice.'[20]

Since Campbell was married to the daughter of James Scarlett, Lord Abinger, Bankes's old adversary from Cambridge elections, the Buckingham libel and 1833 trials, this connection was particularly intriguing. Campbell, the son of a minister who studied theology at St Andrews, was a sound, careful and industrious lawyer who, according to contemporaries, was 'insensitive, self-satisfied and ambitiously worldly', hardly the sort of man predisposed to give William Bankes a sympathetic hearing. Yet there could be no clearer indication of how close William Bankes was to men at the heart of the British establishment and source of power yet who were unable, or chose not to, ameliorate his sentence. A charter of pardon from the Crown was another remote option but Bankes never pursued it.

These were heady days in Venice, too. May 6 1854, the day after William wrote to his sister and his steward, saw the triumphantly successful performance of Verdi's ground-breaking opera *La Traviata* at the Teatro San Benedetto. Fourteen months earlier it had had a disastrous première at La Fenice, but now, reworked and with new singers, it held the audience spellbound with its scandalous subject matter of love without marriage. Lovers attended in droves, some returning several times to hear the opera's dramatic plea for free love. *La Traviata* soon became a symbol of revolt against current sexual conventions and Bankes, even had he not attended the opening night, would surely have been caught up in the excitement of controversial new ideas gaining momentum through an artistic medium. Much of Bankes's adult life had been ruled by a narrow interpretation of sexual convention. No one living in Venice in May 1854 could have failed to be stirred by this new desire for change.

Having adjusted to the possibility of returning, Bankes decided not to arrive openly and face an almost certain trial but to make a secret visit. He wished to see his house and his collection. He had nothing to lose except his freedom, which he now risked. There is a convincing case to be made that sometime in the spring and summer of 1854 Bankes made at least one voyage from Cherbourg to Studland – the most direct route. Studland, as Bankes would be well aware, had been a favourite landing stage for eighteenth century smugglers on this stretch of coastline and descendants of the most famous smuggler of all, Isaac Gulliver, probably ensured Bankes's safety from arrest when he made his return trips.

Early in the nineteenth century, Gulliver's granddaughter, Ann Fryer, had married Edward Castleman of Chettle, a solicitor. Castleman's brother Charles was also a solicitor. Ann's father, Gulliver's son-in-law, and her brother owned the Fryers and Castleman's Bank in Wimborne. When in 1847 Emily Castleman wed Thomas Hanham, the clan could count among its relations one of the oldest Dorset landowning families whose impeccable connections in the law and the church had been secure in the county since the fifteenth century. The Hanhams were among the 140 guests at Frances and Henry Bankes's 1791 ball. Thomas Hanham himself was a magistrate and Provincial Senior Grand Warden of Dorset. The Bankes would have been acquainted with the Fryers and Castlemans, all diehard country Tories, through various routes. Isaac Gulliver, who died in 1822, had grown fat pursuing his illegal activities for generations on Bankes properties. Doubtless he had supplied William's father with some of his finest brandies and wines.

William would have been especially aware of their power once he started work on Kingston Lacy since they controlled all the shipping through Poole, the port of disembarkation for his treasures from abroad. William Castleman, on the payroll of both William Bankes and his father Henry, wasted little time demanding an increase from William once he inherited Kingston Lacy on the grounds that he now had 'additional duties . . . and had managed to reduce estate expenditure. The present management arrangements offer much security,' he concluded.[21] According to Castleman family lore, William, not trusting his brother George, decided early in his exile to throw in his lot with this rich and powerful local nexus and asked the Castlemans to keep an eye on his affairs. When the time came to arrange a visit home they repaid an old favour by ensuring that no warrant would be served on him while he was in England.[22] There is every reason to believe the story. This Wimborne-based clan, alone in the British establishment, did not ostracise the erstwhile Member of Parliament. After all, the Castlemans had always aspired to be, like the Bankes, true gentry.

Channel crossings were often extremely rough in the nineteenth century with strong south-westerly winds. Since William could not swim and the need for secrecy was great, his weak and nervous state can only be guessed at. Yet his excitement at seeing the four-mile sandy beach where he had played in childhood must have been overpowering. Seymour would have to meet him from the larger boat at anchor in the bay, no doubt rowing out in a small dinghy kept in George's boathouse under the cliffs, and convey him quickly to Kingston Lacy.

Although the two men had not previously met they had established a strong rapport and Bankes had to trust him not to gossip among the servants. There were many unfinished projects and crate-loads of still unused marble and alabaster to be discussed in haste. Seymour was involved with the Baron and the Corfe Castle bronzes, repairs to picture frames, ceiling girders so that paintings could be erected, general work on the water and heating system for the house and myriad other smaller schemes. Much pleased William but, as he told Seymour, he aimed for perfection and had no hesitation in stating what did not meet his exacting standards. In one undated note William had written of how 'extremely vexed' he was that nothing was done in Osborne's time as to staining of the deal carved work on the shutters, which he had ordered.

For a while, William had used both Osborne and Seymour for projects, sending home detailed drawings and urging them both to reply immediately. For example, he told Osborne, probably early in 1847, 'to draw to scale the whole pier and pilaster between the drawing room and saloon door on the marble landing with dimensions also figured . . . give me the dimension in figures of the square which forms the top of the capping to the pedestal, you need not return this paper but let me know what progress Seymour has made.'[23] But soon the dynamics changed as Seymour proved his worth and in 1854, after Osborne's death, William wrote: 'it is quite melancholy to see some of the mistakes that have been made in poor Osborne's time'[24] – a note not in itself proof of a visit as it is possible he was commenting on samples and drawings sent over for his comments.

How to finish the great marble niches in the saloon was the main project Bankes wished to discuss in situ with Seymour. In addition to overseeing the design of the niche floor, William had procured some fine marble and wanted to see for himself how it would work in place. He had become an expert on Italian marble in the last fifteen years, travelling widely to vet colour and quality, rarely relying on middlemen. He feared there was not quite enough of the finest marble for the niches. He wrote to Seymour from France on 25 August, presumably after the visit:

> The green and white marble for the lining of the niches cannot be had. Open therefore the two great cases (*which you shewed me*) [author's italics] containing blocks of purple and white marble and see whether slices shaved off from them might not serve the purpose. The quality of that marble being very rare and precious it must be used with the least waste possible that much may remain over for the capping of the dining room dado ... but this is all guesswork as I have no memorandum with me at all of their dimensions. If applicable to the niches, saw from such faces of the block as have the purest and brightest colours, purple and white with as little of the greenish as may be. Turn your attention to this at once and let me have your report at soon as may be, before I quit France.

A few months later he wrote again, an undated note marked by Seymour on the back 'read Dec 30th 1854' which offers the most conclusive proof that he had indeed visited his still unfinished ancestral home.

Nothing can be more unfortunate than the manner in which the saloon dado, doors etc have been painted . . . white in a cold aspect such as the north room has the worst effect possible. I had particularly directed that only a wash in distemper should have been given to the woodwork in that room. There has been the gross folly also of passing oil paint over that finely carved oak capping which was not only primed for gilding but was actually gilt and required nothing but retouching here and there . . . but what is worse than all . . . *it appeared to my eye* [author's italics] that the plaster cornice round the saloon (which was never intended to be painted but to remain pure white and gold) had been picked out with the same abominable colour and the beautiful stuccos in relief over the side window. Let this be examined and inquired into and, if my eye has not been misled, see if it be possible to scrape the ground white again.[25]

Bankes had no option but to rely on the hard working Seymour, who seems to have proved himself more than worthy of his trust. One instruction that summer contained the master's usual detailed directions: 'The iron girders should be 9" thick . . . but I will not object to 10" thickness' and concluded: 'judge this for the best on the spot without consulting me further.'[26] Seymour had become his close collaborator. Bankes never treated his domestic staff other than as hired hands – which may also indicate why, unlike other homosexuals of his day, he needed to look outside his own household to satisfy his sexual urges. But there is a suggestion that he took Seymour further into his confidence than he had others.'The very first point in preparing for the alterations in the library ceiling will be not to inconvenience Lady Falmouth. Get the girders ready therefore and all the woodwork ready and cut out before the work is commenced. If several hands be put upon it this may be done very shortly when all is actually ready for commencing write up to Spring Gardens [Lady F's home] and inquire if her ladyship would be coming down shortly. If not, commence immediately that you get the answer and carry this as quickly as is possible all the noisy and knocking part.'[27]

Even so, William eventually lost his élan. Exhausted, he decided not to plunge ahead with the library ceiling, only partly for his sister's sake. According to an inventory of 1841, the library contained

2,442 volumes as well as sixteen large books and four portfolios containing prints. No wonder William baulked at the thought of moving all these.

> I have somehow taken it into my head that the change in the library ceiling, though so ordered and contrived that it should not interfere one day with you in the doing, might yet have somehow the effect of disgusting you with it and giving you a distaste for what seems to suit you so well. I have therefore at once decided on counter ordering it all and can assure you in all sincerity that I feel more actual pleasure and satisfaction if doing so from such a motive and from the prospect of knowing you to be comfortable and at your ease than I could possibly have felt from carrying out my plans.[28]

Surviving letters to Anne make it clear that the collaboration with Marochetti was his inspiration until the end of his life. The four marble 'upright vases' which he had made by Bartolomeo Barrini in 1847 were each supported by four bronze tortoises cast by Marochetti in 1853. 'Think of my carrying a live Tortoise in a bag all the way from the Palais Royal!' he had written to Anne from Paris.[29] A few months later Marochetti told Bankes that the bronze tortoises – now numbering sixteen – were 'multiplying at speed'. William's fondness for tortoises as an ornament is curious since none of the usual symbolic meanings of the creature – constancy, hell, the phlegmatic temperament, the modest woman's devotion to housework – seem applicable to him. However, he might have enjoyed a mundane interpretation of the creature as one who hides in his shell, carrying his house on his back – or rather, in his mind. In choosing the tortoise Bankes may unwittingly have hit upon an apt image of one who upon embarrassing himself, knows it and retreats.*

Did Marochetti never meet Bankes during his fourteen years of

---

* According to Alastair Laing of the National Trust there is however an intriguing little Elizabethan or Jacobean picture at Syon House of the Princess Elizabeth, but now called Arabella Stuart, which is actually a depiction of Cesare Ripa's personification of secrecy, save that she stands on a tortoise rather than a toad – might this be an explanation of William's love of the tortoise?

exile when both were moving around the continent? Or was it that a meeting could not be referred to? According to a letter from Marochetti's financial adviser after William's death, the Baron had 'executed a plaster model of a bust of Mr Bankes which has not been settled for, Mr Bankes not having decided upon the materials in which it was to be ... marble or bronze.'[30] Could Marochetti have sculpted this from memory, or did Bankes sit to him during the months in autumn 1853 and September 1854 when he stayed at the Hotel Choiseul in Rue St Honoré, Paris? And what happened to the plaster bust?

William died in Venice on 15 April 1855, probably in a rented apartment within a palazzo: receipts from the previous year exist for 'two months rent on a flat from February to April 1854' and for a further three months. The address of this flat (given, presumably by mistake by his English shipping agent unless William had ceased caring for secrecy) on another letter was Calle de Marenil, a small street that is longer so-called. He was still there in the summer but there were discussions about spending the following winter seeing George and Georgina in the South of France. Spring in Venice is delightful and his small apartment is probably where the British Vice Consul, Alexander Malcolm, came to certify his death having been notified by one Edward Williams, to whom no other reference survives in the Bankes papers. The cause of William's death is also unknown and never referred to in family letters or diplomatic records. But Malcolm surely knew and conveyed the information to William's family. On his last letter to her, Anne noted that 'her dear kind brother was taken ill on April 2nd he died on the 15th of that month in the morning, quite conscious to the very last moment'. He possibly succumbed to cholera: in June, the British Consul had informed his superiors in the Foreign Office that, although an epidemic had flared up in Venice in April, 'it was only yesterday that the existence of the Evil was publicly recognised in the non-official colours of the Venice Gazette.'[31]

There is an account of Cardinal Mazarin walking through his fine art collection shortly before he died, muttering repeatedly, 'All this must be left behind.' The prospect of relinquishing a painstakingly acquired collection taunts many collectors. In *Utz*, a novel about a multi-million pound porcelain collection assembled by Rudolf Just, Bruce Chatwin, an author-collector himself close to death, weaves a drama around the possibility that since the collection could not be preserved after Just's death it had been destroyed. The story brilliantly posits the collector's dilemma: how to face parting from his collection and what was the point of amassing it? This was one dilemma William was spared, since he had never lived among his objects and he understood his purpose with painful clarity. During his exile and for much of his life William had given considerable thought to posterity and how he might be judged, as well as how the house could be preserved for future generations. When Thomas Robson, the steward who had helped William in the dark days of 1841, fell ill, William insisted to George that upon Robson's imminent death 'I wish you to obtain all my letters from his executor and to have them all preserved. Nowhere will so much be found as to my all over views as to the house.'[32] To Anne, also, he sent instructions that she must keep letters of interest (by which he meant those referring to the house) so that they 'can afterwards be laid up with my other papers that regard Kingston Lacy'.[33]

Shortly after his flight, William had unequivocally stipulated his burial wishes to George. 'After so much said on the uncertainties of life, it may be as well to mention here that whenever it may please God to release me I wish to be closed up in lead and buried with our forefathers in the vault at Wimborne.'[34]

Wimborne Minster, largely Norman in origin, was built on the site of a Benedictine nunnery in about AD 705 and for all the time that William knew it was a Royal Peculiar (a title abolished in 1846) which exempted it from all diocesan jurisdiction and entitled choristers to wear distinctive scarlet robes. William's affinity towards the place is confirmed by his donation of some glass, reputedly fifteenth century and probably looted from a Belgian convent during his early travels in Europe. 'The gift of WJ Bankes' is how the Minster recorded the glass.

In his desire to have his body returned home William may have had in mind a comparison with Byron, who died of fever at Missolonghi but whose embalmed corpse was shipped to England for a second funeral. To preserve Byron's body during the voyage home, holes were bored through the layers of wood and tin and the coffin set in a large outer cask containing 180 gallons of spirits. Without this treatment (there is no evidence of embalming) Bankes's remains must have thoroughly mouldered by the time they were returned to Dorset in the middle of the summer of 1855.

Instead of urns containing the heart, brain or intestines, a more poignant memento was sent home either with or after the body: a leather writing box with concertinaed sides, worn but still in good condition, embossed with a broken consular seal stamped VENICE, indicating either that it was sent home via the consulate or perhaps that other missives of William's had occasionally found their way home in the diplomatic pouch. Inside is a strap and a pocket for pencils; a few of William's charcoals and chalks remain as he must have left them. Two other objects inside the box eluded the family censorship: a calling card from somebody with the surname Harris and a lock of long, shiny chestnut-coloured hair tied in the middle with a piece of string and wrapped up in a twist of paper on which it is identified, in William's writing, as 'Mr H. a.' In addition to sorting out the affairs of their dead countrymen, the main task of the consul and his deputy in 1855 had been to send provisions from Venice to the Crimea for the use of HM forces established there for the previous year. And so, when it came to organising for William's body to be returned home, the Vice Consul was ideally placed to know which vessels were passing through Venice on their way to London and when.

But if Malcolm ensured William's body was sent home, surely it was Edward Bankes who facilitated burial in the family vault at Wimborne Minster, thanks to his connection with Queen Victoria and his high position in the Church. According to family lore, special permission in the form of a private Act of Parliament was required for William's burial in the family vault, not merely on account of his being a fugitive from justice, criminal and outlaw, but because intramural interment was no longer legally permitted. However, there is no such private act and a clause in the Burial Act allowed for a discretionary power, vested in the Secretary of State for the Home Department, to grant a licence in specified cases for interments in vaults. The licence would be granted only if there was no likely detriment to public health, which ridiculously required that the application be made before the death of the party to be interred. Clearly in William's case this would not have been possible; more probably, Canon Edward quietly arranged with someone influential to ensure his brother could be buried alongside his Bankes ancestors. At least he could satisfy one of his brother's dearest wishes in death if not in life.

The family also managed to ensure that William Bankes's funeral – two months after his death on 13 June, according to parish records – was held in total secrecy. The Rev. Charles Onslow MA, Hon. Canon of the Cathedral Church of Sarum and for thirty-four years one of the Presbyters of the Minster, officiated, probably at a ceremony in the crypt chapel. None of the local papers reported the event, although there had been a brief announcement of his death in Venice in the Dorset County Chronicle for 10 May 1855. A sanitised column in the *Gentleman's Magazine* of August 1855 which mentioned his parliamentary career and his translation of Finati's book and concluded flatly, 'for the last few years, Mr Bankes had chiefly resided at Venice,' was the only obituary. William's body was the last in his family to be interred in the vault. A brass plaque placed outside the vault in 1856 states below the family motto, *Velle Quod Vult Deus* (Desire That Which God Wishes), 'This vault from henceforth being for ever closed.'*

Returning the body may have been the most urgent matter but there were also outstanding commissions to sort out and, as the bills flooded in, Malcolm was the obvious person for the family to turn

---

* In 1905 the vault was opened up for the ashes of William's descendant Walter Ralph to be deposited there inside the gold cup he had won at Ascot.

to. First to claim was Francesco Vason, artist and mirror-maker, who sent a bill for 3,400 lire. He gave a detailed breakdown of the costs incurred in restoring two ceilings in the Lombard style, commissioned by William Bankes. There was a list of paintings on each ceiling with notes of work done or still to be done. 'All the work is in progress,' he wrote, 'and should be ready in eight months.'[35] Costante Traversi, artist, sent a bill dated 16 August 1855 for 767 Austrian lire citing work done on ceilings A and B (A referred to the state bedchamber and B the library) 'commissioned by William Bankes and halted at his death by the English Consul Malcolm. The old woodwork is nearby partly untreated and partly worked as it was to be . . .' Daphne Bankes noted in 1932 that parts of these ceilings were sent to England and parts retained – presumably in lieu of payment. In Paris Lady Warrender, sister of the late Earl of Falmouth and a longstanding family friend, paid Louis Roguet, a worker in mosaic, for two black marble pilasters.[36] And in September 1855 a bill arrived from Scotney and Earnshaw to Countess Falmouth for carriage and duty on marble work.

When William had reassured his sister that work on the library ceiling would be cancelled immediately to ensure her peace of mind, he had turned his attention instead to the state bedchamber – the room in which he would have slept had he lived at Kingston Lacy. He had long been engaged in collecting materials to put together a beautiful ceiling in that room; in his final months he was also organising for a 'fine bed . . . which I trust will in process of time be completed.'[37] It never was. William would have been saddened less by its incomplete state at the time of his death – only details were still to be worked on – than by the reaction it received.

'The state bedstead', as Bankes referred to it, was carved in walnut and holly by Vincenzo Favenza, the gilder and woodworker also patronised by Edward Leeves whose treasures for Kingston Lacy included the carved boxwood doors in the dining room. The doors, with their exquisite carved cherubs and angels, some copied from Renaissance sculptors, are among Bankes's most successful Venetian commissions. The ornate four-poster, however, was dark, fussy and heavy and incorporated a confusion of styles, periods and symbols including pre-Raphaelite nymphs, winged Roman soldiers, tortoises, shields, Old Father Time, bats (which Italians considered messengers of good luck) and the Bankes coat of arms. Eventually, George dispatched his son Edmund in the summer of 1855 to help Malcolm sort out the mess. It was probably this nephew of William's who, while Malcolm was away, went through his uncle's personal effects, including letters and papers, and brought them home. The list of objects found in Bankes's wardrobe gives little away: twelve collar-less shirts and twelve collared, thirty-seven pairs of socks, four ties. Everything, from his vests to his coats, five razors and a Fedora, was listed. There was also a miniature of Lord Byron, painted by Sandars just after Byron was at Cambridge, which William bought in Venice in October 1848 at the height of the siege and which seems to have found its way back to Kingston Lacy. Daphne Bankes came across a note in her father's hand, copying one by WJB: 'Lord Byron presented it about 1819 or 1820 in Venice to the Countess Albrizzi, (signed on the back inside), her son sold this to me in October 1848 in Venice. W.J.B.'[38] The original note and the miniature are now missing.

By August, Malcolm was back in charge and in despair. He wrote about the carved bed 'as the artist proposes to finish it . . . I cannot but say that if it is carried out as intended it would be throwing away money and I believe your brother was fully aware of the mistake in design and taste. I have caused the artist to make an estimate of the lowest he would take to finish the bed as proposed by him and consequently submit the whole for your approval or not.'[39] Malcolm made it plain to George that

> it is a great inconvenience to me to have to look after all these artists – in addition to the bed there were several parts of ceilings, a carved marble fireplace, carved shutters and marble bas reliefs, all being made by different men – and it is quite impossible for me to dedicate sufficient time to superintend the proper carry out and finishing of these works of art.[40]

George was conciliatory, agreeing to all of Malcolm's suggestions and not haggling over money. He asked only 'you will have the goodness, as I hope, to continue some degree of superintendence over these works and to convey an intimation to me as soon as the balance now in your hand shall be exhausted.'[41] Six months after William's death, Malcolm was still negotiating. One artist wrote of his astonishment to learn that the heirs of the 'noble William Bankes' intended to deprive him of his commission to restore paintings and finish a ceiling that he had dedicated himself to. He insisted he would continue working on it as he had heard that William Bankes had provided in his will for the artists he employed. Not so.

The bed eventually arrived plus an unexplained extra pole for one corner. Far from the creation of a bitter or sad man, in its opulence and exuberance it is rather the confident if confused statement of someone bursting with artistic ideas. But other commissions were halted in mid-execution. Malcolm informed George of a carved marble fireplace being made by Pegrassi in Verona of which two pieces were finished. Edmund had suspended the work.*

There is an interesting postscript to the Malcolm story. Throughout the years he was honorary Vice Consul his name hardly crops up in any surviving Foreign Office records. However, as recorded in correspondence shortly after William's death, in August 1855, the

---

* This fireplace could be the one at Canford Manor, home since 1846 of Sir John and Lady Charlotte Guest – a rather incongruous piece of un-Italian Biancone marble amidst the heavy Gothic of the staircase and the rest of the house. Although signed and dated 'Pegrassi 1866' as authenticated by Pevsner it could be that when William's heirs suspended work in Verona on what might have been Pegrassi's masterpiece for William, it was subsequently offered to or taken over by the 1st Lord Wimborne, son of Sir John and Lady Charlotte, who may have already been familiar with Pegrassi's work at Kingston Lacy first hand or through Charles Barry, commissioned by Lady Charlotte to give Canford the touches of grandeur she craved. The Guests were to employ other Venetian craftsman recommended by Lord Wimborne's brother-in-law, Sir Henry Layard (1817–94) British archaeologist and politician who grew up in the Palazzo Rucellai and returned to live in Venice in the 1850s. He was in Italy almost annually from 1855–9, picture hunting, fresco copying and occasionally advising John Murray for his hand-book. Much of Layard's collection is now in London's National Gallery. He might have informed Lord Wimborne of the magnificent half-finished Pegrassi chimneypiece in Verona.

Acting Consul, Mr Harris, took leave and Malcolm was in charge. This led him to request a salary for the tasks he was now undertaking, which the Foreign Office declined, leaving Malcolm no option but to resign altogether in December 1855.[42] Malcolm continued to live in Venice, however, his dealings a clear illustration of the shady and mysterious side of the city. Two years after Bankes's death he was again acting for the British Government, now arranging the purchase from the Pisani family of Veronese's *La Tenda di Dario*, and was able to pull the necessary strings to obtain permission to remove it to London. He also exported to England fragments of rare marble removed from the southern façade of San Marco during restoration and as late as 1886 Enid Layard, Sir Henry's wife, recorded in her journal that she and her husband had been taken by Mr Malcolm 'to Madonna dell'Orto to see a palace where doors and ceilings were for sale'.[43] Bankes and Malcolm must have known each other long before 1855 yet their friendship has gone unrecorded.

George, William's heir, and Edward had to sort out the contract with Marochetti themselves. Just as William might have guessed, they curtailed as many optional extras as they could. In the contract, William allowed for two pairs of six-foot high symbolic lamps, the effect of which would have been to turn the Loggia into a sort of Royalist shrine dedicated to the King's memory. William's intention was probably a more basic desire to express for posterity his place within a brave and loyal family; but the theatricality of a chapel-like area would have appealed to his sense of drama. More than a year after William's death, Marochetti was still applying to the Bankes family for the extra £500 which he maintained there was 'never any doubt that Mr Bankes intended to have paid' for the three statues. Surely Edmund, to whom the letter from Marochetti's financial adviser was addressed, could not have refused payment and surely Marochetti's workshop could not have allowed the bust of William to be smashed? Perhaps it was quietly 'lost', like the embalmed head of which William had written to Byron. Kingston Lacy has no record of either head ever having existed.

William was to die intestate and as Gregory predicted, the Estate passed unmolested to George, who enjoyed it for one year after which it passed to his eldest son, Edmund George, who lived only for another four years. Even these extra years were not enough to sort out everything his uncle had had shipped over. An eight-page inventory made in 1858 indicates that Edmund had been stockpiling William's superfluous purchases throughout his stewardship. More than two hundred items are listed as stored throughout the house, shop and storerooms at Kingston Lacy. Some were put in the wash-house, others over the brewhouse or in the stable yard and further boxes tucked away in closets. They included three lumps of 'serptine' marble, pieces of antique Verona, Baincone, Ravacone and French marble, a slab of vein marble, polished, two panels carved and gilded, alabaster, Egyptian granite, Portland stone, carved oak panels, lengths of boxwood, pieces of scrolling in oak, etc, etc. The list, which occasionally refers to 'Beautifull carvings', or a piece of 'very' antique marble, makes for sad reading. William's buying habits had, at the end, become a compulsion. With no devoted relation to install them they languished unattended, an embarrassing reminder of the exiled collector.

But the settlement of the property in 1841, renewed in 1855 as soon as William died, was effective. The trustees carried out extensive draining work on the Dorset land and the Government made no claims on it. In 1855 the family must have breathed a collective sigh of relief as, once again, the estates were settled into the traditional trusts so beloved of the English landed gentry, which were to stabilise the Bankes succession for the next five hundred years. Or so they thought.

Epilogue

~

'Good Taste is to my mind little else but a refined good sense
and a nice perception of propriety'

William Bankes to Anne Falmouth

14 JULY 2002, 6 p.m. Early evening brings a welcome slight
breeze after one of the hottest days of the year. The unusually fine weather swelled the crowd of visitors to this gem of a country
house in Dorset but all have now departed. Kingston Lacy, its flag
of St George fluttering behind the cupola, is left briefly alone again.

Within an hour, a small army of National Trust volunteers and
helpers arrives, this time not to work but to party, joined by families who live on the estate. Soon the lawns are awash with panama
hats, picnic hampers and folding chairs; champagne bottles perch
precariously on ledges of the magnificent well heads William shipped
from Italy. From an open-sided marquee on the hillock overlooking
the south lawns, the Stour Valley Stompers jazz band blasts out its
rhythm and blues repertoire.

As the sun drops behind the large cedar trees, obelisk-shaped
shadows fall across the great lawns, reminders of the man who shaped
the house. The musicians, echoing the emotion of a day's end, strike
up the melancholy 'St James' Infirmary'.

The celebrations marked the centenary of the birth of (Henry
John) Ralph Bankes, the great, great nephew of William John Bankes
and the man who bequeathed the Kingston Lacy Estate to the National
Trust in 1981 – one of the most generous gifts in its history. The

party was also the National Trust's thanks to all those who had devoted themselves to the house and grounds for the previous twenty or so years. It echoed the more spectacular party given by Ralph's parents, Walter and Henrietta, to celebrate his birth on an even hotter July day in 1902. On that occasion a band from the Royal Marine Artillery at Portsmouth was brought along to entertain 1,500 guests, whole oxen were roasted, bonfires lit and brilliant fireworks let off into the warm air, so thrilled were the parents at the birth of a male heir and the tenants at their continued security.

Both Ralph and his father Walter were solitary men, as indeed was William. But they had brought stability to the Estate after fourteen lacklustre years. After William's death, one Bankes followed another in short order; George, then Edmund for just four years, followed by Edmund's son, Henry John, who died without heirs in 1869 aged nineteen. Walter, Henry's younger brother, inheriting unexpectedly, remained at the helm for the next thirty-five years. But stability came at the price of any spark of originality. None of the Bankes after George cut a dash in London political life; after six generations, whatever their local importance, Bankes were no longer even Members of Parliament. Walter oversaw various changes to the house, garden and park, including the erection of a new stable block in 1880. But these were necessary rather than inspired. His passion in life came from sport, especially riding. He died suddenly aged fifty-one in 1904, two years after celebrating the birth of his son, a stranger to his young family as much as his servants, with whom he communicated by written notes. His widow, Henrietta, a well known international beauty boasting charm and a full bosom, supervised the Estate with the help of an agent, until Ralph inherited, in July 1923, aged twenty-one.

Fifty years on, Ralph Bankes, aged seventy, decided that the only way to preserve the 16,000 acre estate with its famous herd of Red Devons, as well as the house with its idiosyncratic art collection, was to will it to the National Trust for Places of Historic Interest or National Beauty. The gift was magnificent not only for its size but also for its history, quality and variety. It comprised, in addition to Kingston Lacy, one of the most private houses in the country, Badbury Rings, the famous Iron Age hill fort; Corfe Castle, the ruin steeped in romantic history atop the Purbeck Hills; Hartland Moor, Studland Heath and the monumental rocks known as Old Harry. The last two are both Grade One nature reserves of international status while Studland is home to one of Britain's largest nudist colonies. These acres of parkland, farmland and heathland were all areas of outstanding and unspoilt natural beauty as the Bankes family had been remarkably stringent in refusing all offers to buy the land for development. From the 1920s until the 1970s various proposals were suggested to Ralph Bankes involving golf courses, country clubs, marinas, luxury hotels or private airstrips. He turned them all down, needing neither the money nor the bother such a transaction would bring. In this way the Bankes family preserved for the nation large areas of unusual tranquillity with vistas often unchanged for centuries. Would the British government, had it confiscated the estates after William's flight in 1841, have been able to hold firm in the same way?

Having been promised that total secrecy about his intentions would be maintained throughout the remainder of his life, Ralph Bankes arranged in 1972 for the entire property, which had been in the private possession of the Bankes family for the last 300 years, to be left to the Trust. The gift became public knowledge only after his death on 19 August 1981. Few people knew what Kingston Lacy contained, deterred equally by No Trespass notices posted all around the estate and rumours about the reclusive owner's solitary lifestyle.

Ralph Bankes was an extremely handsome man, barrister and Justice of the Peace who also adopted many of his ancestor's ancient titles such as Lay Bishop of Wimborne, hereditary Lord High Admiral within the Castle Lordship and Manorship of Corfe and the Isle of Purbeck by Charter of Queen Elizabeth. This apparently entitled the holder to take command of the fleet if anchored in the bay – a sinecure William John might have found useful had he not been stripped of all privileges. In 1935 Ralph married Hilary Strickland-Constable, daughter of an old Yorkshire family, and the couple had two children, John and Mary, who had an unusual and sheltered upbringing at Kingston Lacy. During the Second World War an American military hospital was built in the park and the flower garden given over to vegetable production. Shortly after the War, Hilary developed multiple sclerosis which confined her increasingly to a wheelchair. She died in 1967, the children grew up and left, and, as most family ties had been severed, Ralph's only companion was his housekeeper, Mrs E. E. O'Connell, who had nursed his invalid wife for years. The state rooms were mostly closed off to conserve heating.

There are many stories about Ralph's eccentricity during these years, some of which his older sister Viola recounted with gusto. One day Lord Pembroke, a contemporary of Ralph's at Eton, telephoned to say that the Queen Mother was staying with him and would like to see the Bankes's collection of pictures.

'The house is open to the public at weekends,' Ralph shot back, as indeed it was from 1954 to 1968 in order to fulfil the conditions of a Government loan to help repair the roof.

'But Ralph, this is the Queen Mother!'

'Oh, all right!' said Ralph reluctantly.[1]

Ralph's dislike of the outside world was legendary. There was the time a coachload of Commonwealth VIPs arrived to visit the house, as arranged by written agreement between Ralph and the Department of the Environment.

On ringing the front doorbell, they saw a window thrown open; Ralph put his head out saying, unbelievably, 'Not in here.' The coach was obliged to return to London.

Ralph did however produce a small *Official Guide to Kingston Lacy* (price one shilling) which is neither patronising nor uninformative, although occasionally misinformed. It recounts all the well-known anecdotes, such as Dr Johnson's famous visit to Kingston Lacy, and states unambiguously that the *Judgment of Solomon* is by Giorgione.

Some Bankes cousins with children the same age as John and Mary remember being invited over one day for tea and family games. 'We were terribly excited at all the other cars in the entrance driveway, thinking it was a party, only to find we had been asked on one of the rare days when the place was open to the public. John came out to greet us and his enthusiasm was infectious. But the day became a great family joke because as he took us down for tea in this bare and chilly basement all the cups were laid out and we were asked to pay 10 pence for tea just like all the other punters. That was the only time we ever went although we lived nearby.'[2]

The tenants and employees had many other tales, mostly about Ralph's lack of concern for material possessions and largely benevolent neglect of Kingston Lacy. Nonetheless, few doubted his genuine feelings for the estate. Requests for improvements and even maintenance were often ignored, but equally he seldom bothered to raise rents, which were sometimes as low as £50 a year. Both Ralph and his father Walter were deeply private, solitary men. In this way the estate was effectively frozen throughout the twentieth century, making it something of a historical curiosity. Although the 330 cottages on 40 farms were mainly built in the sixteenth and seventeenth centuries, they occupied sites dating back to before 1500, fronting common land where the medieval poor grazed their animals. Much of the land has been tended by the same families for generations.

After Ralph's death newspapers reported that the Trust had been left its biggest bequest, valued at between £23 and 30 million. He left smaller bequests of £50,000 each to John and Mary and Mrs O'Connell. The latter was also left the use of the stable flat and old garage at Kingston Lacy as well as a house in Lancelot Place, London. All the rest, residue and remainder went to the National Trust absolutely. It would have amused William to note that the will was drawn up and the entire Bankes properties and lands conveyed by Gregory Rowcliffe and Co of 1, Bedford Row. Most of those millions were tied up in a severely rundown property that could neither be sold nor mortgaged. But the Trust was able to sell off a parcel of land for building development near Wimborne, which financed much of the restoration, and the estate brought in a useful annual income of at least £750,000. It was recognised that restoration of the house, the near derelict gardens and most buildings on the estate would require massive expenditure of at least £1 million and that four or five years would be needed before this 'monumental doll's house of grey stone', as Tim Knox, the Trust's Chief Curator, called it, could open to public viewing.

The architects Caroe and Martin were responsible for the exterior and fabric of the building. The decaying roof, with timbers the consistency of dry meringue, was the most urgent problem. Although the roof had been re-leaded in 1957 and limited repairs carried out in the early 1970s the house had suffered from inadequate care for decades. Dry rot was endemic – leaking pipes and condensation the usual cause – with the most serious outbreak extending throughout the length of the western cornice. Some ceilings had gaping holes, some walls had mushy patches while deathwatch beetle and wood-worm rampaged.

Dangerous defects in the very structure of the house were also uncovered and the architects believed some of these had been deliberately concealed by Sir Charles Barry in the 1830s. Why? Possibly out of frustration with his client's continual barrage of instructions. William Bankes truly saw himself as the guiding architectural spirit behind the project but did not have the training. Perhaps Barry simply decided when Bankes fled to Venice in 1841 that he had had enough.

Caroe and Martin discovered serious cracking in the side walls of the main stair, caused by interference with a complex series of structural trussed partitions which Barry had formed within apparently simple stud partitions. Thirty feet of steel had to be introduced to reduce continuing movement in an original beam which had already deflected six inches and sagged eight inches when concealed by Barry and was now in a perilous state. Barry's projecting cornice was also a highly dangerous structure: 'Temporary removal of one stone, weighing a third of a tonne, showed the factor of safety to be nil.'

A minor problem that gave the house its baleful smell of neglect was lack of ventilation; by 1981 only three windows in the entire house would open. Most had been painted solid for years, and the fetid atmosphere and plague of flies gave the interior a melancholic ambience. 'It felt like a stagnant pool with no air,' recalls Dudley Dodd, former Historic Buildings Advisor for the Trust, who organized visits for curatorial advisors to the Trust and acted as liaison officer between remaining members of the Bankes family and Kingston Lacy. 'It was not squalid but rather sad. So few rooms had been used latterly. Ralph had lived almost entirely downstairs. The ropes were still there from the days when the government had tried to help.'[3]

There were excitements and discoveries as the house was packed up for the builders to take over. Hidden in the garden fernery, abandoned and face down, was an important and previously unknown statue of the little known Egyptian god Hetep-baqef, presumably William's. Inside the house part of an eighth century bible from Northumbria, made at Wearmouth or Jarrow in Abbot Ceolfrith's time and described by the Venerable Bede, was found in a damp box in the boot room.

Hidden away in the attic rooms were great quantities of carved woodwork and dusty panelling, presumably purchased by William. Some may have been intended as part of a complicated scheme for new garniture, or as a model for new work: 'among the carvings at Kingston Lacy as models there is a broken and worm-eaten sunflower that is of no value at all except for the freedom of style,' he once wrote to Osborne. 'This you will look out, and carry it up with you when you go to London.'[4]

Another 'find' was the stash of letters from floor to ceiling in the Muniment room, which today has a large lock dated 1862. This extraordinary cupboard of a room contained about seventy 'tills' or pigeonholes of material, much of it damp and damaged, on numbered shelves. There were also several trunks, boxes and bundles of papers. In the nearby estate office were thousands of estate records about rents and repairs, leases and land sales, negotiations and settlements kept by generations of Bankes, some dating from medieval times. There were hundreds of bits of paper from William to Osborne and Seymour as well as packages of letters to his family about his efforts to transform the house; and page upon unpublished page of his thoughts about art and architecture in England and Europe.

Not quite pristine, these, as Daphne, Walter's unmarried daughter, had 'sorted and arranged' many of them in the long days of enforced leisure before World War Two. She retyped a selection with occasional annotations but it is impossible to know to what extent she changed the context or removed or destroyed any with embarrassing content. Some surviving letters written by William John are severely cut or have lines through, but it seems probable that the cutting was mostly done so that Osborne or Seymour could take away and work on the section intended for them. The blacking out may have been the work of contemporary relatives, Anne or George, rather than Daphne. When the letters were first discovered and before they were moved to the Dorset County Record Office, where they are now, James Lees-Milne, responsible for rescuing so many country houses for the National Trust, contemplated writing William's biography. Approaching 73 and tired by the journeys to Dorset, he eventually declined. One compensation, he said, was getting to know Viola, who regaled him with mildly salacious stories about her eccentric relations, referring always to William as 'The Naughty One'.[5] A strong-minded woman, she too had been banished from the house, in her case by her mother Henrietta when in 1927 she had decided to marry a charming but untitled Australian doctor, Norman Hall.

Lees-Milne was not the only one to fall under Viola's sway at this time. Dodd too found Viola, then in her early eighties, 'a cultivated and highly intelligent woman who could be charming as well as sharp-tongued'. Viola found returning to the revived house now an intensely emotional experience, which triggered an avalanche of memories. She had been back once before with her husband on a public open day and, although she signed the visitors' book, did not make herself known to her brother. 'I don't the least want to see him,' she told a guide who offered to fetch him.[6]

'She was there quite a lot after Ralph's death,' recalls Dodd. 'For her it was a return to the childhood memories which had been denied her. She relived for us just how it must have been, and not much appeared to have changed at all in sixty years.'

When Kingston Lacy entered the National Trust fold, Viola felt herself brought back into a family circle of sorts. 'As the sister of the donor and the author of the only book on the house, *A Dorset Heritage: the Story of Kingston Lacy*, she now enjoyed an importance and a status in the eyes of her friends and literary acquaintances that she had not enjoyed for years,' explained Dodd. Her book, first published in 1953, was reissued to coincide with the opening with a new foreword by her friend, the historian A.L. Rowse in which he paid tribute to William John Bankes as the man who created this veritable treasure house. Shortly before the house was finished in 1986, the Trust suggested that she invite her well-connected friends and as many Bankes relatives as she could muster for an *al fresco* lunch on trestle tables the length of the terrace. It was a memorable occasion when the house took on the air of an Italian palazzo, just as William had intended. Viola's return, after an exile of nearly sixty years, had a resonance that was not lost on the other guests. She particularly enjoyed meeting again the octogenarian gardener Dukes, who had married the maid, Gladys, more than fifty years earlier.

But there was a darker side to the euphoria. Ralph's son John inherited traits of eccentricity and severe shyness, but also a genuine love and concern for the family estate his ancestors had owned and lived in for three centuries. John had grown up at Kingston Lacy, read agriculture at Oxford and, expecting to take over the Bankes properties, studied to become a Chartered Surveyor with a large firm specializing in managing landed estates. He was passionate and knowledgeable about his family home and made it his business to walk around and get to know the tenants and their families. But by the late 1960s, so he told friends, he was persuaded to give up his absolute right to inherit in return for more than adequate financial provision, so as to avoid inheritance tax. When he realised that the Bankes properties would pass into the hands of the National Trust during his own lifetime, he began to experience a sorrow and alienation eerily close to the experience of exile suffered by his ancestor William John. Like him, he too was an original who refused to conform. Denied the pleasure of living as an adult among the treasures of Kingston Lacy, he would spend hours in the Victoria and Albert Museum where he felt safe. Neither John nor his sister Mary returned to Kingston Lacy after its restoration by the Trust.

John had wit, intelligence and a professional training but he dropped out and grew a beard down to his waist. Friends tried to keep in touch, but he invariably reverted to his chosen solitary life. Professional social workers were unable to help him. He was un-communicative if rational, and increasingly immune to those who warned him of the dangers of refusing to wear warm clothes in winter, or scavenging for food.

One friend remembers visiting him in a London hospital and being told by doctors that he was suffering the worst case of frost-bite they had ever encountered. Totally isolated, he behaved as if he were living in exile; in his case it broke him and he gave up on life. He died from cancer, aged fifty-nine, in 1996 and was buried at the fine old Norman Church of St Nicholas at Studland, about half an hour from Kingston Lacy in the shadow of Old Harry. The few relatives who attended remember a moving silence beforehand as the hearse stopped outside Corfe Castle, a favourite childhood haunt of John as of so many of his ancestors.

It is hard to imagine how an estate the size of Kingston Lacy could continue to be run successfully in private hands in the twenty-first century. Descendants of the Calcrafts, the largely Whig polit-ical family who had a number of boundary (and other) disputes with their Bankes neighbours, still live at Rempstone Hall, near Corfe, a beautiful but small Georgian house and a reduced estate now of 4,500 acres. The family acquired it in 1757 along with much of Wareham. Perhaps the Kingston Lacy estate might have tottered on for a few years only to go the way of nearby Encombe House, built by the Pitt family in the shadow of Corfe in the eighteenth century and bought in 1807 by the Earl of Eldon, whose daughter had married William's brother Edward. The Scott family put their house on the market in 2002 with an asking price of £15 million.

It was sold to an American. Such estates can no longer function as private homes and there is limited demand for them from pop stars or business tycoons. Often they lie derelict for years until either an institution transforms them into a hotel or conference centre or the house is demolished. Occasionally, but rarely, a family is wealthy or devoted enough to cherish and nurture such a house. Chatsworth survives in the hands of the hardworking and ever more inventive Duke and Duchess of Devonshire and is open to the public now as it always has been even to 'the humblest individual,'[7] but at the price of developing it into a leisure park.

Kingston Lacy was finally opened to the public on 28 April 1986 and the story of the mansion's rescue was given widespread media coverage. The new accounts gave full prominence to the role of William John Bankes in creating the house, a copy of an Italian palazzo in the heart of rural Dorset. In 1900, when *Country Life* had written about the stately red granite obelisk having been brought back from Philae by Giovanni Belzoni, no mention was made of William. But in 1986, in the authoritative John Cornforth's series of six articles, *Country Life* could admit at last that Kingston Lacy 'owes its present character to William Bankes'.

Generally, the newspapers' reactions vindicated the years devoted to the task by Anthony Mitchell, then the Trust's Regional Historic Buildings Representative, and his cohorts of advisers. Mitchell, having to decide which member of the Bankes family had given the house its overriding character, had no difficulty in selecting William John. But there are also strong touches of Henrietta in the Edwardian-flavoured drawing room and pretty bedrooms.

Impeccable restoration, said the *Financial Times* before launching a small volley of 'minor criticisms'. The author described the use of plate glass for the windows on the stair loggia as 'quite simply looking wrong. It would not have been made in such large sheets in the 1830s.' How wrong he was. A more valid concern, with which the Trust is still grappling, was the decision to remove the Guido Reni *Dawn Separating Night from Day* from the library ceiling. While admitting that the painting was 'rather overpowering', the author went on to comment that its loss was important. 'The impression that the collector William John Bankes was trying to achieve from his continental exile *was* of an exotic and rich palace. The beautifully restored Spanish room has exactly maintained that flavour – a stage set for a passionately conceived collection. Any thinning out of the collection or major rearrangements to suit contemporary taste has to be resisted.'[8]

For me, the tale of the library ceiling is one of the most poignant in the story of William John Bankes. Ralph Bankes's little guidebook explains that this painting was originally a fresco, then transferred to canvas, 'a remarkable achievement and one not attempted before'. During his exile, William's preoccupation with paintings for decorative purposes, especially ceilings, became intense. He bought most paintings with a precise idea of where they would hang and the effect they would have in transforming the room.

He seems to have bought the Reni, which had been removed in 1840 from a ceiling in the Palazzo Zani in Bologna, and had it transferred to canvas early on in his exile, intending to install it in the central oval of the dining room – probably the least successful room in the house. However, the family later found this unsatisfactory and transferred it to the library ceiling where it was much too close to the spectator and the wrong size. William planned to raise the ceiling and put another picture in its place but ultimately capitulated to Anne's distaste for further upheaval. Building work in the library was, owing to the precious nature of the books, particularly troublesome. In one of his last letters to his sister he gave instructions to leave the library ceiling as it was and move the canvas to the stables. 'It will be easy to have all this stowed away safely over the stables, and when we are both gone, those who come after us can apply them if they will.'[9] Yet those in the Bankes family who came after lacked knowledge or drive to do anything with this. It has foxed experts at the National Trust too. Taken down to remedy the effects of its botched transfer from plaster to canvas, the detached fresco is, at time of writing, still in the National Trust workshop awaiting restoration. One glance upward to the unembellished, uncorniced, unpainted library ceiling reveals much about William's gloriously fertile imagination and unbounded vision.

Some of the pictures William bought have turned out to be copies – but his belief that he had found an oil sketch of *Las Meninas* should not be criticised as showing he had a bad eye – 'since most people had never seen the original it was a very "good" mistake to have made and is remarkable and interesting in its own right,' is the view of Alastair Laing from the National Trust.[10] His 'Raphael' too, though no longer thought to be a Raphael, is a magnificent picture which once formed part of the collection of King Charles I and before that belonged to Vincenzo I Gonzaga, 4th Duke of Mantua. In 1853 William commissioned a frame for it from Pietro Giusti in Siena in order to incorporate medallions of the painting's previous owners.

A panel of advisers was established to help decide which paintings needed cleaning or major restoration work, and how and where they should be hung. But the *Judgment of Solomon*, which the Bankes family had always insisted was by Giorgione, presented particular problems because of its several layers of overpainting. The Trust had to decide whether William had had it overpainted or if this was how he had bought it. 'The Great Giorgione', he wrote to his father, in 1821, 'which I continue to like better every time I look upon it,' was to hang in the Saloon, he said. It was clearly always unfinished – there were, for example, never any babies in the picture. But its composition was also unresolved. Ultimately the decision was taken to clean the painting to consolidate the flaking, discoloured paint surface. Restoration experts uncovered several earlier compositions, none of them completed, beneath the extensive later repainting which covered up the more ambiguous areas in an attempt to present a more unified whole. The painting, handed back to Kingston Lacy, is still unfinished, its final form uncertain and still without babies. But it now has a unity and force and one can see the allure that drove William to buy it.

Would the National Trust version of Kingston Lacy have chimed with William's dreams of turning a modest Carolean brick gentleman's house into a semi-Venetian palazzo which nonetheless recalls Inigo Jones and the period of the original house?

'It's a brilliant compromise,' says Alastair Laing. In his view the seeds of William's genius lay in his obsessiveness, the results of which can still be admired today. 'I can't think of another English gentleman owner who paid that amount of attention to every detail from dado rail to door handles, which is crucial for what he acquires.'[11]

The Spanish Room shows his brilliance and originality at its best. Other collectors at the time were not interested in amassing works of one country in a single room but were collecting according to period or artist or mixing. Nor was Spanish art in vogue until the middle of the century, and even then remained an acquired taste. His gilded leather walls might be dismissed as responding to a fashion – the 6th Duke of Devonshire, for example, already had several magnificent leather-clad rooms at Chatsworth before William organised his. But William, concerned with the dynamics of how a painting would function within a particular room, was using the leather to create an overall harmonising effect. Again, each of the Marochetti figures would be lifeless on their own. But between them there is a dynamism, an energy flow, that gives a charge as you enter the landing where they stand.

'And does it add to the richness of effect?' William asked his sister apropos the cartouches or oval medallions over the pictures in the Spanish Room: richness his touchstone of a successful effect. He once described a coffee house in Padua as 'vast in extent, magnificent in every detail and in point of taste is in my opinion the finest work of modern Europe, nobody can conceive anything to exceed the richness of the materials or the propriety of their application and exquisiteness of the work, it is a building after my own heart.'[12] William's artistic heart, his instinct, believed that an ancient Egyptian obelisk could well adorn a lawn which also boasted ancient Venetian well heads and lead into a house where copies of Renaissance cupids coexisted with gilded baroque woodwork.

Not everyone admired William's wildly eclectic taste. Two of the twentieth century's finest arbiters of artistic good judgment, Henry

Moore and Roger Fry, considered the house contained much that was overrated. Viola enjoyed recounting how when she was a child Roger Fry had come to stay and when he saw the *Judgment of Solomon* immediately commented: 'That painting isn't by Giorgione, it's by Sebastiano del Piombo,' of whom Mrs Henrietta Bankes had never heard. 'She said not a word but walked to the fireplace, pulled the bell and said to the appearing footman, "Pack Mr Fry's bag, he is leaving by the next train."'[13] Perhaps the real tragedy of William's fine and idiosyncratic collection is that the one truly great painting, the Velasquez full-length portrait of Philip IV of Spain, was sold in 1896 for £10,000 by Walter Bankes. It is now in the Isabella Stewart Gardner Museum in Boston.

'No eye that is observant to beautiful effect will have been insensible in Italy to the gay and charming contrast produced by those streams of light glittering through the tangles of leaves and blossoms which gush through grated openings pierced at intervals in the northern face of a garden wall . . .'[14] William's eye had always been keenly observant to fine effect and the stacks of boxes filled with his observations on art and architecture wherever he travelled bear eloquent witness to his desire to leave the world more exquisitely adorned than he found it.

Kingston Lacy is William John Bankes's testament to his personal search for beauty.

Notes

~

The following abbreviations have been used:
WJB   William John Bankes
DRO   Dorset County Record Office
JMA   John Murray Archive
KLA   Kingston Lacy Archive
BLJ   *Byron's Letters and Journals* by Leslie A. Marchand, 13 vols, John Murray, 1973–94

CHAPTER 1: Ancestors

1. WJB to Henry Bankes, Cairo, 3 Sept. 1815, DRO.
2. George Birkbeck Hill (ed.), *Boswell's Life of Johnson*, Oxford, Clarendon Press, 1934, 6 vols, I: 145.
3. Sir Joseph Banks, 'A Visit to Kingston Lacy' quoted in Desmond Hawkins (ed.), *Wessex, A Literary Celebration,* Century, London, 1991.
4. WJB to Margaret Bankes, 24 Sept. 1812, DRO.
5. Henry Bankes to Margaret Bankes, 14 Aug. 1779, DRO.
6. Henry Bankes to Margaret Bankes, 28 Sept. 1779, DRO.
7. Henry Bankes to Margaret Bankes, 24 Nov. 1779, DRO.
8. Henry Bankes to Margaret Bankes, 23 Sept. 1779, DRO.
9. Quoted in Antony Cleminson, 'The Transition from Kingston Hall to Kingston Lacy', *Architectural History* 1988, Vol. XXXI: 120.
10. *Gentleman's Magazine*, 1823, p. 641.
11. All information about the ball from Frances Bankes's letter to her mother-in-law Margaret Bankes, quoted in Antony Cleminson, 'Christmas at Kingston Lacy, Frances Bankes's Ball of 1791', *Apollo,* Dec. 1991.
12. WJB, Blue Memorandum Book 1836–1841, DRO.

CHAPTER 2: Education

1. Frances Bankes Notebook, 11 Dec. 1786, DRO.
2. Frances Bankes to son Henry Bankes, 1785, DRO.
3. Public Schools Commission; Evidence of James Mure and R.J. Phillimore, cited by Lawrence Tanner, 'Westminster School', *Country Life*, 1951.
4. Anne Falmouth to Margaret Bankes, 19 Sept. 1799, DRO.
5. Clark, J.W. and Hughes T.M. (eds), *The Life and Letters of Rev Adam Sedgwick,* Cambridge, Cambridge University Press, 1890, 2 vols, I: 259.
6. William Wynne to WJB, 12 Nov. 1804, DRO.
7. Wilfred S. Dowden (ed.), *Journal of Thomas Moore*, Associated University Presses, 1983–91, IV: 1540.
8. WJB to Margaret Bankes, postmarked 1 Nov. 1803, DRO.
9. Byron to John Murray, Ravenna, Nov. 9bre 19, 1820, *BLJ.*
10. Byron to James Wedderburn Webster, 31 Aug. 1811, *BLJ.*
11. WJB to Byron, 2 Jan. 1822, JMA.
12. Byron to John Murray, 9bre 19, 1820, *BLJ.*
13. WJB to Byron, 2 Jan. 1822, *BLJ.*
14. WJB to Byron, quoted in Viola Bankes, *A Dorset Heritage*, Anthony Mott, 1986.
15. Note by J.C. Hobhouse in his copy of Thomas Moore, *The Works of Lord Byron With His Letters and His Journals and His Life*, 14 vols, John Murray, Vol. I, p. 130, courtesy Brenthurst Library, South Africa.
16. *Journal of Mrs. Arbuthnot 1820–1832,* ed. Francis Bamford and the Duke of Wellington, Macmillan, 1950, I:327.
17. Sir William Wynne to WJB, 20 Oct. 1804, DRO.
18. Quoted in Kenneth Bourne (ed.), 'Letters of 3rd Vt Palmerston to Laurence and Elizabeth Sulivan, Camden 4th Series, *London Royal Historical Society*, 1973, Vol. XXIII.
19. Byron to Scrope Berdmore Davies, Newstead, 2 Sept. 1811. Quoted in T.A.J. Burnett, *Rise and Fall of a Regency Dandy*, John Murray, 1981.
20. Byron to Edward Noel Long, 23 Feb. 1807, *BLJ.*
21. WJB to Byron, 3 Mar. 1807, JMA.
22. Byron to WJB, 6 Mar. 1807, *BLJ.*
23. *ibid.*
24. WJB to Byron 18 Mar. 1807, JMA.

25. Byron to Edward Noel Long, 30 Mar. 1807, *BLJ.*
26. WJB to Byron, 18 Mar. 1807, JMA.
27. *The Farington Diary*, ed. James Greig Hutchinson 1924, 6 Apr. 1807, p. 11.
28. Sir William Wynne to WJB, 9 Mar. 1807, DRO.

CHAPTER 3: Travel

1. Sir Nathaniel Wraxall, *Historical Memoirs of his own Time, 1772–1884*, ed. Henry B.Wheatley, London, Bickers and Son, 1884, 5 vols, IV:79.
2. Sir R.I.Wilberforce, *Life of William Wilberforce*, John Murray, 1838, 5 vols, III:438.
3. Lord Broughton (John Cam Hobhouse), *Recollections of a Long Life*, ed. Lady Dorchester, II:125–127.
4. John William Ward (son of Dudley), *Letters to the Bishop of Llandaff*, London, 1840, pp. 203–6.
5. Quoted in R.G.Thorne (ed.), *The History of Parliament: House of Commons 1790–1820.*
6. WJB to Byron, Soughton, 18 Sept. 1811, JMA.
7. Byron to Scrope Davies, 2 Sept. 1811; Burnett, *Rise and Fall of a Regency Dandy*, p. 222.
8. WJB to Byron, 9 Nov. 1812, JMA.
9. Byron to Lady Caroline Lamb, 1 May 1812, *BLJ.*
10. Byron to Anne Isabella Milbanke, 31 Aug. 1813, *BLJ.*
11. Quoted Ethel C. Mayne, *Life and Letters of Anne Isabella, Lady Noel Byron*, Constable, 1929, p. 27.
12. *ibid.*
13. Anne Isabella Milbanke to Byron, 18 Oct. 1814, (*ibid*).
14. WJB to Byron, 9 Nov. 1812, JMA.
15. Sir William Wynne to WJB, 10 June 1814, DRO.
16. Quoted in Benita Eisler, *Byron Child of Passion Fool of Fame*, Penguin, 1999.
17. WJB to Margaret Bankes, 23 Dec. 1811, DRO.
18. A. Brett-James, *Life In Wellington's Army*, Allen and Unwin, 1979.
19. Quoted in Andrew Roberts, *Napoleon and Wellington*, Weidenfeld and Nicolson, 2001, p. 88.
20. WJB to Byron, 20 Jan. 1813, JMA.
21. *ibid.*
22. WJB to Byron, 21 Dec. 1812, JMA.

23. *ibid.*

24. WJB to Byron, 6 Mar. 1813, JMA.

25. WJB to Byron, Lisbon, 16 Mar. 1813, JMA.

26. *Heber Letters 1783–1832*, ed. R.H. Cholmondely, London, Batchworth, 1950, pp. 255–6.

27. *Diary and Correspondence of Charles Abbot, Lord Colchester*, ed. Charles Lord Colchester, 1861, 25 Nov. 1813, Vol III, p. 46.

28. William Buchanan, *Memoirs of Painting*, London, 1824.

29. 22 Nov. 1822 in *Private Letters of Princess Lieven to Prince Metternich 1820–1826*, ed. Peter Quennell, 1937, p. 155.

30. WJB to Frances Bankes, Galicia, n.d. 1813, DRO.

31. Anne Isabella Milbanke to Byron, n.d. 1814, quoted in Mayne, p. 470.

32. Quoted in F. Haskell, *Rediscoveries in Art*, 1980, p. 78.

33. WJB to Henry Bankes, Cairo, 3 Sept. 1815, DRO.

34. WJB to Henry Bankes, Alicante, 17–20 Oct. 1814, DRO.

35. WJB to Henry Bankes, Cairo, 3 Sept. 1815, DRO.

36. WJB to Henry Bankes, Alicante, 17–20 Oct. 1814, DRO.

37. WJB to Henry Bankes, Cairo, 3 Sept. 1815, DRO.

38. WJB to Henry Bankes, postscript Alicante, 20 Oct. 1814, DRO.

39. WJB to Henry Bankes, Cairo, 3 Sept. 1815, DRO.

40. WJB to Henry Bankes, Alicante, 17–20 Oct. 1814, DRO.

41. WJB to Henry Bankes, Alicante, 17–20 Oct. 1814 and WJB to Henry Bankes, Cairo, 3 Sept. 1815, DRO.

CHAPTER 4: Exploration

1. WJB to Henry Bankes, Cairo, 3 Sept. 1815, DRO.

2. *ibid.*

3. Byron to John Murray, Ravenna, 7 Aug. 1820, *BLJ.*

4. WJB to Henry Bankes, Cairo, 3 Sept. 1815, DRO.

5. P. Usick, *Adventures in Egypt and Nubia: The Travels of William John Bankes*, 2002.

6. William Turner, *Journal of a Tour in the Levant*, John Murray, 1820.

7. Henry Salt to Bessy Morgan, 22 May 1819, in J.J. Halls (ed.), *Life and Correspondence of Henry Salt*, London, 1834.

8. WJB to Henry Bankes, Cairo, 3 Sept. 1815, DRO.

9. All unnumbered quotes in this chapter taken from Giovanni Finati, *Life of Finati*, ed. W.J. Bankes, John Murray, 2 vols, 1830.

10. Unpublished account by WJB on or after his first journey in 1815, seen in BM; to be lodged at DRO.

11. *Life of Finati*, 1830.

12. Clifford Bosworth (ed.), *Some Correspondence concerning J.L. Burckhardt and Lady Hester Stanhope*, John Rylands University Library of Manchester, 1972.

13. Usick, *Adventures in Egypt and Nubia*.

14. WJB to Henry Bankes, n.d. *c.* 1817, DRO.

15. *Gentleman's Magazine*, 1855.

16. *Quarterly Review* No. 52, Jan. 1822.

17. Undated statement by WJB, DRO.

18. J.S. Buckingham to J.L. Burckhardt, c/o Henry Salt, 1816, DRO.

19. *ibid*.

20. Lady Hester Stanhope to WJB, 14 May 1816, DRO.

21. Lady Hester Stanhope to Michael Bruce, 21 Mar. 1816, quoted in Ian Bruce, *The Nun of Lebanon*, Collins, 1951.

22. Lady Hester Stanhope to Sir Joseph Banks, Mt Lebanon, 3 Jan. 1817 (courtesy of Natural History Museum).

23. Lady Hester Stanhope to M. Bruce, 5 Mar. 1816, quoted in Bruce, *The Nun of Lebanon*.

24. WJB to Lady Hester Stanhope, Tripoli, 17 June 1816 (courtesy of Wellcome Institute).

25. *ibid*.

26. *ibid*.

27. Lady Hester Stanhope to Dr Meryon, 23 June 1816 (courtesy of Wellcome Institute).

28. *ibid*.

29. *ibid*.

30. J.S. Buckingham to WJB, Feb. 1816, DRO.

31. *ibid*.

32. J.S. Buckingham to WJB, 30 Apr. 1816, DRO.

33. Lady Hester Stanhope to WJB, 14 May 1816, DRO.

34. J.S. Buckingham to Lady Hester Stanhope, 21 June 1816, DRO.

35. J.L. Burckhardt to WJB, July 1816, DRO.

36. WJB to J.L. Burckhardt, Cyprus, 15 Oct. 1817, DRO.

CHAPTER 5: Discovery

1. J.L. Burckhardt to WJB, 15 July 1816, DRO.
2. Quoted Usick, *Adventures in Egypt and Nubia*, p. 61.
3. WJB to Burckhardt, 15 Oct. 1817, DRO.
4. J.L. Burckhardt to WJB, quoted T.G.H. James, *Egypt Revealed*, 1997.
5. C.L. Irby and J. Mangles, *Travels in Egypt*, 1823.
6. *ibid.*
7. *ibid.*
8. Henry Salt to Julia Hanson, quoted J.J. Halls (ed.), *Life and Correspondence of Henry Salt FRS*, 2 vols, London, 1834.
9. Henry Salt to Mrs Hamilton, quoted Halls, *Life and Correspondence of Henry Salt*.
10. Henry Salt to Mrs Hamilton, 22 May 1819.
11. Charles Barry quoted Manley and Rée, *Henry Salt,* 2001.
12. Henry Salt to Mrs Hamilton, 22 May 1819, quoted James, *Egypt Revealed*, 1997.
13. WJB to William Hamilton, July 1819, quoted James, *Egypt Revealed*, 1997.
14. Bankes Collection of Drawings at Kingston Lacy, DRO and British Museum, includes many unsigned drawings and also considerable work paid for by Bankes undertaken by others, especially Linant and Ricci.
15. Quoted James, *Egypt Revealed*, 1997, p. 91.
16. Charles Barry, Diary of Travels (MS), RIBA Drawings Collection, London. Quoted Alfred Barry, *Life and Works of Sir Charles Barry*, 1867, p 67.
17. *Quarterly Review*, Oct. 1822.
18. Hyde Journal BL Add Mss 42102 f 91.
19. WJB to J.S. Buckingham, Thebes, 12 June 1819, DRO.
20. Belzoni to WJB, 22 Aug. 1819, DRO.
21. WJB to Nathaniel Pearce, Alexandria, 11 Oct. 1819, BL MSS.
22. Quoted Usick, 'Drawings of Egypt and Nubia', p 59.
23. WJB to Henry Bankes, n.d. 1817, DRO.
24. Byron to John Cam Hobhouse, Ravenna, 2 Aug. 1819, *BLJ.*
25. Byron to WJB, Venice, 20 Nov. 1819, *BLJ.*
26. Quoted Eisler, *Byron Child of Passion*, p. 647.
27. Byron to WJB, Venice, 20 Nov. 1819, *BLJ.*

28. Byron to WJB, 19 Feb. 1820, *BLJ*.
29. *Journal of Thomas Moore*, ed. Dowden, 1983–91, III:1191.
30. *ibid*.
31. *ibid*.
32. Byron to John Cam Hobhouse, Ravenna, 3 Mar. 1820, *BLJ*.
33. Byron to Richard Hoppner, Ravenna, 31 Jan. 1820, *BLJ*.
34. Byron to WJB, 19 Feb. 1820, *BLJ*.
35. *ibid*.
36. Byron to WJB, Ravenna, 26 Feb. 1820, *BLJ*.
37. Byron to John Murray, 14 Apr. 1817, *BLJ*.
38. John Murray's *Handbook for Travellers in Northern Italy*.
39. Byron to WJB, Ravenna, 26 Feb. 1820, *BLJ*.
40. From occasional diary of Frances Bankes, 1820, DRO.
41. Byron to John Murray, Ravenna, 8 octbre 1820, *BLJ*.
42. Richard Hoppner to WJB, Venice, 19 Mar. 1823, DRO.
43. Extracts from diary of Frances Bankes, 1820, DRO.

CHAPTER 6: Society

1. WJB to Byron, 2 Jan. 1822, JMA.
2. Wellington to Charles Arbuthnot, 18 May 1820, Wellington MSS quoted in Longford, *Wellington*.
3. *Maria Edgeworth in France and Switzerland: Selections from the Edgeworth Family Letters*, ed. C. Colvin, 1979.
4. *Private Letters of Princess Lieven*, 22 Feb. 1822.
5. *Recollections of the Table Talk of Samuel Rogers*, ed. Alexander Dyce, 1856.
6. Stanley Lane-Poole, *Life of Stratford Canning*, Longman, 1888, Vol. II.
7. WJB to Henry Salt, HJ1/227, DRO.
8. Annesley BL ADD Mss 19347 f 169.
9. Henry Salt to WJB, Cairo, 6 Jan. 1822, DRO.
10. *ibid*.
11. Quoted Manley and Rée, *Henry Salt*, 2001.
12. *ibid*.
13. WJB to Henry Bankes, postmarked 16 Oct. 1821, DRO.
14. *ibid*.
15. *Illustrated London News*, 18 Apr. 1868.
16. Baillie to WJB, Naples, 24 Jan. 1820, DRO.

17. Peel MS BL Add 40372, 27 Jan 1825.
18. WJB to Henry Bankes, 1824, DRO.
19. Quoted in K.W. Jones-Robertson, *Historic Houses in Ffestiniog and District*, Merioneth Historical and Record Society, 1959.
20. WJB to Mr Conway, 23 July 1826, Bankes family archive (BFA).
21. WJB to Martin, 12 Dec. 1831, BFA.
22. WJB to Martin, 18 Dec. 1831, BFA.
23. *ibid.*
24. David Blisset, 'Veneerer-in-Chief to the Nobility' in *The Victorian Great House*, ed. M. Airs, 2000.
25. WJB to Frances Bankes, undated, DRO.
26. *Journal of Mrs. Arbuthnot*, June 1822.
27. Sir H. Maxwell (ed.), *Life and Letters of GWF, 4th Earl Clarendon*, 1913.
28. *The Times*, 29 Nov. 1822.
29. Clark and Hughes (eds), *Life of Sedgwick*.
30. *Palmerston–Sullivan* letters.
31. *Clarendon* ed. Maxwell, p. 37.
32. The Rt. Hon. Charles W Wynn to the Duke of Buckingham, 30 Dec. 1822, *Memoirs of George IV*, p. 401.
33. *Clarendon* ed. Maxwell.
34. Diary of Hudson Gurney, April 1823, quoted in unpublished draft biography of WJB for *History of Parliament* by D.R. Fisher.
35. Clark and Hughes (eds), *Life of Sedgwick*.
36. *The Journal of the Hon. Henry Edward Fox 1818–1830*, ed. Earl of Illchester, Thornton Butterworth,1823.
37. Mrs Arbuthnot to WJB, undated but watermarked 1821, DRO.
38. WJB to Byron, 2 Jan. 1822, JMA.
39. WJB to John Murray, 24 Nov. 1821, JMA.
40. *Gentleman's Magazine*, 1823, p. 469.
41. WJB to Duke of Wellington, 8 Nov. 1823, University of Southampton Library Archives.
42. *Farington Diary*, ed. Hutchinson, 1824.
43. *The Times*, 1 Dec. 1823.
44. WJB to Hobhouse, 4 Mar. 1825, in Broughton, *Recollections*, ed. Dorchester, 1909–11.
45. *Journal of Mrs Arbuthnot*, 1822 and 1824.
46. Undated but paper watermarked 1824, KL folder.
47. *Journal of Thomas Moore,* ed. Dowden, Feb. 1829.

48. WJB to George Bankes, in Daphne Bankes notes, KLA.

49. WJB to Byron, 2 Jan. 1822, JMA.

50. *Journal of Thomas Moore*, ed. Dowden, III/1042.

51. *Journal of Henry Edward Fox*, ed. Illchester, 1823.

52. Jasper Ridley, *Lord Palmerston*, Constable, 1970, pp. 85–7.

53. Quoted in unpublished draft biography of WJB for *History of Paliament* by D.R. Fisher.

54. *Journal of Mrs. Arbuthnot*, 15 Nov. 1826.

55. *The Journal of Sir Walter Scott*, ed. W.E.K. Anderson, Oxford, Clarendon, 1972.

56. WJB to John Murray, 24 Nov. 1821, JMA.

57. *Quarterly Review*, Vol. 52, Jan. 1822.

58. *The Times*, 6 June 1825.

59. WJB to J.S. Buckingham, 12 June 1819, DRO.

60. *Journal of Thomas Moore,* ed. Dowden, III:976.

CHAPTER 7: Arrest

1. Anon, *Don Leon*, 1830s, published 1866 then by Fortune Press in an edition of 1,000 copies.

2. WJB to John Murray, 8 Nov. 1929, JMA.

3. John Barker to WJB, 29 Oct. 1827, DRO.

4. Parliamentary Report, 23 July 1832.

5. WJB to Henry Bankes, see Daphne Bankes notes, p. 306.

6. Henry Bankes to Georgina Bankes, 2 Aug. 1829, DRO.

7. Note by WJB, 6 Oct. 1829, DRO.

8. *Journal of Mrs. Arbuthnot*, Sept. 1830.

9. WJB to Henry Bankes, 18 Sept. 1830, DRO.

10. Broughton, *Recollections*, ed. Dorchester, Vol. IV, 5 July 1832.

11. *Dorset County Chronicle and Somersetshire Gazette*, undated cutting 1832, DRO.

12. All the above account taken from *The Times*, 8 June 1833.

13. *Punishments and Particularly that of Death*, HM Law Commissioners British Sessional Papers, 1836.

14. *The Times*, 3 Dec. 1833.

15. *ibid*.

16. *ibid*.

17. *Wellington Political Correspondence*, ed. Brooke and Gandy, Vol. I.
18. C. Skinner Matthews to Byron, 13 Jan. 1811, quoted in Louis Crompton, *Byron and Greek Love*, 1985.
19. Quoted in A.H. Manchester, *Modern Legal History*, Butterworth, 1980.
20. *Gentleman's Magazine*, 1835.

CHAPTER 8: Punishment

1. Quoted by David Blissett, 'Veneerer-in-Chief to the Nobility' in *The Victorian Great House*, ed. M. Airs, 2000.
2. WJB undated notes, Memorandum Book, DRO.
3. Charles Barry to Henry Bankes, 18 July 1829, KLA.
4. WJB to George Bankes, postmarked 29 May 1844, DRO.
5. WJB Memorandum Book, DRO.
6. *ibid.*
7. *ibid.*
8. WJB, undated notes, DRO.
9. WJB to George Bankes, Kingston Hall, 11 Dec. 1837, DRO.
10. WJB Memorandum Book, DRO.
11. WJB to George Bankes, 11 Dec. 1837, DRO.
12. Clerk of Works, Kingston Lacy to WJB, n.d., DRO.
13. WJB Memorandum Book 1836–1840, DRO.
14. WJB to George Bankes, 11 Dec. 1837, DRO.
15. WJB to Margaret Bankes, n.d., DRO.
16. Charles Barry to WJB, 6 Jan. 1840, DRO.
17. Charles Barry to WJB, 9 Jan. 1840, DRO.
18. George Bankes to WJB, n.d., DRO.
19. WJB to Duke of Wellington, 27 Sept. 1840, DRO.
20. Broughton, *Recollections*.
21. WJB 'Observations on Art and Architecture' n.d., DRO.
22. Parliamentary Papers: Reports from Committees/Minutes of Evidence, 8 June 1841, pp. 54–57.
23. *ibid.*
24. Bennett's statement as quoted in 1841 indictment and charge, *Queen v. Bankes*, DRO.
25. Hobhouse letter (1841) quoted in unpublished biography of WJB for House of Commons section of *History of Parliament* by D.R. Fisher.

NOTES

26. *Solicitor's Journal and Reporter*, 1860, p. 783.
27. Falmouth to J.S. Gregory, 5 Oct. 1841, DRO.
28. Unsigned, 14 Sept. 1841, DRO.
29. WJB to George Bankes, quoted Daphne Bankes, KLA.
30. Falmouth to J.S. Gregory, 25 Sept. 1841, DRO.
31. Falmouth to J.S. Gregory, 30 Sept. 1841, DRO.
32. WJB to Henry Falmouth, Florence, 4 Dec. 1850, refers to separate explanatory memorandum.
33. *The Times*, 10 May 1842.
34. *ibid*.
35. Falmouth to J.S. Gregory, 6 Oct. 1841, DRO.
36. J.S. Gregory to Falmouth, 5 Oct. 1841, DRO.
37. *ibid*.
38. *The Times*, 10 May 1842.

CHAPTER 9: Venice

1. Byron to Scrope Davies, 17 Dec. 1818.
2. Byron to John Murray, Ravenna, 3 Mar. 1820, *BLJ*.
3. Ann Radcliffe, *The Mysteries of Udolpho*, 1966.
4. Frances Trollope, *A Visit to Italy*, Richard Bentley, 1842.
5. John Pemble, *Venice Rediscovered,* 1995.
6. Frances Trollope, *Visit to Italy*.
7. *Effie in Venice*, ed. Mary Lutyens, Pallas Editions, 1999.
8. *Handbook for Travellers in Northern Italy*, John Murray, 1842.
9. WBJ to Anne Falmouth, Padua, 16 Sept. 1847, DRO.
10. John Ruskin, *The Stones of Venice*, Everyman, 1898.

CHAPTER 10: Family

1. J.S. Gregory to WJB, 3 Nov. 1841, DRO.
2. J.S. Gregory to WJB, 31 Dec. 1841, DRO.
3. WJB to Henry Falmouth, undated, approx. 1844, DRO.
4. *ibid*.
5. *ibid*.
6. George Bankes to WJB, 26 July 1845, DRO.

7. WJB to Henry Falmouth, undated, approx. 1844, DRO.
8. *ibid*.
9. WJB to J.S. Gregory, 21 Sept. 1844, DRO.
10. *ibid*.
11. WJB to George Bankes, Rome, 15 Oct. 1844, DRO.
12. WJB to George Bankes, undated, DRO.
13. *ibid*.
14. Bankes family papers.
15. John Latimer, *The Annals of Bristol 1887–1900*, 3 vols. reprinted Bath, Kinsmead, 1970.
16. WJB, undated (top cut off), DRO.
17. WJB to George Bankes, Rome, 15 Oct. 1844, DRO.
18. WJB to George Bankes, 23 Jan. 1844, DRO.
19. WJB to George Bankes, 30 May 1845, DRO.
20. WJB to Osborne, undated, DRO.
21. WJB to Osborne, undated, DRO.
22. WJB Memorandum, 30 Jan. 1849, DRO.
23. WJB to George Bankes, 5/12 May 1844, DRO.
24. *ibid*.
25. *ibid*.
26. *ibid*.
27. WJB to George Bankes, 15 Oct. 1844, DRO.
28. *ibid*.
29. WJB to George Bankes, Perugia, 30 May 1845, DRO.
30. Agreement for coasting voyages etc. schedule A PRO 1848.
31. Quotes from Seymour, undated, KLA.

CHAPTER 11: Memory

1. WJB to Anne Falmouth, Verona, 11 May 1846, DRO.
2. WJB to Francesco Vason, 13 Mar. 1848, DRO.
3. WJB to Francesco Vason, 26 Mar. 1851, DRO.
4. Bill for October 1852, DRO.
5. WJB to Anne Falmouth, Verona, 11 May 1846, DRO.
6. *Foglie de Verona*, No. 34, 1846, DRO.
7. *Foglie de Verona*, No. 228, 1849, DRO.
8. Quoted in Pemble, *Venice Rediscovered*, 1995.

9. WJB to Seymour, undated, DRO.

10. WJB to Anne Falmouth, undated *c.* 1853, DRO.

11. WJB to Seymour, undated *c.* 1847, DRO.

12. Flagg, *Venice*, 1853.

13. Edward Leeves, 15 Apr. 1848 in *Leaves from a Victorian Diary*, ed. John Sparrow, Secker and Warburg, 1985.

14. Leeves, 11 May 1848, *ibid*.

15. WJB Memorandum, 2 May 1849, DRO.

16. Daphne Bankes notes, 1932, KLA.

17. Effie Ruskin to her mother, quoted *Effie in Venice*, ed. Lutyens.

18. WJB to George Bankes, Venice, 3 May 1851, DRO.

19. WJB to Anne Falmouth, 27 Nov. 1850, DRO.

CHAPTER 12: Pride

1. *Art History*, Journal of the Association of Art Historians, Vol. 24 No. 2, Apr. 2001.

2. James Lees-Milne, *The Bachelor Duke*, John Murray, 1991.

3. WJB to Anne Falmouth, 29 Mar. 1855, DRO.

4. WJB to Anne Falmouth, 18 Nov. 1853, DRO.

5. WJB Instructions, undated approx. 1853, DRO.

6. WJB to Anne Falmouth, Venice, 14 June 1851; extracts only survive. DRO.

7. *ibid*.

8. WJB to Anne Falmouth, Venice, 1 July 1853, DRO.

9. WJB to Lady Burghersh, 11 Sept. 1840, quoted Viola Bankes, *A Dorset Heritage*, p. 173.

10. WJB to George Bankes, Rome, 15 Oct. 1844, DRO.

11. *ibid*.

12. WJB to Anne Falmouth, Venice, 22 Mar. 1853, DRO.

13. *ibid*.

14. *ibid*.

15. *ibid*.

16. Quoted in Philip Ward-Jackson, 'Monuments by Marochetti', *Journal of Warburg and Courtauld Institutes*, 1990, Vol. 53.

17. WJB to George Bankes, 21 Nov. 1852, DRO.

18. *ibid*.

19. WJB to J.S. Gregory, 26 Sept. 1853, DRO.
20. J.S. Gregory to WJB, 8 Oct. 1853, DRO.
21. William Castleman to WJB, 18 Apr. 1838, DRO.
22. Information from Edward Bourke, Chettle Estate, conversation with author, 12 June 2003. There is no written evidence of any connection between the Bankes and Castleman families but their assistance to WJB was well known among Castleman descendants.
23. WJB Memorandum, undated, DRO.
24. WJB to Seymour, 5 May 1854, DRO.
25. WJB to Seymour, marked *read Dec 30th 1854*, DRO.
26. WJB instructions to Seymour, marked *arrival july 4 1854*, DRO.
27. WJB to Seymour, undated, DRO.
28. WJB to Anne Falmouth, 5 May 1854, DRO.
29. WJB to Anne Falmouth, Paris, 28 Oct. 1853, DRO.
30. On behalf of Baron Marochetti to Edmund Bankes, 2 Dec. 1856, DRO.
31. Public Record Office (PRO) Kew, fo7466.
32. WJB to George Bankes, 1844, DRO.
33. WJB to Anne Falmouth, 11 May 1846, DRO.
34. WJB to George Bankes, undated Memorandum, DRO.
35. Francesco Vason to WJB, 15 May 1855, DRO.
36. Note dated 11 June 1855, DRO.
37. WJB to Anne Falmouth, 5 May 1854, DRO.
38. Daphne Bankes notes p. 338, KLA.
39. A. Malcolm to George Bankes, 26 Aug. 1855, KLA.
40. *ibid.*
41. George Bankes to A. Malcolm, 3 Sept. 1855, KLA.
42. Public Record Office (PRO) Kew fo7466.
43 Pemble, *Venice Rediscovered*, p. 126.

EPILOGUE

1. Viola Bankes, *A Dorset Heritage*, 1986.
2. Betke Zamoyska, descendant of Albert Bankes, conversation with author, 21 Mar. 2002.
3. Dudley Dodd, conversation with author, 22 July 2002.
4. WJB to Osborne, undated Memorandum, DRO.
5. James Lees-Milne, 11 Feb. 1984, in *Holy Dread, Diaries 1982–1984*, ed.

Michael Bloch, John Murray, 2001.

6. James Lees-Milne, 16 Mar. 1984, *ibid.*
7. Chatsworth Guide Book, 2002.
8. *Financial Times*, 2 Sept. 1985.
9. WJB to Anne Falmouth, 5 May 1854, DRO.
10. Alastair Laing, conversation with author, 23 July 2001.
11. *ibid.*
12. WJB to Anne Falmouth, 16 Sept. 1847, DRO.
13. Recounted in James Lees-Milne, *Holy Dread*, ed. Bloch.
14. WJB 'Observations on Art and Architecture', DRO.

Bibliography

~

The principal archive on which this book was based is the Bankes Collection at the Dorset County Record Office (DRO) in Dorchester. Of the papers and drawings at Kingston Lacy, most have now been deposited in the County Record Office. There are two leather-bound manuscript volumes containing Bankes's travel notes from Egypt at the British Museum presented in 1923 by G. Nugent Bankes, but most of the Egyptian drawings on temporary loan to the Department of Ancient Egypt and Sudan at the British Museum are being relocated with the main collection. Other unpublished sources include the John Murray Archive at 50, Albemarle Street, London W1.

All books in the following edited list were published in London unless otherwise stated.

Airs M. (ed.), *The Victorian Great House*, Oxford University Department for Continuing Education (OUDCE), 2000

Anglesey, Marquess of, *One Leg: The Life and Letters of H. W. Paget, 1768–1854*, New York, William Morrow, 1951

Bamford, Francis and the Duke of Wellington (eds.), *The Journal of Mrs. Arbuthnot 1820–32*, 2 vols, Macmillan and Co., 1950

Bankes, George, *The Story of Corfe Castle*, John Murray, 1853

Bankes, Viola, *A Kingston Lacy Childhood*, Wimborne, Dovecote Press, 1986

——*A Dorset Heritage: The Story of Kingston Lacy*, Anthony Mott, 1986

Bankes, W. J., *Geometrical Elevation of an Obelisk from the Island of Philae*, John Murray, 1821

Barry, Rev. Alfred, *The Life and Works of Sir Charles Barry*, John Murray, 1867

Beazly, E., *Maddocks and the Wonder of Wales*, Faber & Faber, 1967

Belzoni, Giuseppe, *Narrative of the Operations and Recent Discoveries within the Pyramids, Temples, Tombs and Excavations in Egypt and Nubia*, 2 vols, London, 1822

Bloch, Michael (ed.), *Holy Dread, Diaries 1982–1984* by James Lees-Milne, John Murray, 2001

Bond, Thomas, *History and Description of Corfe Castle*, London, 1883

Brett-James, A., *Life In Wellington's Army*, Allen and Unwin, 1979

Brigtocke, Hugh, *William Buchanan and the 19th Century Art Trade: 100 letters to his agents in London and Italy*, London, Paul Mellon Center for Studies in Art, 1982

Brooke, J. and Gandy, J. (eds.), *The Prime Minister's Papers: Wellington Political Correspondence*, London, HMSO, 1975

Buchanan, William, *Memoirs of Painting*, 2 vols, London, 1824

Buckingham, J.S., *Travels Among the Arab Tribes . . .* Longman and Co, 1825

Burnett, T.A.J., *The Rise and Fall of a Regency Dandy: The Life and Times of Scrope Berdmore Davies*, John Murray, 1981

Cleminson, Antony, 'The Bankes' Fifty Year Search for an Adequate Dining Room' in *Architectural History* (Journal of the Society of Architectural Historians of Great Britain), 1988, XXXI

——— 'Frances Bankes 1791 Letter' in *Apollo* Magazine, Dec. 1991, p. 405

Colchester, Lord (ed.), *Diary and Correspondence of Charles Abbot, Lord Colchester*, 3 vols, John Murray, 1861

Crompton, Louis, *Byron and Greek Love: Homophobia in 19th Century England*, Berkeley, University of California Press, 1985

Davenport-Hines, Richard, *Sex, Death and Punishment: Attitudes Towards Sex in Britain Since the Renaissance*, Fontana, 1990

Dorchester, Lady (ed.), *Recollections of a Long Life* by Broughton, Lord John Cam Hobhouse, 6 vols, John Murray, 1909-11

Dowden, W.S. (ed.), *The Journal of Thomas Moore*, 6 vols, Associated University Presses, 1983–91

Eisler, Benita, *Byron Child of Passion Fool of Fame*, Penguin Books, 1999

Elsner, John and Cardinal, Roger (eds.), *The Cultures of Collecting*, Reaktion Books, 1994

Finati, Giovanni, *Narrative of the Life and Adventures of Giovanni Finati*, ed. W.J. Bankes, 2 vols, John Murray, 1830

Flagg, Edmund, *Venice*, New York, Sampson Low, 1853

Ginsborg, Paul, *Daniele Manin and the Revolutions of 1848*, Cambridge, Cambridge University Press, 1979

Gould, Cecil, *The Trophy of Conquest,* Faber & Faber, 1965

Grattan, Thomas Colley, *Beaten Paths and Those who Trod Them*, 2 vols, Chapman and Hall, 1862

Haskell, F., *Rediscoveries in Art*, Phaidon, 1976

Hayter, Alethea, *A Sultry Month: Scenes of London Literary Life in 1846*, Faber & Faber, 1965

Hermann, Frank, *The English as Collectors*, John Murray, 1999

Hutchings, Rev. John, *The History and Antiquities of the County of Dorset*, 1774 and other editions

Irby, C.L. and Mangles, J., *Travels in Egypt and Nubia, Syria and Asia Minor*, London, 1823

James, T.G.H., *Egypt Revealed: Artist-Travellers in an Antique Land*, London, Folio Society, 1997

———— 'Egyptian Antiquities at Kingston Lacy, Dorset', *Apollo* Magazine, May 1994

Jameson, Mrs Anna, *Companion to the Most Celebrated Private Galleries of Art*, London, 1844

Laing, Alastair, *In Trust for the Nation*, National Trust, 1995

Laven, David, *Venice and Venetia Under the Hapsburgs*, Oxford, Oxford University Press, 2002

Lees-Milne, James, *Venetian Evenings*, Collins, 1988

———— *People and Places: Country House Donors and the National Trust*, John Murray, 1992

———— *The Bachelor Duke*, John Murray, 1991

———— *William Beckford*, Century, 1990

Longford, Elizabeth, *Wellington: The Years of the Sword* and *Wellington: Pillar of State*, Weidenfeld and Nicolson, 1969 and 1972

Lutyens, Mary (ed.), *Effie in Venice: Mrs John Ruskin's Letters Home 1849–52*, Pallas Editions, 1999

MacCarthy, Fiona, *Byron: Life and Legend*, John Murray, 2002

Maclarnon, Kathleen, 'WJ Bankes in Egypt', *Apollo* Magazine, August 1986

————'William Bankes and his Collection of Spanish Paintings at Kingston Lacy', *Burlington Magazine*, Feb. 1990, pp. 114–25

Manley, Debra and Rée, Peta, *Henry Salt, Artist, Traveller, Diplomat, Egyptologist*, Boston, Ars Libri Publications, 2001

Marchand, Leslie A., *Byron's Letters and Journals*, 13 vols, John Murray, 1973–94

Martin, George, *Verdi: His Music, Life and Times*, Macmillan, 1965

Mayne, Ethel Colburn (ed.), *Life and Letters of Anne Isabella, Lady Noel Byron,* Constable, 1929

Mitchell, Anthony, Kingston Lacy Guide Book, The National Trust, 1987

Mowl, Timothy, *William Beckford,* John Murray, 1998

Muensterberger, Werner, *Collecting: An Unruly Passion Psychological Perspectives,* Princeton, Princeton University Press, 1994

Norwich, John Julius, *Paradise of Cities, Venice and its Nineteenth-century Visitors,* Viking, 2003

Ollard, Richard, *Dorset,* Wimborne, Dovecote Press, 1999

Pemble, John, *Venice Rediscovered,* Oxford, Clarendon Press, 1995

Pine Coffin, Sydney, *Bibliography of British and American Travel in Italy to 1860,* Biblioteca di Bibliografia Italiana, Florence, 1974

Quennell, Peter, *Romantic England: Writing and Painting 1717–1851,* Weidenfeld and Nicolson, 1970

———— *Byron, a Self Portrait: Letters and Diaries 1798–1824,* Oxford, Oxford University Press, 1990

———— (ed.), *The Private Letters of Princess Lieven to Prince Metternich 1820–1826,* John Murray, 1937

Radcliffe, Ann, *The Mysteries of Udolpho,* Harmondsworth, 1966

Read, Ben, *Victorian Sculpture,* New Haven, Yale University Press, 1982

Reitlinger, Gerald, *The Economics of Taste,* New York, Hacker Art Books, 1982

Rogers, Samuel. *Recollections of the Table Talk of Samuel Rogers,* ed. Alexander Dyce, E. Moxon, 1856

Rowse, A. L., *Homosexuals in History,* Weidenfeld and Nicolson, 1977

———— 'Byron's friend Bankes: a Portrait', *Encounter,* March 1975

Ruskin, John, *The Stones of Venice,* 2 vols, Orpington, 1898

Siegel, Jonah, *Desire and Excess: the 19th Century Culture of Art,* Princeton, Princeton University Press, 2000

Sparrow, John (ed.), *Leaves from a Victorian Diary* by Edward Leeves, Secker and Warburg, 1985

Starkey, Paul and Janet (eds.), *Travellers in Egypt,* London and New York, IB Taurus, 1998

Tanner, Tony, *Venice Desired,* Oxford, Blackwell, 1992

Trollope, Frances, *A Visit to Italy,* 2 vols, Richard Bentley, 1842

Usick, Dr Patricia, *Adventures in Egypt and Nubia: the Travels of William John Bankes (1786–1855),* British Museum Press, 2002

———— 'William John Bankes' Collection of Drawings of Egypt and Nubia', from *Travellers in Egypt,* ed. P. & J. Starkey (above)

Waagen, Dr Gustav, *Galleries and Cabinets of Art in Great Britain*, London, 1857

Ward-Jackson, P., 'Expiatory Monuments by Carlo Marochetti in Dorset and the Isle of Wight', *Journal of Warburg and Courtauld Institute*, 1990

——— 'Carlo Marochetti and the Glasgow Wellington Memorial', *Burlington Magazine*, Dec. 1990

Wasserman, Jack Gumpert, 'William John Bankes', *The Newstead Byron Society Review*, July 2000

Williams Wynn, Frances, *Diaries of a Lady of Quality 1797–1844*, Longman, 1864

Wilson, Richard and Mackley, Alan (eds.), *Creating Paradise: the Building of the English Country House 1660–1880*, Hambledon and London, 2000

Acknowledgements

~

My chief thanks must go to The National Trust and in particular to the Curator of Kingston Lacy, James Grasby, the Collections Manager, Kate Warren and her colleagues, especially Carolyn Anand, the Honorary Archivist. Their constant enthusiasm for this book, willingness to help and ability to point me in new directions so that I could better understand William's character and achievements were unbounded. They tirelessly ferreted out material of interest and shared with me the benefit of their own researches. I am also grateful to other members of The National Trust including Alastair Laing, Curator, Pictures and Sculpture and Tim Knox, Head Curator. I should like to thank everyone at the Dorset County Record Office in Dorchester, which is now responsible for the vast Bankes Archive, still in the process of being catalogued, as well as Sarah Bridges, formerly of the Dorset County Record Office, who undertook much of the early cataloguing of the Bankes papers. I am particularly grateful to Antony Cleminson, who has been unfailingly helpful and informative and has generously shared his vast fund of knowledge, as well as Anthony Mitchell for his guiding hand at the beginning.

Staff at the London Library, British Library, Cambridge University Library, Hartley Library (University of Southampton), Wellcome Library for the History and Understanding of Medicine, Westminster Archives and my local library at Richmond upon Thames have all gone out of their way on several occasions to locate material I needed. I was also grateful to see copies of Thomas Moore's *Letters and Journals of Lord Byron*, annotated by J. C. Hobhouse, from the Brenthurst Library in Johannesburg. Warm thanks are due to John and Virginia Murray for unselfish access to the John Murray Archive at Albemarle Street, to Paul Seaward, Director of the History of Parliament, to staff at Canford School for a fascinating guided tour of the main house, to my editor Caroline

Knox for improving the shape of the book, and to Douglas Matthews, prince among indexers.

Other people I should like to thank include Jaynie Anderson, John Anderson (Gregory Rowcliffe and Milner), Val Andrew, Dottore Paolo and Signora Donatella Asta (Palazzo Mocenigo), Ariane Bankes, David and Muriel Bankes, John and Althea Bankes, Nicholas and Sheri Bankes, Steven Brindle (English Heritage), Alan Brown, Edward Burke, Sir Michael Burton, Harry Clark, George Clarke, Lady Clarke (President of the Venice in Peril Fund), Kenneth Curtis, Richard Davenport-Hines, Dudley Dodd, Victoria Datnow, C. J. Dawkins, Bruce Dixon, Viscount Falmouth, Christopher Fergusson, Knoll House Hotel, Lalage Hall, Frank Hermann, Guy Holborn (Lincoln's Inn), John Hubbard, Hugh Jacques, Nick Jeans (St Michael, Penkivel), Simon Jervis, Philip Joseph, Professor Jeffrey Hackney, Lee Langley, David Laven, Christopher Lee, Mary Moore, Fiona MacCarthy, Dr Paul Mitchell, Anthony Mott, Professor W. T. Murphy, Dr Annette Peach, Canon David Price, Roy Price, Joseph Rykwerts, Dr Luigi Sera, Christopher Symons Q. C., Richard Ryder, John and Rosemary Rodenhurst (Soughton Hall Hotel), Robert Sandell, Andrew and Sally Salmon, Charles Sebag-Montefiore, David Smith, E. A. Smith (Westminster School Archivist), Dr Christopher Tyerman, Dr Patricia Usick, Professor Richard Wilson, John Winstanley, Philip Ward-Jackson, Dr Maurice Whitehead, Betke Zamoyska, Dr Piera Zanon.

Finally, I owe a particular debt of gratitude to my agent Clare Alexander, who has always been passionate about William Bankes's story, and to my husband and family, who have lived with every twist and turn of discovery as well as the frustration of dead ends and have done so with their usual understanding and encouragement. Thank you.

Index